Auditions

D0139603

Auditions are an integral part of every performer's life. From getting into drama school, through to a successful career in an overcrowded industry, *Auditions: A Practical Guide* offers crucial advice, resources and tried and tested techniques to maximise success before, during and after each audition.

Written by an established casting director and former actor with thirty years of experience on a wide range of productions, this book offers a wealth of personal and professional insights, covering:

- drama and theatre schools
- classical, contemporary, physical and musical theatre
- television and radio drama
- screen tests and commercial castings
- voice work
- recalls and workshops
- handling job offers, and rejection.

From training to triumph, nerves to networking and camera to casting couch, *Auditions: A Practical Guide* is an entertaining, accessible and indispensable read for every performer.

Richard Evans CDG has cast a wide variety of productions in all media since 1989 and, prior to this, worked as an actor for ten years. He has devised and presented audition and career development workshops at the Actors Centres in London and Manchester, and at many top drama and theatre schools, as well as writing 'A Casting Director's Perspective' for *The Actors' Yearbook, 2005*. He is a member of The Casting Directors' Guild of Great Britain and Ireland.

Auditions

A practical guide

Richard Evans CDG

Routledge
Taylor & Francis Group

LONDON AND NEW YORK

First published 2009
by Routledge
2 Park Square, Milton Park, Abingdon, Oxon OX14 4RN

Simultaneously published in the USA and Canada
by Routledge
270 Madison Avenue, New York, NY 10016

*Routledge is an imprint of the Taylor & Francis Group,
an informa business*

Typeset in Univers and Avant Garde by
Keystroke, 28 High Street, Tettenhall, Wolverhampton
Printed and bound in Great Britain by
TJ International Ltd, Padstow, Cornwall

British Library Cataloguing in Publication Data
A catalogue record for this book is available from the British Library

Library of Congress Cataloging in Publication Data
Evans, Richard, 1967–
Auditions : a practical guide / Richard Evans.
p. cm.
Includes index.
1. Acting–Auditions. I. Title.
PN2071.A92E93 2009
792.02'8–dc22
2008047997

ISBN10: 0–415–47034–X (hbk)
ISBN10: 0–415–47035–8 (pbk)
ISBN10: 0–203–87832–9 (ebk)

ISBN13: 978–0–415–47034–6 (hbk)
ISBN13: 978–0–415–47035–3 (pbk)
ISBN13: 978–0–203–87832–3 (ebk)

Contents

Introduction		ix
Acknowledgements		xi
PART 1 BEFORE		**1**
1	Where to find Auditions	3
2	Preparation and Research	11
3	Submitting Yourself for Work	28
4	Agents	47
5	Audition Log	56
6	Audition Wardrobe	60
7	Perceptions	63
8	The Power of Positive Thinking	68
9	Gatecrashing	72

PART 2 DURING   77

10 Entrances and Exits   79

11 Nerves   82

12 Drama and Theatre Schools   86

13 Theatre   99

14 Musical Theatre   121

15 Actor/Musicians   137

16 Recalls and Workshop Auditions   141

17 Television   146

18 Films and Screen Tests   154

19 Commercial Castings   160

20 Roleplay   170

21 Corporate Training Films   173

22 Radio Drama   176

23 Voice Work   179

24 Presenting   188

25 Interview Technique   194

26 Awkward Questions   209

27 Is Timing Everything?   212

28 In the Mood   214

29 Friend or Foe?   215

30 Actors Who Know Too Much   219

31 Same Old Faces   222

32	Recasts	226
33	The Casting Couch	228

PART 3 AFTER — **231**

34	Red Letter Days	233
35	Success	236
36	Negotiation	240
37	Rejection	245
38	Follow Ups	248
39	Turning Down Work	251
40	Help! What if . . . ?	253
41	A Diary of an Audition	256
42	Final Thoughts	260
	Index	264

Introduction

Love them or hate them, auditions are an integral and necessary part of every performer's life – yes, *every* performer. No matter at what stage of your professional life you are, whether looking to train at drama school, a graduate or newcomer struggling to get on to the first rung of the ladder, or someone further up it, who is more experienced, successful, well respected or even a famous star, auditions will always be part of your life. 'A star?' I hear you cry, 'Surely these doyennes are exempt from the whole sordid process.' A few indeed are, but even well-known names (who might be completely unknown to producers and directors from other countries), and those who have been well known in the past, sometimes don't have offers flooding in fifty-two weeks a year, and find themselves having to audition, screen test, interview, read, sing and dance in order to keep working.

Performers from all aspects of the Industry have always been fascinated and mystified by the casting process and the secrets of successful auditions – the kind of things you're not taught during your training, or would necessarily even think about. Wherever I go I am always asked for tips on how to get cast as a working actor (or how to become an international superstar by people from other walks of life). The subject intrigued me during my ten years as an actor, and since I made the transition into casting in the late 1980s, I have kept a close eye on how people have auditioned and thought back to how I could have improved my own technique. While there is sadly no magic formula, no hard and fast rules or even perfect auditions which will work every time, knowledge is power and to be forewarned is to be forearmed. This book contains proven techniques and inside information that will not only give you food for thought, but will also radically improve your chances of getting work, as well as the often ignored practical aspects and background information, all of which can contribute to success.

When reading this book, you might think it is largely a book of *don'ts*. This is intentional and far from negative, as I am a firm believer that much can be learned from other people's mistakes. Hopefully, the advice that lies within – which I have liberally peppered with stories and anecdotes, seen or heard over the years, and which I have chosen to keep anonymous to protect the innocent – will inspire you not to repeat the common errors that can often hamper success. While much of the information and advice is tailored to finding work in the British marketplace, many of the techniques included are universal and can be adapted to suit the working practices of performers all around the world. Some information is also repeated in several chapters, as there is much overlap between genres, so please bear with it – repetition is a useful tool and it is therefore well worth reading through all the chapters, whether or not you feel they apply to you at this point in time, as you never know what tips you may pick up. Once you have read the book, you can quickly refer to the memory-refreshing points at the end of each chapter, as well as the help section at the back, as and when you need them.

So read on, absorb and improve your auditions. Here's to success!

Richard Evans
2009

Acknowledgements

I would like to express my heartfelt gratitude to everybody who has made this book possible by so freely giving and sharing their encouragement, guidance, belief, expertise, knowledge, experiences, stories, talent and time. I'll spare their blushes by not mentioning everyone by name (and my own should I inadvertently overlook anyone). You know who you are and your help and support are greatly appreciated – *thank you!*

PART 1

Before

CHAPTER 1

Where to find Auditions

Before we start talking about auditions in earnest, it would be useful to think about how the actual process of casting happens. First, a production company will either be approached by moneyed people, or decide to produce a play, film, television series, commercial, etc. This can happen at short notice (a matter of a few weeks) or way ahead (sometimes several years) before the actual production is to be mounted. The producers will then appoint a creative team to oversee the production, which will include directors, designers, a choreographer, their assistants and possibly a casting director, all employed for their specialist areas of skill and knowledge. The production will be budgeted, dates firmed up and casting requirements confirmed. This phase is known as pre-production.

A casting brief will then be issued and circulated by whoever is responsible – a casting director or production assistant – either to selected agents, or more widely, via one or more of the casting information services. Availability checks may also be made for suitable artists already known to the creatives and casting personnel. An availability check is made by phone and, as the name implies, is a call to check whether an artist will be available for certain dates. That is all it is at this stage, so if you receive one, it does not mean you have got a job, or even necessarily an audition, so don't get excited (most agents will not consider it worth mentioning to their clients). If a casting director has a list of artists in mind who they want to bring in for each part, they may not bother advertising the project if all the artists turn out to be available and interested. The person in charge of casting will schedule the necessary auditions and the short-listed artists will be invited to attend – this may be a great many or just a handful for each character. I always aim for the latter approach – quality rather than quantity – bringing in a few selected artists who fit the brief and can deliver what is required, rather than vast numbers, many of whom will not be suitable for the part, or even good actors – this practice is known derogatorily as a 'cattle call' and can waste everybody's time. If necessary, there will be one or more rounds of recalls (callbacks), after which the director and fellow creatives will go through the lists and put their choices in order of preference (there may be several choices for each character, which can sometimes change as time goes on). Then artists may be pencilled in to keep them available for the dates – this will be discussed in more detail in Chapter 19 – and offers made to the first choices. If the first choice declines, the second choice will then be offered, and so on, if needs be. If there is no second choice, further auditions will have to be held, which can also happen if the casting requirements change during the process. Once all the offers have been accepted and deals negotiated, contracts are issued and signed and then the fun really begins. Sounds simple, doesn't it?!

So, how do you find out about auditions? You might have an agent who will submit you for suitable roles in return for a percentage of your earnings if you are successful in getting the job. If so, that's great – keep in touch with them (though not over regularly, as this will do you no favours) and ideally cultivate a good working relationship with them. Whether or not you have an agent – and, while very useful people, they are far from the be all and end all of life – it always pays to do your own legwork too. After all, nobody can work as hard for you as you can for yourself. My personal rule is always to do at least one thing every day for my career. That might be to call or write to a person or company that might need my services (especially if I have heard rumour of a specific project coming up); perhaps I will do some research on the internet, read a trade magazine or phone a colleague to see what's going on. Whatever it is (and it need not take long at all), I like to feel at the end of each day that I've done something to increase my chances of getting my next job and make myself better at what I do. Whenever I hear about a job lead which is especially suited to my skills and areas of knowledge, I feel a real sense of purpose and am motivated to leap into action, applying for the job as soon as possible (having first done any necessary research) in the hope of getting a meeting and offer of employment.

It is important to keep your ear to the ground as auditions can come from a variety of sources, some not so obvious, and sometimes when you least expect them. These days, the majority of casting information is dealt with through *Spotlight Link*, an excellent and effective online service provided for current subscribers of the *Spotlight* casting directories (www.spotlight.com). Casting personnel and other work-givers circulate character breakdowns via the service and receive suggestions for each role from agents, who respond electronically sending in their clients' *Spotlight* CVs. The breakdown sender can choose to send the information to all the agents on the list, or just to agents specialising in certain categories (those representing children or presenters, for instance) or they can hand pick the agents they wish to receive it. Work-givers can also elect to send their breakdowns via the Link directly to those subscribing artists who are not represented by any agent, thus enabling them to submit themselves for suitable opportunities. If this situation applies to you (which it will if the contact details are through *Spotlight*, rather than an agent), be sure you request to receive this information. If you are with an agent, however, you will not be sent breakdowns directly, as they will be receiving them, and should be suggesting you for suitable parts.

There are regular casting publications that are widely available. *The Stage* is the most well known, published every Thursday and available from newsagents, postal subscription and at some public libraries. *The Stage*'s website (www.thestage.co.uk) publishes the online recruitment section from 12 noon every Saturday, where the week's auditions are posted. Keep in mind if you are replying to a *Stage* advertisement that advertisers often get besieged with many hundreds of letters, especially when the edition is first published, so, unless there is a deadline, it may be worth waiting a few days before posting your submission as it may arrive in a delivery with fewer letters and stand a greater chance of being more fully read and considered. However, as *The Stage* only publishes adverts that companies have paid for, the quantity and selection of jobs in each issue can vary radically, so it's a good idea to spread your net wider and also use more specialist services and publications.

Another good and free web resource is the casting section of www.mandy.com – an international website mainly devoted to vacancies on the production side, but which has diversified into auditions. Equity members who are in benefit can use Equity's Job Information Service free of charge by logging on to www.equity.org.uk and entering the required details. Both these sites are worth checking regularly. There are other web-based and postal subscription services, which charge you a monthly or annual fee to receive their information. Online, *Castweb* (www.castweb.co.uk) provides an excellent service, emailing up-to-the-minute casting information direct to your inbox as it happens. While the daily volume is sometimes massive and very encouraging, often the briefs will be very specific and may be unsuitable for you, so just head straight into the recycle bin. The European equivalent is *Stage Pool* (www.stagepool.com), which covers work throughout the EU and could be useful for those living or wishing to work abroad. A word of warning though, the information provided is not given in the English language, but translation websites such as www.google.com/language_tools or www.freetranslation.com can help. Those in North America should check out www.nycasting.com and www.lacasting.com for casting news in New York and Los Angeles respectively, as well as www.actorsaccess.com, www.castingworkbook.com and www.backstage.com/bso/production_listings/nyc.jsp. For casting news and networking for British and American independent films, Shooting People (www.shootingpeople.org) should be explored. You can register with *Casting Call Pro* (www.castingcallpro.com) free of charge, which not only gives you limited access to casting information but also enables you to create your own web page containing your profile, CV and photograph. Film and television production news can be found in the weekly bulletin *Advance Production News UK* (www.CrimsonUK.com) which is only available by annual subscription, as well as the magazines, *Screen International* (www.Screeninternational.com) and *Broadcast* (www.broadcastnow.co.uk). The American magazine *Variety* (www.variety.com) is by far the best source of news from across the Atlantic. All these magazines can be found in some public reference libraries.

Another UK internet service is *Castnet* (www.castingnetwork.co.uk) which not only disseminates information and includes your details in a directory but, for an extra fee, will also match subscriber profiles to current casting briefs and submit your details to the people concerned when a match is made. While useful to a degree, this is quite a basic service and can result in large bundles of not brilliantly accurate submissions, with lists of names as opposed to enticing letters. You may be better off submitting yourself using the information that *Castnet* provides. *Actors Inc* (www.actors-inc.co.uk) provides basic information in exchange for a modest monthly or quarterly subscription, and offers a month's free trial.

The oldest and best-known postal service (although they now also offer an online service and updates for subscribers) is *PCR – Production and Casting Report*. Delivered every Monday, this newsletter provides a good knowledge base for current and future casting. Some of this information is very premature (sometimes months or even years ahead) and the odd rumour slips through from time to time, so always obey their instruction to hold contact on certain projects until casting actually commences and checking whether it is actually worth your while writing at that time if you are unsure. Some years ago, *PCR* published information about an impending production on which I was booked to work with the emboldened words *'please hold contact'* clearly at the bottom. I received 212 letters from that mention, many of which were completely wrong for the piece, as no breakdown had been included, and ironically some weeks later the whole project was shelved.

Try to keep up to date with the production plans of the regional repertory companies. Some will include season information and casting breakdowns on their websites; others may put you on an email list to receive details if you ask nicely. Otherwise, phone the theatres to find out what their forthcoming productions will be, asking when specific shows will be casting and if you can keep in contact every few months. By keeping records of the names of those you speak to – who may be the people responsible for the casting – you can hopefully build up a rapport over time, which may give you a slight advantage when audition lists are being drawn up.

Other resources to check out if you are in central London are the notice boards at the offices of *Spotlight* (7 Leicester Place, London WC2) and the Actors Centre (1a Tower Street, London WC2), though you have to be a member or buy a ticket for a show at the Tristan Bates Theatre to gain access to the Actors Centre (visit www.actorscentre.co.uk for details on both). Similar information can be found at the Actors Centre in Manchester (www.actorscentre north.com).

Another less obvious way which can reap dividends is to look out for stalls of theatres and professional theatre companies at fairs and carnivals. These will usually be there to publicise the companies' work to the potential local audience and therefore may be staffed by the marketing team or volunteers, but it is worth chatting with them and asking if they know who does the casting. Several times the response has been 'Him/her' and I have been pointed in the direction of the artistic director or production assistant, with whom I have been able to chat (much easier if I've actually seen their company's work) and ask if they minded my sending details for consideration. I did this some years ago at a big festival in London and was told that writing would not be worthwhile as their company consisted of a core group of performers and no outsiders were ever employed. I thanked them, wishing them well, and was about to walk away when a man who was sitting quietly asked me to tell him about myself. I did so and he explained that he was an assistant to a well-known casting director, asking me to send my CV and photograph to her office as they were about to start work on a major new movie. I duly did so – reminding him of our meeting in my letter – and was called in for a screen test, and subsequent recall, several weeks later for the second lead. Although unsuccessful, they did see me for another project some while later and I was told that I would never have even got through the door in the first place if he had not met me on that Sunday afternoon.

A great way of finding out what is happening is to keep in touch, or network, with friends and share information. This is probably best done with those who are so different from you that they do not pose any threat to you (you will be less likely to mention a job that someone else might get instead of you than one for which you are not remotely right). When I was in my early twenties, I had two friends with whom I kept in touch regularly. One was male and about fifteen years my senior, the other female in her mid-forties, and we all used to look out for each other. If one of us heard about, or got, an audition for something in which there was a part for one of the others, they would immediately call and tell us to make contact with the people concerned. Sometimes we used to try to gatecrash an audition for which we knew we were suitable if one of our trio had an appointment for a different role (we'll talk more about gate-crashing in Chapter 9). It was a wonderful feeling the time my friend got a part in a West End play, for which he was perfect, as a result of my hearing about an urgent casting call. Our system was an excellent one, working for each other and not waiting for the phone to ring, as we each also had a good agent working on our behalf. Even outside our trio, if another friend sprang to mind for a part, I would let them know, and they would often return the compliment when they heard about things. This ethos of resource pooling was the basis that led to the formation of many actors' co-operative agencies (an agency formed and run by a group of actors, who represent each other by taking turns in the office when they are not working, in order to take more control of their own careers). If you have a friend who is a member of a co-op agency, you can always ask them to keep a look out for any suitable casting for you, as they will receive breakdowns and information that may not be available to individual actors. I have fond memories of those times and whole-heartedly recommend any group of like-minded friends to give it a try. The practice of calling theatres is time-consuming and subscribing to several of the information services (many cost upwards of £20 a month) can be expensive, so consider sharing the labour, as well as the costs.

So remember to . . .

- ✓   Do at least one thing every day for your career.
- ✓   Read *The Stage* every week and regularly check the free websites.
- ✓   Keep your eyes open and an ear to the ground.
- ✓   Be motivated and act quickly on job leads which are suited to you.
- ✓   Keep in touch with theatres and build rapports with casting contacts.
- ✓   Share information and pool resources with like-minded friends.

CHAPTER 2

Preparation and Research

So, what is the one secret of a good audition then? Talent, many might say, and while right in some respects, it is not what I would answer. Being right for the part is another strong contender, and plays a large part in my answer, which is . . . *confidence*. Easier said than done, I hear you cry, but there are tricks to boost that all-important confidence. So what can we do?

Well first, knowledge and truth are an important key. When you write to suggest yourself for jobs, and even more so if you are offered an audition, make sure you know as much as possible about the part and project concerned. Think seriously about your suitability, bearing in mind the brief you have been given. If, for instance, you are not convincingly in the stated age range (there is a vast difference between twenty-five and forty, or even twenty-five and thirty) or to the required standard of a skill – outstanding tap dancer; competent guitarist; excellent horseman; fluent in a language or native in a dialect; singing within a specified range, etc. – *please be honest and truthful*, do yourself a favour and leave this job well alone. It is a mistake to think that you can learn tap dancing in a week; ride a horse because you once had a donkey ride on Blackpool beach when you were five; bluff your way in a language or listen to a dialect and immediately imitate it; and sing a top C when you can barely reach a B. As far as skills are concerned, they should be honed and ready to demonstrate now if someone asks. The age-old excuse of 'I can do it with a few days' practice' really does not wash and will knock your confidence if you make claims that you cannot fulfil. The trick is to offer less and give more. That will make you look good and earn respect in the process.

Do your homework about the director and other creatives (writer, composer, choreographer, musical supervisor and/or director, casting director, etc.) you will be meeting. Do you have any mutual friends or contacts that you can ask for information or pass on regards? Find out what they have done in the past. Have you seen any of their work which you could drop into a conversation or talk about, if asked, during your interview? The internet is a useful tool for this research, using the search engines of such sites as www.google.co.uk, www.imdb.com, www.tv.com, www.dggb.org, www.thecdg.co.uk, www.whatson stage.com and www.geocities.com. Old theatre programmes are another excellent resource. Always try to buy one whenever you see a show and keep them on file for this purpose. Back issues of the *Radio Times* and *TV Times* can also be good, if a little laborious to look through, and can be found in most public libraries. *The Actors' Yearbook*, edited by Simon Dunmore (www.acblack.com), contains in-depth information about companies and creatives.

Also think about whether you actually want the job on offer and are indeed available for the dates concerned – it is a waste of everyone's time if you go through the audition process only to decline an offer – especially if you are already committed to another job that conflicts. Please do not go to auditions for the sake of it, even for practice, if you have no intention of actually taking the job. Let someone who wants it use the valuable space.

As any boy scout will tell you, be prepared, and this also applies with auditions – be prepared for absolutely *anything*! As well as know-ledge, preparation is a great confidence booster. Do you know the correct address and how to get there? I know actors who do a dummy travel run to the audition venue prior to the day, so they are not panicking trying to find the right place with only minutes to spare. These days, internet mapping programs, such as www.multimap. com allow you to pinpoint the exact location of an address by entering the postcode (so it's a good idea to make sure you ask for it, or research it, using the Royal Mail postcode finder at www.royal mail.com) as well as detailed directions from your own postcode or the local station. Another reason for a dummy run is to find out timing, and always allow plenty of it in case of delays. If the audition is in London or another major city, I would urge you to use public transport and not to drive. There has been many a time when an actor has run into the audition room, yelling 'Keep an eye on my car!' over their shoulder, which happens to be double parked in a warden-filled street. They rarely get the job. There is nothing more nerve-wracking, especially when you may already be a little nervous, as knowing you're going to be late – and lateness and rushing does your performance and stress levels no favours either. The only saving grace can be when the casting session is running late, as some do, but there is no guarantee of this. There's nothing so reassuring for me when arriving at a casting as to see the first appointments either sitting in the waiting room (it is always worth checking if you can arrive early to look over sides of script that you will be asked to perform – another very valuable piece of preparation) or walking around near the venue as they are way too early themselves. Sometimes, sessions run early, if a director takes less time with each candidate than has been allotted, or people drop out with little or no notice, which happens with alarming regularity. I always try to make provision for this in various ways, but there is nothing so irritating – or embarrassing for the casting director – than long gaps of nobody. Even if you do arrive early, be prepared to go in as soon as you arrive, if necessary, so calmness and confidence – of which you will have more by being early – are the key.

Before the day itself, try to make sure you have arranged necessary care for your children and even dogs. Some actors bring their children with them to castings (especially if they are looking after them during school holidays) and this is generally not a problem if they are well behaved and there is adequate room for them to safely wait. The one downside of doing this is that looking after them and ensuring they are behaved and settled can be a major distraction from the job in hand – your actual audition. I have seen many parents who are more worried about their misbehaving toddler – or crying newborn, in one man's case – than getting the job. The same goes with dogs, as while these lovable pets invariably make hearts melt in casting suites and production offices, they can sometimes be a nuisance and sapping to your attention. It is often said that children and animals upstage actors, and at any audition it's you who should be the star, so be on the safe side and organise alternative care whenever possible.

Speeches

While you will not be asked for one at 90 per cent of all the auditions you go for, always ensure that a selection of monologues are fresh in your mind and you know them so well that you can adapt them into whatever accent or emotion is asked of you, without fluffing the lines or repeatedly having to start again. If you do happen to forget the lines of your speech, don't be afraid to ask if you can start again from the beginning. If the answer is yes, compose yourself (a deep breath through your mouth, held and sharply exhaled should help with this, as well as alleviate some of the nerves), quickly run through it mentally and start again. However, if they respond 'No, we don't need to see any more', accept this as they've seen enough to make a decision – you may have already got the job. I never cease to be amazed by the actors who bumble and fumble when asked if they have a piece – even recent graduates who should have a vast selection. Make sure this is not you! Monologues are far more prevalent at auditions across the Atlantic, so be especially prepared if auditioning for an American director.

When asked to prepare a piece, especially at short notice, most unprepared (dare I say lazy) folk will dive straight for the trusty

'Popular Audition Speeches for Men/Women' anthologies such as *Award Monologues for Women/Men*, edited by Patrick Tucker and Christine Ozanne, which feature selected pieces from award-winning plays, separated by age range and accompanied by sound background information. These are great, well-researched guides, which offer a quick solution, but there are two important points to bear in mind. First, speeches in these books are tried and tested and will be performed more and more the longer the volume has been on the bookshelves. The majority of panellists will know these monologues backwards and invariably compare your rendition to the best they have seen, even on the same day – great if you are utterly outstanding or totally original, but unless you are absolutely convinced you are, it is wiser to avoid them. Second, many books of this nature only print the speech and play title, so should you be asked for an explanation about the play or character you are performing, you will be left floundering – like reviewing a play you have never seen – another major confidence shatterer. Some volumes have now got wise to this and print a short synopsis and character details with the speech, but to be on the safe side, if it is a piece that really suits you and you intend to use it regularly, do yourself a favour and get a copy of the actual play from which it is drawn and read it several times from cover to cover until you know it intimately, as the panellists may. You might also find other speeches in the same play which are not seen so often. One other factor to keep in mind when choosing speeches is bad language. While our society is far less prudish nowadays, and people in the entertainment industry more open minded than most, excessive swearing, especially for the sake of it, can be off putting and there are a couple of expletives that some still consider taboo and unacceptable. Keep this in mind when choosing pieces as it may be a turn off.

Sight reading

Far more often you will be asked to read some of the script, and this is very much a skill in itself. Sight reading can make or break whether you get the job, so it is a skill to practise regularly and hone. The Actors Centre in London offers a variety of classes on the subject by different tutors, as I am sure do many other localised training centres, so do look around for something near you. The undoubted guru of sight reading is Nina Finburgh, who has taught the greats. She works privately with people (her details are in the Drama Training, Schools and Coaches section of *Contacts*) and regularly does weekly group sessions at the Actors Centre in London. A group is often better to work with, as you can learn from other people's mistakes, as well as your own, though you get less specific attention. Be warned, these are ongoing and you need to book to return week after week, rather than just one session, as I discovered as a young actor over twenty years ago. I remember sitting in the room, feeling utterly terrified as everyone was so good, some, unbeknown to me, having been study-ing with Nina for years, and there was me, having my confidence knocked by every word as she criticised the piece I had attempted in front of the entire agreeing group. I quickly left the Actors Centre at the end with head bowed, not daring to look or speak to any of my ultra talented classmates and never found the courage to return. More fool me! Miss Finburgh, while formidable, is a genius. Her 1993 book, *Hot Tips for Cold Readings – Some Do's and Don'ts for Actors at Auditions*, co-written with Anne McArthur, is available from www. amazon.com and other bookstores, and is another great resource as a supplement, or for those who cannot work with the lady herself.

At the end of this chapter, there are some fake television scripts that I wrote and use for mock auditions with drama students, which will be useful to practise your sight-reading techniques. The five *Plods* scripts are a good example of small one-scene or episode parts found in series with a high turnover of guest artists, such as *The Bill*, *Casualty* and *Doctors*. The title 'Plods' is named after an old-fashioned slang term 'PC Plod', used for a policeman who plods (walks slowly) on his beat. Each character is specifically defined and written so that his or her status and class is obvious. *My Garden Gnomes Are Aliens*, on the other hand, while it may seem far fetched, is not only an example of an off-the-wall children's TV series, but also holds with the theory of being prepared for anything, as this is probably one of the toughest scripts you will ever be asked to sight read. The only thing I tell the candidates when giving out the Garden Gnomes scripts is there are no tricks and all the gobbledygook words are pronounced exactly the way they are written (if you are not told this and have any doubts in a real situation, don't be afraid to ask to make sure).

The scripts are presented as most television scripts will be, with exterior and interior shots and directions. There are more precise directions in my scripts than most others, because while the lines are important (in a television script they will have been written precisely to ensure the episode's running time is exact to the second), the major point of these scripts is the directions, each of which require quite different emotions, often several in the same short scene. Also bear in mind that these shots may be close-ups and your face will be extremely exposed, with every little twitch or movement obvious to the audience. At a casting you will probably be sitting stationary on a chair with a camera close on you, so tailor your performance to the right degree. Less really is more in this instance, both physically and vocally. Watch other actors on screen to see how they do things and adapt the techniques you see into your own performances. Try reading both characters in each script with a friend to get the contrast between them. Think how you are going to achieve the emotions, feeling each and keeping them real and totally believable, even in close-up on camera. Recording yourself on a camcorder and studying the playback can be a great help, and very revealing. If the script is your own (a play script you have bought, for instance), mark it up with emphases and emotions for easier learning. You can mark your lines with a fluorescent highlighter pen, but be sure to ask permission before making any marks if the script belongs to the company, as other people may have to use it after you.

The major technique of sight reading, regardless of the medium, is to know roughly what you are going to say, by reading the piece through several times before entering the audition room, and then memorise each line before you speak, rather than reading the words off the page as you are saying them. This can be done while someone else is speaking or possibly making the character pause for thought before looking up from your script. Whatever you do, take your time and try not to gabble your way quickly through the piece, which is often a sign of nerves. A dangerous trap which some fall into is learning the script while waiting and then giving a finished performance without holding the pages. While this can free up your body to act the scene, it can backfire, for not only might you look over confident, but if you should rearrange or forget lines, or even totally dry, it will do you no favours. Learn the piece by all means, but *always* keep the script in your hand, regularly referring to it as and when necessary, as a newsreader would during a broadcast, despite using autocue.

Dyslexia and disability

It is a well-known fact that there are a significant number of artists who are dyslexic to some degree and this can hamper performances, especially when asked to sight read. If this condition affects you, please don't be brave and suffer in silence – there's no stigma attached and it is your right to have exactly the same chance as everybody else. If your dyslexia is mild, ask if you can arrive earlier to take the script away to a quiet place for as long as you need to learn it (perhaps taking a friend along to help you). If it is more severe, don't be afraid to ask if pages of script can be emailed, faxed or posted to you prior to the audition day to enable you to work on it beforehand, politely explaining the reason, lest you be thought arrogant. If you have an agent, please tell them so they can also do this on your behalf. The British Dyslexia Association (www.bda dyslexia.org.uk) can help you with information. I am amazed at the amount of artists, and agents, who fail to mention this vital information until it is too late to do anything about it, or the reading has been blown, especially easy to do in the case of comedy scripts, where the delivery needs to be spot on to convey the sense, and get the laughs.

Some companies may also be able to offer scripts in other formats, such as Braille, large print or audio, so check if you need them. Graeae Theatre Company (www.graeae.org), Artsline (www.artsline.org.uk) and Skill (www.skill.org.uk) – The National Bureau for Students with Disabilities – may also be able to help and advise on this, as well as with access issues.

And finally. . .

If you are going for a theatre audition, it is always a good idea to carry the music for a couple of songs that suit your voice, you know well and can sing at the drop of a hat, even unaccompanied, as you never know when you will be asked. We'll talk more about musical theatre auditions in Chapter 14, but it is essential to ensure the music is in the right key for your voice – please *never* ask the pianist to transpose for you, even though most can. Your singing teacher may be able to do this for you, or put you in touch with someone who can. Also make sure that the sheets are collated and taped together so they are able to stand up on the piano for the pianist to read. I remember auditioning a young actor, who, when asked for his music, reached into his trouser pocket pulled out a crumpled sheet of paper, folded into six, and handed it to the pianist. How we stopped ourselves from laughing I will never know – and, needless to say, he was not successful.

One other item always to keep in your bag – and many performers I know have a special bag or case just for auditions – is a couple of copies of your résumé and photograph. You will put yourself a cut above the competition for this if the panel are without them for any reason, as many people do not think of carrying them. Ensure the CV is up to date, both items are firmly stapled together, and your name and contact details are clearly on the back of the photograph.

**PLODS EPISODE 21 SCENE 9
(FEMALE AUDITIONEE – ROLE OF ROSIE COBURN)**

EXT DAY

WPC HARRIS walks along Ainwick Street towards Ainwick House. She goes up the stairs, across the first floor balcony, stopping at number 14. She knocks hard and loudly on the door. There is no response, so she knocks again as the door of number 12 opens and ROSIE COBURN pokes her head out.

> **ROSIE**
> He's not there you know.

> **HARRIS**
> Sorry?

> **ROSIE**
> He's not there.

> **HARRIS**
> Who's not there?

ROSIE looks at HARRIS with smug defiance.

> **ROSIE**
> Whoever you're looking for. The bloke who lives there. He's not there.

> **HARRIS**
> When did you last see Arthur Lucas? Today? Yesterday?

ROSIE looks confused.

> **ROSIE**
> Lucas? (Realising HARRIS may be trying to trick her) Oh! I get it. You're not getting me like that. I'm not a nark; specially with you damned coppers.

> **HARRIS**
> We urgently need to speak to Arthur Lucas of 14 Ainwick House, so could you please tell me . . .

> **ROSIE**
> I'm not telling you nothing cos I told you I'm not a nark. Go on, bog off!

ROSIE slams the door. HARRIS looks bewildered before walking away.

FADE INTO SCENE 10

PLODS EPISODE 11 SCENE 19
(MALE AUDITIONEE – ROLE OF JAMES BUSH)

INT DAY

Front doors of Oxlow Police Station open and JAMES BUSH enters. The camera pans with him as he walks to the front desk and rings the bell for attention. SGT CLARKE finishes his conversation and walks over to the desk.

CLARKE
Can I help you Sir?

BUSH
You've got my Dad in there. Arthur Bush. I want to see him.

CLARKE
I'm sorry Sir, Mr Bush is being questioned by our officers at the moment and is therefore unable, at present, to see any visitors.

Close-up on BUSH, who looks tense at SGT CLARKE's response.

CLARKE
Might I suggest you go home and call the station later when we may well have more news?

BUSH
I said I want to see my Father.

CLARKE
And I heard you Sir, though obviously you did not hear me. Do yourself a favour Mr Bush and just go home.

Pause as BUSH stands and stares at SGT CLARKE, enraged and bewildered, not knowing what to say for the best.

CLARKE
Go home!

BUSH turns to go.

BUSH
You've not heard the last of this.

BUSH walks towards the door, pushes it violently and exits. Camera pans back to SGT CLARKE, who smiles, shakes his head and walks away from the desk.

FADE INTO SCENE 20

PLODS EPISODE 11 SCENE 9
(FEMALE AUDITIONEE – ROLE OF LAURA FAIRMAN)

INT DAY
SGT CLARKE unlocks the door of Cell 2 with a large bunch of keys. He opens it and ushers LAURA FAIRMAN in.

LAURA
Thank you Sergeant. I'll knock when I'm ready.

CLARKE
No problem Mrs Fairman.

SGT CLARKE closes and locks the cell door behind her. LAURA turns and sees ROY BILLINGS sitting on the bench. She goes over to him, hand outstretched.

LAURA
Hello Roy, I'm Laura Fairman, your lawyer.

BILLINGS sits motionless. He does not look up at her. She retracts her hand.

LAURA
I think we've got some talking to do. These are pretty serious allegations against you. Now have you thought what your plea will be?

BILLINGS does not look up, but speaks quietly.

BILLINGS
I'm innocent. Innocent, ya hear. I was set up by them Jones Brothers. Scumbags!

BILLINGS thinks for a second, rises and looks straight at LAURA.

BILLINGS
Here, it wasn't them that sent you, was it? I can't afford no fancy brief.

LAURA
I'm not at liberty to reveal that, Roy.

BILLINGS
It bloody was, wasn't it? I don't need you. Get out of here. I'd prefer to go down than take their charity. Go on, get off out of it!

BILLINGS turns his back on LAURA. She pauses for thought, then walks calmly towards the door and loudly knocks twice on it.

CUT TO SCENE 10

PLODS EPISODE 11 SCENE 6
(MALE AUDITIONEE – ROLE OF RAY MOLONEY)

INT DAY
Front doors of Oxlow Police Station open and RAY MOLONEY enters. The camera pans with him as he nervously walks to the front desk and apprehensively rings the bell. SGT CLARKE finishes his conversation and walks over to the desk.

CLARKE
Can I help you Sir?

MOLONEY
I didn't do it ya know.

CLARKE
I cannot be sure of the accuracy of your statement, Sir.

Close-up on MOLONEY, who looks terrified.

CLARKE
Unless you tell me in detail what exactly IT is, I cannot make any judgement upon whether your statement is right or wrong now can I? Would you care to elaborate Sir?

MOLONEY (Speaking fast and in an agitated manner)

I din't do it, Mrs Ross said I did but I din't honest! It was all her cat's fault. I told it not to scratch me, I bleedin' told it, but cats is thick. It woun't listen, stupid animal! I told it what would happen if it scratched me and I'm not a person to be messed with, as my brother Steve will tell ya, so it was its dumb fault not mine OK?

CLARKE
Are you saying that you killed Mrs Ross's cat, Sir?

MOLONEY stands looking confused, not knowing what to say. As he thinks, he starts to cry.

MOLONEY
I din't kill it. It scratched me. Got to defend myself. My right, yeah?

SGT CLARKE looks exasperated.

CLARKE
Wait there please Sir.

SGT CLARKE shakes his head and walks away from the desk.

FADE INTO SCENE 7

**PLODS EPISODE 11 SCENE 4
(FEMALE AUDITIONEE − ROLE OF JOANNE PRINGLE)**

EXT DAY
WPC HARRIS walks along the balcony to 38 Ainwick House. With apprehension, she presses the doorbell. After a few seconds, JOANNE PRINGLE comes to the glass-panelled door and answers it.

> **HARRIS**
> Good afternoon. I'm WPC Harris from Oxlow Police. Are you Joanne Pringle?

> **JOANNE**
> Yes, what's wrong?

> **HARRIS**
> Can I come in please, Mrs Pringle?

JOANNE nervously ushers HARRIS through the front door, down the passage and into the living room. As they are walking she starts to rant at speed.

> **JOANNE**
> For God's sake, third time this week. You might as well set up a cop shop outside, you'd have less far to travel. Jeez! You lot must like it round here, can have my flat if you give me enough. Mind the bike, it's new! How'd you like it if I kicked your kids' toys? No respect! (Pausing to think) Why you here? It's not my Dave is it?

> **HARRIS**
> You'd better sit down Mrs Pringle. I'm afraid . . . I'm afraid it's your Mother.

She sits. Close-up as JOANNE shoots a terrified look to HARRIS.

> **HARRIS**
> She was shopping in Jamestown Street Market when she keeled over. Somebody called an ambulance which came as quickly as possible . . .

The realisation of what has happened begins to dawn on JOANNE. She stares numbly into space, and involuntarily cries silently.

> **HARRIS**
> . . . but she'd had a massive heart attack and was pronounced dead at the scene. I'm so sorry Mrs Pringle.

> **JOANNE** (Through her tears)
> But she was only fifty-six. She had loads more living to do.

CUT TO SCENE 5

MY GARDEN GNOMES ARE ALIENS EPISODE 1 SCENE 9 (FEMALE AUDITIONEE – ROLE OF JOOMFLANA)

INT DAY
EMMA SMITH opens her bedroom door, enters and shuts it. JOOMFLANA is sitting on the floor by the window. She is a very shy gnome and looks nervously at EMMA, not wanting to be noticed. EMMA sees her and jumps back in surprise.

> **EMMA**
> W-who are you?

> **JOOMFLANA**
> Nidda crulchit.

> **EMMA**
> What?

JOOMFLANA looks even more nervous.

> **JOOMFLANA**
> Eddalonco fratipani . . . jofflo?

> **EMMA**
> That's not English . . . or French. (Smiling and outstretching a hand) Hello, I'm Emma. Emma Smith. What's your name?

JOOMFLANA cowers and looks confused.

> **JOOMFLANA**
> Mittakoo frop frop edch pomfrani. Dresh Joomflana. (Pausing) Emmasmiff?

> **EMMA**
> Yes! Yes! Emmasmiff! . . . Smith . . . So is your name Dresh Joonflana then?

> **JOOMFLANA** (Jumping up excitedly and grinning broadly)
> Edch! Edch! Edch! Joomflana! Joomflana!

> **EMMA**
> Well nice to meet you Joomflana!

JOOMFLANA beams at EMMA, grabbing her tightly round the waist.

> **JOOMFLANA** (Contentedly)
> Joomflana!

FADE INTO SCENE 10

MY GARDEN GNOMES ARE ALIENS EPISODE 1 SCENE 7 (MALE AUDITIONEE – ROLE OF NEDDAREEG)

INT DAY
JONATHAN SMITH is asleep in bed. He stirs, opens his eyes, rubs them and yawns. He sits up and is confronted by NEDDAREEG, a confident, jolly gnome, sitting at the bottom of his bed, playing with one of his shoes and grinning.

NEDDAREEG
Hespa rildy edch crulchit.

JONATHAN
Say what? Who are you and what are you doing on my bed? . . . with my shoe?

NEDDAREEG
Hoofla jupp jupps? Inta fringoo dresh Neddareeg!

JONATHAN
Umm no, we speak English here . . . you know? Eng-er-lish?

NEDDAREEG looks bewildered and baffled.

NEDDAREEG
Nedd-arrrrrrr-eeeeeeeeg! Hifly idlarp edch?

JONATHAN
Listen right, I dunno who you are or what you're doing in my room but I'd be grateful if you'd go please (Pointing towards the door) . . . erm . . . Like now!

NEDDAREEG looks sad, then jumps off the bed and excitedly points to the door.

NEDDAREEG
Iffly froop hensp! (Jumping up and down) Neddareeg! Neddareeg! Neddareeg!

JONATHAN
Like what's with all this Neddareeg stuff?

NEDDAREEG stares quizzically and unnervingly at JONATHAN for a few seconds.

JONATHAN
Man you're freaky! (Goes to the door, opens it, looks back and exits)

NEDDAREEG (Saddened that he's all alone)
Neddareeg.

CUT TO SCENE 8

So remember to . . .

✓   Be confident and prepared for ANYTHING.
✓   Be honest and truthful about yourself and your current capabilities.
✓   Know where you're going and allow enough time for everything.
✓   Use public transport instead of driving in London and other major cities.
✓   Ensure you have made any necessary provision for child or pet care.
✓   Research the company and people you will be meeting.
✓   Keep your skills, speeches and songs honed and learn new ones.
✓   Be adventurous, but realistic when choosing speeches.
✓   Practise your sight reading regularly.
✓   Inform all concerned if you are dyslexic and need time with the script.
✓   Check facilities for the disabled, if you need them.
✓   Always carry your résumé, photos and sheet music.
✓   Ensure your music is in the correct key and able to be easily read.

CHAPTER 3

Submitting Yourself for Work

How you respond to the casting information you receive can seriously affect your chance of being selected to audition. You will doubtless read many chapters on this subject during your career, so without wishing to bore you, here is some basic advice from one who opens thousands of letters every year.

When you are asked to write, that does not mean merely sending your enveloped résumé and photograph via the nearest post box. I find receiving just these two items without any written communication rude, and, depending on my mood and the usefulness of the artist concerned at the time of writing, it is the quickest way for a piece of post to find its way straight into the round file (waste paper bin). Call me old fashioned, but in these days of *Spotlight Link* and email submissions, it is refreshing to receive a succinct, well-crafted and presented letter through the post. By succinct, I mean three short, easily readable paragraphs explaining what you want, rather than page after page about your life story and career history (as many do). The paragraphs should be ordered as follows, and should be no more than two sentences each:

Dear name of person (or company if you *really* cannot find or research a contact name). How should we address the person? Dear John Smith? Dear Mr Smith? Dear John? All are acceptable, although nowadays the use of first names is prevalent in our industry, so you should probably avoid Mr Smith as it is considered rather formal, and you may wish to leave just the first name until you have actually met the person concerned. Therefore, Dear John Smith is your safest bet.

1   Why you are writing (e.g. I have heard that you are casting {name of production} and I am enclosing my details as I'd like to audition for the part of {name}).

2   Why they should see you above the other hundreds, or thousands, of people who have written in (e.g. I fit the character perfectly, as I am not only the correct age, height and look that you described in the breakdown/is in the script, but I also have excellent juggling skills (x balls and clubs), play the violin to grade x standard and speak fluent French, having lived for x years in Paris).

3   Why you are interested in working with the company and sign off (e.g. having seen several of your productions/ heard good things about your Company's work, I'd be interested in working with you and hope we can meet at your auditions).

Yours sincerely (as you will know or have researched the name of the person to whom you are writing, though if you really have to address a letter to the company name, 'Yours faithfully' should be used).

Your signature (always sign a letter, as if you send a printed or typed one, your signature is the only personal thing about you that the reader will see). Ensure your signature reflects you and avoid illegible squiggles – we often play guess the name in the office when the squiggle bears no relation to the person's actual name. When I started in business, I made the conscious decision to change mine from an appalling set of hieroglyphics to a more stylish and readable signature, for which I regularly get complimented. Using a coloured and/or thicker pen when signing letters will make a greater statement. Your name, both written and spoken, should be the most memorable detail about you, so ensure that it can always be easily read.

Your full professional name (typed or legibly written underneath your signature).

Present your letters and résumé on good quality paper (the same type and colour for both is advisable to create a firm corporate image) and use a good quality laser or inkjet printer.

Let's imagine that the following breakdown has been placed in one or more of the numerous casting information services:

XYZ Theatre Productions are currently casting a UK tour of a new musical, SONG OF SYRACUSE, and are looking for a male actor/musician in his mid–late twenties to play the role of 'Graham'. He should be at least 5'10" tall, have a strong tenor singing voice, up to a top B, a convincing American accent and should play guitar and saxophone to performance standard. A full, clean driving licence and experience of van driving is also an advantage. The production rehearses from 2 February, opens on 19 February and tours small- to middle-scale venues in the UK and Ireland until 4 April. Please send CVs and photos by 11 December to The Artistic Director, XYZ Theatre Productions, 41 Main Street, London WC2E 8TN.

Three friends from drama school, Tom, Robert and Sam, see this breakdown and all think about applying for the job.

Tom is 23, 5'8" tall, has a bass baritone singing voice, a passable American accent, drives and played guitar and drums in the school band as a teenager, but has not really played or practised since.

Robert is 26, 6'1" tall, has a strong tenor singing voice up to a top C, a good American accent, having lived in New York for six months before going to drama school, has driven delivery vans when not working as an actor and regularly plays trumpet, saxophone and lead guitar with a local jazz band.

Sam is 28, 5'10" tall, has a strong singing voice within easy reach of the top note, is a native of Florida with dual nationality, has driven large vans for a removal company, plays six musical instruments to performance standard, including lead and bass guitar and saxophone, and – is female.

So who should apply for this job? There will be a school of thought that says Robert and Sam, as the part may be able to be adapted into female. There will be another that believes that all three should apply, as the brief may be adaptable or changeable, or it is worth telling a few little white lies, as 'They're bound to change their minds about everything as soon as I walk through the door.' Lovely though that would be, if it were to happen, the harsh reality is that if specific criteria are clearly stated in a breakdown, they should be strictly adhered to. It is a waste of your time and resources, and the time of the company concerned, to apply.

Irritating though it may be, it is far more effective to wait and target the projects you actually do fit perfectly rather than waste time on those you do not, which will also gain you more respect among work-givers. I am not only dismayed by the amount of actors who don't suggest themselves appropriately, but amazed by the number of agents who do exactly the same and cannot, or choose not, to read a breakdown correctly. If you have had experiences like this with your agent (I once had an agent who thought I was six inches shorter than

I was, and therefore received strange looks and remarks that I was 'very tall' whenever I walked into a room), always check the brief with them, and if you do not fit the bill, tactfully tell them so and ask to be withdrawn from the session. After all, it is *you* that will look bad on the day, and not them.

So, back to *Song of Syracuse*, the three friends, being sensible, decided that only Robert should apply for the job, so he set about the task. When he reread the breakdown it said 'Send CVs and photos', so he initially just thought of putting his CV and photo in an envelope, but thought that might appear rude, so sat down at his computer and wrote the letter on the opposite page.

He printed his letter and was just about to post it when his flatmate, who worked in recruitment, walked in and read it. She pointed out to him that not only was his letter grammatically incorrect ('Yours sincerely' is only used when you know the name of the person to whom you are writing. If you use Dear Sir or otherwise 'Yours faithfully' is then the correct phrase) but it was also rather dull and uninspiring, and would fail to stand out from the other letters which they would doubtless receive. The phrase 'To whom it may concern' is not exactly endearing either (in fact it is the worst thing you could ever write in a letter to me and my concern for the writer immediately vanishes whenever I read it). 'After all, why should they see you above all the others?' she asked. 'Because I am absolutely perfect for the part,' replied Robert. 'Well make yourself stand out from the crowd and tell them exactly why you are so right.' So Robert sat again at the computer, reread the breakdown and set about thinking of what made him perfect for the part.

To start with, he wrote a keynote plan of the essential information he should include. This comprised the following:

- *Age* (the brief said mid–late twenties and he is 26)
- *Height* (at least 5'10" tall was required and he is 6'1" tall)
- *Vocal range* (a strong tenor singing voice, up to a top B was requested, and Robert's range more than fits the brief)

Robert Bloggs
17 Olivier Street.
London
W1A 1AB
07999 997799
bobdabloggs@hotmail.com

10 December 2009

To whom it may concern

I heard you are casting for Song Of Syracuse and an enclosing my
CV and photo for an audition.

I look forward to hearing from you.

Yours sincerely

- *Accent* (Robert has a good American accent, having lived in New York for six months)
- *Musician* (he plays both guitar and saxophone to performance standard with the jazz band)
- *Driving* (his driving licence is full and clean and he has driven delivery vans when not working as an actor)

He then started to write.

Robert Bloggs
17 Olivier Street.
London
W1A 1AB
07999 997799
bobdabloggs@hotmail.com

10 December 2009

Dear Sir/Madam

I heard that you are casting for the part of Graham in Song Of Syracuse. Well, you can stop looking right now, cos I am your man! No kidding, I really am and here's why.

OK where shall I start? Well the first thing you want is a bloke in his mid–late twenties, and I am 26, nearly 27, so I am mid-twenties, but getting later every day. The next thing you ask for is somebody over 5 feet 10 inches tall. Well I fit that one too, as I am 6'1", so there is tick number 2 on the list! Next, you said you wanted a strong tenor voice that can go up to a top B – well mine can easily go to a top C (well, not really early in the morning, but you know what I mean!), so once again, I am so right for you.

As for a convincing American accent, well that's me too, as I spent six months in New York in my gap year, and god what a laugh that was! I had an absolutely wicked time, with lots of nice girls, masses of food and an amazing social life, the beer sure did flow there (though it is not as strong as the beer in Belgium, man is that stuff lethal or what?, but that's another story!!!) While I was there though I did take the opportunity to do something positive for my career and learnt to speak the accent so everyone thought I was a native New Yorker, so that's another point to me!

Then you ask for a musician who can play guitar and saxophone, which I do (completely brilliantly, if I'm honest) in a local jazz band. I have been playing since I was a kid at school and play the trumpet well and drums fairly badly as well (especially after a few pints!!!) if you need them. I am sometimes amazed at my own versatility!!!

Last, but not least, I also drive delivery vans when I am not working as an actor, which let's face it is most of the time, as despite my huge talent and potential, this business is very unfair and I don't get seen for most of the stuff that I write off for. I really wonder why I bother sometimes, as most of these people don't deserve someone as good as me anyway, but I hope you will have more sense than those other tossers and give me the job (after all, you'd be bloody fools not to!!!) Needless to say, my van driving skills are really good though, after so long doing it. Life really is very unfair.

Anyway, I am enclosing my CV and photo for you to read and marvel at and I look forward to getting a call telling me where and when to come for an audition. You can write or email instead if you want, I really don't care how you do it – just do it, OK?

I can't wait to meet you and show you exactly what I can do and how amazingly brilliant I really am. See you then!

Yours faithfully

Robert's flatmate read this second draft and looked aghast. She told him that not only was the letter far too long and wordy, it was unprofessional, extremely negative and made him sound like an unemployable, big-headed alcoholic – not someone that a small company would wish to employ, especially if touring in a van.

She mentioned the points for good letter writing that I have outlined and told Robert to reconstruct his letter, keeping them firmly in mind. He was about to start, when he came across a major stumbling block – he didn't know the name of the artistic director, and, as he wanted to maximise his impact by addressing the letter personally, set about researching the information. He looked in *Contacts* under Theatre Producers, but there was no name, just a website, so he went online to see if the name was there. Looking in the 'Contact Us' section, he immediately found what he was looking for. The name he needed was Pat Jones, but another dilemma now faced him, was Pat male or female? He thought of playing safe and writing 'Dear Pat Jones', but instead picked up the phone and called the company's office. When the phone was answered, he asked 'I wonder if you can help me please? Is Pat Jones still your Artistic Director?' 'Yes she is', came the reply. Bingo! He thanked them and set about honing his letter, referring regularly to our paragraph guides and the essential information about himself. As he had a computer, he decided to smarten his image by creating a very simple letterhead as well as highlighting some key facts using bold type, thus making them stand out and the letter easier to read. His third attempt is opposite.

Both Robert and his flatmate agreed this was by far the best draft and it should be posted, as well as used as a basic template which could be tailored to suit future applications. He printed the letter and his résumé on some good quality paper to maximise the effect.

Surprising as it may sound, I receive letters similar to all three drafts through my letterbox every week. In fact, the second draft is rather tame compared to some that come through, which can be peppered with frustration, angst and even expletives, and somewhat longer

ROBERT BLOGGS

17 Olivier Street, London W1A 1AB
07999 997799 bobdabloggs@hotmail.com

Agent: John Smith at Premier Actors Management
020 7321 5678

10 December 2009

Ms Pat Jones
Artistic Director
XYZ Theatre Productions
41 Main Street
London
WC2E 8TN

Dear Pat Jones

I heard recently that you are casting a tour of '**SONG OF SYRACUSE**', so am enclosing my CV and photograph as I'd like to audition for the part of **Graham**.

Reading your brief, I fit all the aspects well, being in my **mid twenties** and **6 feet 1 inch tall**. I also have a **strong tenor voice, up to a high C**, I **play guitar, saxophone** and **trumpet** regularly in a local jazz band and, having lived in New York for six months as a student, have a **convincing American accent**. I also have extensive **van driving experience** and would happily do my share of the driving.

Having seen your production of '**A Midsummer Night's Dream**' a few years ago, I admire the way you work and would be very keen to be part of XYZ. I do hope we can meet at your auditions.

Yours sincerely

ROBERT BLOGGS

than the one printed here (the record is six A4 pages). Actually, no letter needs to be more than one page in length and often no more than the first sentence or paragraph will be read, so say what you want and be as concise as possible.

Before posting, always ensure that you have paid the correct postage for the weight and size of your letter, which can be done at your local post office, or online at www.royalmail.com. I regularly receive cards through my door telling me that an A4 envelope is awaiting my collection at the local sorting office (over a mile away), which will cost me £1.24 in additional charges to receive, as stamps of insufficient value have been attached. Not being made of money, I rarely pay for these and the post office's policy is return them to the sender.

When applying for work, always enclose a CV or résumé with your letter. This should be no more than one side of A4 paper in length, concisely written and well set out, ensuring it is easy to read. Essential information to include is: your name (perhaps in larger letters as a heading at the top), contact details, agent's details (if you have one), height, hair colour, eye colour, build or clothing size and measurements (though these are more useful in the case of models), age or playing range (this is optional, and can be contentious, but sometimes useful), skills at which you excel (including native dialect), perhaps a paragraph entitled background, if you have entered the business late or are returning to it after a break, and your credits. The credits should be neatly presented in readable columns, the headings of which should include: Company/Venue, Production, Part and Director. You could also include the years in which you did the jobs, but this is far from essential and can be awkward to explain if you have suffered long periods of unemployment between jobs. Always ensure that names of companies, plays, roles and directors are spelt correctly, as many people within the Industry will spot your mistakes and you will lose brownie points – especially if it is the misspelt director themselves. Here is an example of a well-presented résumé.

ROBERT BLOGGS

Agent
John Smith
Premier Actors Management
72 Covent Garden Street
London WC2A 2AA
Tel: 020 7321 5678
john@premact.co.uk

Home
17 Olivier Street
London W1A 1AB
Mobile: 07999 997799
bobdabloggs@hotmail.com

Spotlight page: 1234/View PIN: 1234–5678–9012–3456
Equity Member (M001234567)
Playing range: 23–29

Height: 6'1" (185cm); Hair: dark brown; Eyes: blue/grey; Build: medium

TRAINING
ABC Academy of Drama, London, 3-year BA Hons course (graduated 2005)

THEATRE includes:

Company	Production	Role	Director
Kent Stage Co	**DEATH OF A SALESMAN**	*Biff*	John Bell
Loft Theatre	**RETURN TO THE FORBIDDEN PLANET**	*Bosun Arras*	Chris Wade
Theatre for Schools	**A IS FOR APPLE**	*Tom*	Derek McBride
Packet Theatre	**THE RIVALS**	*Bob Acres*	Winnie Clinch
ABC Academy	**ROMEO AND JULIET**	*Romeo*	Keith Graves
ABC Academy	**ANIMAL FARM**	*Benjamin*	Chris Black
ABC Academy	**BLOOD BROTHERS**	*Perkins*	Keith Graves

TELEVISION

BBC	**DOCTORS**	*Mr Hatchett*	Leonie Smith

SHORT FILMS

Nail Productions	**SHE'S THE ONE**	*Nick*	Al Francis
Kent Film School	**LEFT WITH THE WIND**	*Joe Parks*	Rufus Tweddle

SKILLS
- Vocal range: tenor (two octaves to top C), plays guitar, trumpet, saxophone and kazoo to performance standard, basic drums, sight reads music.
- Native accent: Kent, excellent American accents (lived in New York), RP.
- Strong swimmer (swam for Kent County), plays tennis, football, lacrosse.
- Full, clean driving licence, including Heavy Goods Vehicles.

As you can see, it is easy to read with the credits in clear columns, well spaced and different styles of lettering used for the productions and roles played. Use this as a basis for experimenting with the design of your own CV.

When it comes to photographs, the rule is simple: the picture on someone's desk should be a clear image of you that will be instantly recognised as soon as you walk into any audition room. If you have several looks (hair up and down, clean shaven or bearded, smart or casual, etc.) make sure the look you portray corresponds with your attire on the day. Keep your photographs up to date – it can be amazing how quickly you change without realising it yourself. Changing photographs at least every three years, if not more frequently, is advisable. Advertisements of theatrical photographers, often containing sample shots, can be found in *Contacts* and a good selection of portfolios is available for perusal at *Spotlight*'s London office. When choosing a photographer, ask yourself whether studio or outdoor shots would suit you best, as well as colour or black and white. Personally, I prefer outdoor shots, as these show you more as you really are. Studio sessions are often more glamorous and can be touched up with various shades of paint or computer programs by the photographers to remove blemishes. As you get older, please steer clear of soft lens shots that blur away lines and wrinkles. While we would all like to be thought of as younger than we are, a sharp photo showing exactly what you look like is far more effective, especially as faces invariably get increasingly interesting the older they get. Ageing is a journey – it shows you have lived.

When you get your photographs reproduced, they should be of good quality, but size is unimportant. The traditional size to send is 10×8, but prints and postage can be expensive, so you may choose to go smaller, or, as long as it is of reasonable quality, a scanned photo on your résumé will suffice (use white and not coloured paper in this case). If you are going to send more than one photo, make sure they are different looks, as I am always amazed how many people send several versions of the same shot – boring to the eye and a waste of money. If anyone wants a big glossy pic they will ask, so ensure you keep some in your audition briefcase, together with an up-to-date résumé.

Lastly, please ensure everything is stapled together (avoid using paperclips) and that your name and contact details are clearly visible on *everything* you send – letters, résumé and the back of photographs – in case items get separated. This can be handwritten, done with your own computer-generated labels or reasonably priced printed labels can be ordered from www.able-labels.co.uk or most good stationers. Some casting personnel prefer the résumé to be stuck or stapled on to the back of a 10×8 photograph, making it easier to read. This is standard practice in North America.

If you have done some work on camera, you may want to get clips of your appearances edited into a short showreel, which you can then send out on DVD (especially when suggesting yourself for a part on television or film) or have linked to your website or *Spotlight* Interactive page. You could do this yourself using editing software, or use one of the many showreel companies that advertise in *Contacts* and other trade publications, many of these are good, but can be expensive. By far the best showreels I have seen have been made by the London-based actor Bill Thomas (www.billthomas.biz), who provides a personalised, reasonably priced service – when acting work permits – and comes highly recommended.

Another way to get yourself into the minds of work-givers is to let them know when they can see you in action, either on stage or screen. I very rarely invite an artist to audition for my employers without having first seen their work. The only time I take risks is when we are looking for a very specific type or skill and there are a limited number of artists to choose from. I always try to see people's work beforehand so that I can speak honestly and accurately about the person concerned to the creatives, using knowledge gained from first-hand experience – as I've mentioned before, the contents of a résumé can be deceptive. So, what are the best ways of inviting people to see you, and what should you keep in mind?

First, ensure the part that you are playing is worth people coming to see or tuning in to watch (asking people to see you play a non-speaking part will rarely help your career). Keep in mind that people's diaries can get booked up quite a way in advance and they are rarely willing to travel too far from where they are based, even if you volunteer to pay their travel expenses. If you know that you will be in a stage show for a limited run, or on the television on a certain date, make sure that you give them enough notice. Two or three weeks before a theatre run starts is probably the best time to write, and a few days before the transmission date of a television episode (or first episode if you are in more than one) is the most effective timescale. Some people make contact far too early (sometimes three to six months ahead), while others post a letter on Thursday informing of a show that ends that Saturday. Both of these are not worth sending, so find a happy medium. Next, think about the type of people you want to target and what you want to achieve from them seeing you. You might want to invite agents to see you with a view to repre-senting you; there might be certain theatre companies that you are keen to work with; people you have met and wanted to keep in touch with, or you may just want to get your face known and remembered by casting directors, in the hope that they will bring you in for their future projects. Write lists of those you want to invite or inform ahead of time, which you can always add to or amend later. Then, try to make your invitation as appealing as possible. I receive upwards of three invitations every day to see shows, showcases, understudy matinees, films and television programmes, and as much as I would like to, I am unable to see everything. Take time to think of the selling points of your production, these might include: the length of the piece (short is good, especially as some of us are out several nights a week), a large cast with a good mixture of types may be more alluring than watching a one person show, perhaps a piece that is more comic than tragic may appeal more after a long hard day in the office, a venue that is easily accessible by car or public transport and comfortable to sit in is always welcome, as possibly is the offer of a drink or refreshments on arrival, in the interval or after the show.

Think of what would make you go to see your show rather than all the others that are around. Always offer complimentary tickets to those you invite, even if you have to pay for them yourself. They are tax deductible against any money you earn and a very worthwhile career investment, as it may lead to future work. There is advice in Chapter 36, 'Negotiation', about how to ask for tickets for those you wish to invite from the Industry.

In the case of television appearances, make it easy for the viewer to spot you: in addition to your character's name, succinctly describe the character and what he or she does in the episode concerned. I have frequently watched a full episode only to realise when looking at the credits that the actor I liked was the same person who wrote to me. If you can, always offer to send a DVD copy if anyone is unable to watch your episode and wants to see it.

While contacting people by email is effective, quick and cheap, your invitation will be more noticeable if it is sent through the post, as more action is required to open a letter than an email, and a piece of paper has to be stored as opposed to quickly getting lost in a bulging inbox. Rather than writing an ordinary letter, you may choose to make your invitation eye-catching, which will increase people's memory and awareness. I have had some brilliantly imaginative invitations over the years, such as my own hospital appointment card for *Casualty* and a note asking me to watch a series about horse racing that was printed on an actual betting slip. These still stick in my mind for their originality and wit, though they have now been done and so please don't copy them. If you want to invite people using this method, think of your own ideas and execute them as artistically as you can. Perhaps you can think of something as a company, in the case of a show, and send out a mailshot from you all rather than many individual letters.

If you can persuade people to stay for a drink after a theatre show, it is a great way of meeting, and for them to get to know you. If you have an agent, you can ask them to bring casting directors to see you while you are working, as the people they bring may be more inclined to stay behind with your agent, than just with you, if you invite them personally. If your agent does come to see you, bringing people with them, or not, and you also have family or friends there on the same night, your agent and their guest(s) must be your first priority – after all, this is business and could lead to castings and work in the future. It will also give them an opportunity to get to know you the person, as well as you the performer. Inform your friends that your agent is also in and you will need to spend some time chatting with them before you will be free to socialise. Ask those people who have come to support you to wait (however long this may take) in a bar or restaurant that you have pre-agreed and spend as long with your agent and whoever they have brought as necessary, letting them decide when it is time to go. They may only stay and chat for a couple of minutes (as they will doubtless have had a long day in their offices beforehand, and may have long journeys back home), which is fair enough, but they may invite you to join them for drinks or supper and keep you talking for far longer. Whatever you do, do not cut the meeting short yourself, or greet them with 'Thank you all for coming and sorry I can't stop, but I've got friends in' – this will not go down well with any of them. If you advise work-givers you invite to call your agent for tickets on your invitation, do make sure that your agent is primed for this and be prepared to pay for the tickets, if necessary. You should also include contact details for yourself as well as your agent, in case of any problems. Adhere to these rules and you can have an extremely effective marketing tool indeed, which may keep you working for years to come.

Finally, a few thoughts about publicising your career and yourself online. If you are going to email work-givers, ensure you have something pertinent to say, rather than just emailing for the sake of it. This might be news of a television appearance or an invitation to a show, or, for example, the launch of your online showreel or website. As I have already mentioned, spam and viruses are a worry, so the more you can reassure those you send to that this is not the case, the better. Avoid sending large attachments – or any attachments, if you can – and, as the majority of spam is sent in the middle of the night and downloaded into inboxes at the start of each working day, your email will stand a better chance of being read if it is sent during office hours (which are normally between 10am and 6pm in our industry). Always make sure it has a relevant subject heading (I am always dubious of mails without a subject, or subjects that sound like disguised spamming) and that your email address contains your full professional name (rather than your real name or a pseudonym, no matter how wacky or clever you may think it is). You can easily set one up via the free web-based email services, which can often be used with Outlook Express (Windows Mail) and other email programs, or investigate buying your own domain name, to which you can then attach a website.

On the subject of websites, if you are going to include a link to yours in email correspondence, or attach it to your *Spotlight* page, always be sure that not only is your site complete and contains up-to-date information, but also that the link and address actually work. I regularly click on hyperlinks, or type an address only to find that the site in question is still under construction, or worse still, the page cannot be displayed, which is irritating to say the least. While they may take a little more effort to create, websites are far easier to view and all your information and photographs, including production shots, can be kept in one place. Avoid sending links to your MySpace, YouTube, Facebook and other social networking pages; and do not invite potential employers you have never met to be your online friends or tag them. This happens increasingly often, so prevent this from accidentally occurring by creating two separate email address books – one for business and one for pleasure.

So remember to . . .

✓ Research as much as you can about the project and people.
✓ Be honest and don't waste your time if you do not fit a specific brief.
✓ Make a checklist of the requirements and how you fit them.
✓ Be specific and concise when writing letters – one page is enough.

✓ Always address letters by name and end them correctly.

✓ Print letters and CVs on good quality matching paper.

✓ Ensure each photograph is different, if you must send more than one.

✓ Staple everything together.

✓ Ensure your name and contact details are on every item you send.

✓ Always affix the correct postage for your letter's size and weight.

✓ Invite people to see your work with a view to future employment.

✓ Make invitations appealing and possibly eye catching.

✓ Always offer complimentary tickets, even if you have to pay for them.

✓ Ensure your agent and guests have priority over friends after shows.

✓ Email during office hours, avoid attachments and include a subject.

✓ Ensure links are active and websites constructed before mentioning.

✓ Keep separate address books and contacts for business and pleasure.

CHAPTER 4

Agents

As I have mentioned, agents are not the be all and end all of an actor's career and you should always be proactive in your own career and explore suitable work opportunities whether you have an agent or not. There are advantages to having one though. A good agent can be an excellent help in guiding your career and procuring auditions on your behalf, as it is their job to have an ear firmly pressed to the ground, hearing about many projects of which you will be totally unaware until they are released in the cinema, transmitted on television or had their opening night. An agent should, hopefully, also have enough personal contacts, respect and influence to receive breakdowns that are not in the public domain and then either remind those responsible for casting of your existence or persuade them of your suitability and get you through the door to meet the work-givers. This will be achieved by building good relationships and rapport with the casting directors, resulting in trust in their judgement and taste in actors, which might take years to gain, or may never happen at all. However, since the deregulation of the closed shop, *anyone* can set up as an agent and represent artists, and I am afraid to say that a great many do, with minimal knowledge, few contacts and little previous experience. You could even do so yourself, with whatever skill you have – though please don't, as it really is not as easy as it sounds. The best agents are those who trained with another agent as an assistant and have therefore amassed the experience to sell their clients and effectively negotiate deals on their behalf. Those agents who are members of the Personal Managers' Association (www.thepma.com) are all experienced – one prerequisite of joining is trading for at least three years – but, as with the Casting Directors' Guild, membership is not obligatory, and many good and well-established agents do not belong. There is now a vast list of agents spread over sixty-odd pages in *Contacts* and, worryingly, in twenty years of casting, I have still to receive any form of communication from a fair percentage of them.

So how do you find the right one? First, think about what you are looking for in an agent. Do you want someone with whom you will have a strictly business relationship, someone you can talk to on a friendlier level or a mixture of the two? The latter is the most common option, but each to their own. Would you feel more comfortable with a man or a woman and someone younger or older? Think about these factors before looking around and making approaches. If possible, you can ask any casting directors you know and who have invited you in for auditions for their thoughts on specific agents (if they have not heard of them it's worth steering clear) or if there is anyone they could recommend (keeping in mind, however, that they are not free information services). Some will not commit themselves and will not answer the question, which is fair enough and should be accepted; others, if they know you very well, might offer to speak to suitable agents on your behalf. Either way, it's worth asking. Also, if you are working in a show, ask your fellow cast members who represents them and what they think of their agents (as with networking, it's best to ask those who are not in direct competition with you). If the agent intends to come and see the production in which you are both appearing, you can write to them saying you are looking for representation and asking them to keep a lookout for you when they come. While *Spotlight* has sadly stopped running their free specialist advisory service, one of their former advisors, John Colclough, (www.johncolclough.org.uk) now offers experienced, expert and impartial guidance for a small fee. Having known John as an actor and during his twenty-plus years at *Spotlight*, I highly recommend his knowledgeable service.

Agents receive many requests from prospective clients and take on relatively few new artists every year, so while getting interviews with them is not easy, it's worth persevering and preparing for when they occur. When meeting an agent to discuss representation, ask straight and pertinent questions. These should include how long they have been trading, questions about their background and progression (if they worked as an assistant before they started their own agency), how many clients they represent, how they perceive you and where they see you fitting into their list, how many clients are currently working and in what sort of productions and with which casting directors and production companies they enjoy good relationships. They will ask you questions too, such as the type of work that you are looking for and what you hope they would do for you, who knows and likes you, what sort of auditions you have had in the past and where you see yourself fitting into the entertainment industry? Any agent who takes you on must feel confident that they will be able to sell you and, more importantly, make money out of you, as the only income that most receive is a commission (a percentage, usually between 10 and 15, plus VAT or other local tax, of the money you earn while you are working). In other words, when you are not working, they're not earning. If an agent asks you for a joining fee, book fee or any other kind of payment over and above their commission, think hard and ask advice before agreeing to pay.

The vast majority of agents will want to see you in action in theatre or on screen before committing to representing you. While this may be a catch-22 situation – how do you get a job without an agent, and vice versa – it is fair, as the agent needs to know that you can deliver the goods in addition to interviewing well. If this is not possible at the time, ask if you can keep in touch, especially if you both get on well, and make contact in the future when you have some work to show them. A few ask to see audition pieces and songs in their offices and may take you on as a result, if they like what they see, though it can be daunting, standing in what could be a small and cramped space trying to be dramatic or tuneful. However, always play along as you never know where it could lead. If an agent is interested but unsure, they may volunteer to look out for suitable jobs for you, perhaps suggesting you for them, without committing to representing you on a sole basis. Accept this, as it may eventually lead to full representation with them, or be a good stopgap until you find yourself another agent. However, this is not something you can ask someone to do – they must suggest it, and they will if they feel confident enough to help you and want to pursue matters.

When you get taken on by an agent, hopefully all will go well, with them working hard on your behalf to keep you being seen and in work. While it may be their job, everyone likes to be appreciated, so always remember to thank them, and their assistants, for their hard work, especially when it results in a job. A card and gift at Christmas is a welcome gesture too, especially if you have had a good year, and a mention in your acceptance speech when you collect your Oscar, or any other award, is also a nice touch, and vital if they are there with you.

An interesting question that often arises is whether commission should be paid to an agent on work that has been obtained directly through your own endeavours or existing contacts. I believe it always should be paid, for three very good reasons. First, they should be working hard procuring you auditions and work for after your contract is finished as well as inviting casting people to see you in action while you are doing it, even bringing them at their own expense. Second, the commission and VAT they charge are tax deductible against your earnings, in other words, deducted from the income on which you have to pay tax, so if you are earning enough to be charged tax, it is surely better to give that money to someone to work on your behalf than to the tax man. Lastly, it may be that you are known to the caster or director as a result of reputation and your agent's hard work in the past (Dame Judi Dench is probably suggested for very little, yet receives offers galore). You are a percentage of your agent's income, however small that may be and, as you may not be in constant work fifty-two weeks a year, while they are spending time and money working for you, they should be allowed to earn from you whenever possible. If, however, you are so unhappy with your agent that you cannot bear to give them any more money, it is better to leave them before accepting the job and go it alone until you find alternative representation.

While unrepresented artists feel their professional lives would be improved immeasurably by getting a good agent, those who are represented are sometimes far from happy. I often hear cries of 'my agent does nothing for me' and 'I have only had x/no auditions from my agent this year'. While the latter statement may be true, the former most probably is not, although your frustration is under-standable, especially if your friends have been seen for juicy jobs galore when you have not. Keep in mind that your agent might well be working tirelessly for you, submitting your details for every job for which you fit the brief (and some you don't), but their labours have not borne fruit. If this is the case, it may put your mind at rest to discuss with them the reasons why this might be happening and strategies to improve your success rate. If you are feeling brave, you could also phone to ask them what they have put you up for (which can be equally depressing if the list is short, or excessively long). If you have heard about a project for which you feel you are right, you could ask if you have been submitted and if it would be a good idea for you to write personally. Do not do either of these too often as it can irritate agents if they feel they are being told how to do their jobs. It has been said that every actor should spend a week working in their agent's office so that they can see the other side of the coin. Having done this, I can vouch that it is very frustrating when someone you totally believe to be perfect for a part doesn't even get a look in – nobody ever said this business was a fair one. Never forget that your agent can only get you the audition or interview. After that, getting the job is up to you and their work is over until you actually receive an offer when they will negotiate your deal and look after the business side. Sadly, agents are sometimes blamed not only when actors don't get seen, but also when they are not recalled or offered the job! Think about this before letting rip – especially to your agent.

Changing your agent is not a decision to be taken lightly, so give the situation a good deal of thought before taking any action. It is said that changing agents is like changing deckchairs on *The Titanic* – you still may not get the auditions you think you should and will be no better off. First, think why you want to change. Are things really that bad, or could they be resolved or at least improved by talking things through? If you have been together for some time, leaving your agent may feel like a divorce and indeed it can be a hard thing to do. Before doing anything, talk to them about the situation, preferably face to face and over lunch, if you can afford it – this way you will be on neutral territory and away from their ringing phones and other distractions. Voice your concerns and listen to their thoughts, asking them how they feel things are going, being open to discussion and suggestion. If, at the end of your conversation, you still feel it would be best to move on, do so amicably, as you can never be sure when you might need their help again – or want to return if the grass elsewhere was not as green as you first thought it would be. Beware of approaching new agents while you are still represented, as agents frequently talk to each other and bad feeling can occur if your agent discovers you are looking to change behind their back – somewhat like dating other people before ending your current relationship.

Conversely, your agent might drop you from their list if they no longer feel they can sell you effectively, or indeed want to do so. In this situation you have no choice but to move on and work hard for yourself, while searching for a new agent to look after you. This may be demoralising at the time – especially if their 'Dear John' letter has been sent together with your remaining photographs, but it is for the best, as if your agent is not prepared to work enthusiastically on your behalf, your photographs will just gather dust in their filing cabinet and nothing will be gained for anyone.

You may be offered representation by a bigger and better agent, while you are still with your current one (this is known as 'poaching') and promised bigger and better things if you move. Beware of this and think seriously about the implications before deciding. While the carrots dangled before you may sound tempting – especially if your contemporaries are doing better work than you are – will the service, care and attention you receive from your smaller agent be as forth-coming from a person or organisation with bigger, higher earning clients than yourself? Sometimes it works, sometimes not. It depends what you want and need at the time. If you are going to be lured away, do it with your eyes open, rather than covered with rose-tinted spectacles, and remember the old Northern adage: 'If it ain't broke, don't fix it.'

Co-operative agencies

As mentioned in Chapter 1, 'Where to find Auditions', many of the early co-operatives (dating back to the late 1970s and early 1980s) were formed by groups of like-minded actors who pooled their contacts and knowledge and represented each other. They primarily did this because they had become frustrated with the service they were receiving from conventional agents and wanted more control over their own careers. The movement was, on the whole, very successful, as many of the members were experienced and could push the newer actors to those employers they knew. Indeed, some famous people started in co-ops: Oscar-winner Julie Walters, nominee Emily Watson and film and television actors Alfred Molina, Pete Postlethwaite, Tim Roth, Michelle Collins, Dougray Scott and Freema Aygeman are just a few of the many well-known and respected actors who have been members of co-ops.

The only potential downside of co-operative agencies is the lack of continuity. To alleviate this problem, some co-ops are now run by paid co-ordinators, assisted by the agency's members, which has helped increase continuity and the building of rapports. Some actors see co-ops as an easier option than getting on to the books of good conventional agents, but this is far from the case: first, a genuine interest and passion for the co-operative movement and its ethos is insisted upon; second, a time commitment for running the office and attending regular meetings in-between acting jobs is essential (which can be tough if you have to earn a living elsewhere to survive); and lastly, the application process is far more stringent. Instead of having to convince one, two or a handful of people that you are the right actor for their list, you will need to persuade the majority, sometimes all, of a co-op's membership that you are for them, which can be a lengthy process. If you are excited and not deterred by these criteria, then this avenue is well worth exploring, when you are seeking representation.

You should start by chatting whenever possible to members of co-ops, asking questions and their advice on applying and being part of one. They may even give you an introduction or recommendation to their agency – after all, it's not what you know, it's who you know. General information can be found by visiting the CPMA (Co-operative Personal Management Association) website (www.cpma.co.uk), where you will also find links to the individual sites of their member agencies. However, like the PMA, membership is not obligatory and not all belong.

Whether you have an agent or not, and whatever stage of your career you are at, you should *never* stop working on your own behalf (in tandem with them), and suggesting yourself for work. It can be reassuring to whoever's casting to receive approaches from both the agent and their client, expressing interest in a part or project. Be sure to ask your agent if they have any criteria when it comes to suggesting their clients (for example, they may not accept commercials that pay below a certain amount or projects for which payment is deferred). Respect their views on these, as they will be taking this stand with their clients' best interests in mind, so don't suggest yourself for jobs that may cause potentially awkward situations to arise.

So remember to . . .

✓ Think about what you are looking for in a prospective agent.
✓ Ask others about their agents, especially when working with them.
✓ Check for experience and contacts.
✓ Ask pertinent questions when meeting agents.
✓ Remember it is you that actually gets the job and not your agent.
✓ Thank them for their hard work and remember them at Christmas.
✓ Talk through concerns, preferably in a neutral place.
✓ Think carefully before you move on – is the grass really greener?
✓ Remember bigger isn't always better – if it ain't broke, don't fix it!
✓ Never stop working for yourself, whether you are represented or not.
✓ Work in tandem with your agent, respecting their criteria for fees.

CHAPTER 5

Audition Log

Some people remember every second of every audition they do – reliving it in their heads – especially if it had, or had not, gone the way they wanted – but it is still a good idea to keep a record on file. This can prove useful if you meet the same company or person again, maybe years later for a different project.

On the following pages, there are some ideas for items to include, which can be tailored depending on the type of audition, what happened and who you met. You can create and customise your own log, or use ours as a template.

Fill in all the details you have prior to the audition when you receive the appointment, being sure to get as much information as possible and the other names and thoughts as soon as you can after the audition, while they are still fresh in your mind.

This is a useful memory tool to keep by the phone, prompting you to ask all the right questions when you are called with an appointment. By keeping this record, you can look back on auditions, perhaps for inspiration if you have a meeting for a similar type of project in the future, as well as monitoring your own progression as your experience and confidence grow.

AUDITION LOG

Date of audition: __/__/__   Time of audition:...................................
Production: ....
Dates: rehearse   __/__/__   open/shoot __/__/__   finish __/__/__
Character name: ....
Character description/Requirements: ....
....
....
Production company: ....
Audition venue: ....
Address: ....
....
Emergency telephone number: ....
Nearest station/Directions: ....
....
....
I got the audition through: an agent/my own efforts/other

Creative team (**names and descriptions**):
Director:..
Choreographer:...
Musical director: ....
Casting director: ....
Writer: ....
Producer: ....
Assistants: ....
Pianist: ....
Cameraman: ....

What I needed to prepare: ....
....

What I read: ....

Which speech(es) I did: ....

....

What I sang: ....

What they asked me to do: ....

....

....

....

....

What I wore: ....

....

How I felt: ....

....

....

....

....

The panel's reaction (including feedback and criticism): ....

....

....

....

....

Was I recalled?...

What would I improve or do differently next time? ....

....

....

....

....

....

Outcome: ....

....

....

....

Finally, a word about assistants. Please do not forget assistant directors, choreographers, musical directors and casting assistants. The assistant of today may be the boss of tomorrow, so be nice to and make an especial note of them, as who knows what the future may bring.

So remember to . . .

✓ Fill in as much information as you can get prior to the day.
✓ Write memory-jogging descriptions of those you have met for the future.
✓ Write detailed notes on your performance and feelings.
✓ Always include assistants. You never know what they will become.
✓ Keep your log on file and refer to it regularly.

CHAPTER 6

Audition Wardrobe

While you will often wear your ordinary everyday street clothes to auditions, we will talk about 'dressing for the part' in later chapters, so think ahead and start to assemble your own audition wardrobe. This may contain items of clothing and accessories that suggest a type, or types, that you are right to play – perhaps things that are plainer, more formal, casual or outlandish than you would normally wear but which make you look different, younger or older than you actually are, or appear to be.

If, for instance, you look young enough for it to be believed that you are in your latter years at school, keep your last school blazer and tie, which you can wear with a white shirt and black trousers or skirt. On the other hand, you may be able to look somewhat older than you are, or ordinarily do (without vast amounts of make-up, prosthetics or alcohol). An actress I know has accumulated a good collection of middle-aged and 'mumsy' dresses, blouses, twin sets, cardigans, etc., cheaply from charity shops and jumble sales, and, while sometimes a far cry from her everyday clothes, they regularly contribute to her getting work.

Small items of jewellery to conjure a style or look can also be useful, and everyone (male and female) should possess a plain gold wedding band, which does not have to be twenty-four carat – costume will do fine, though make sure it doesn't turn your finger green when you wear it.

Wear something to help the panel to pick you out from the rest of the competition. I'm not talking lime green suits or other outrageously coloured clothes, but something bright will get you noticed and act as a memory aide for those you are meeting. A tie, scarf, necklace, brooch or pocket handkerchief that is a little different from the norm will be memorable. Avoid wearing all black, which many people do, while it may look good, it can make you indistinguishable. The same goes for dancers in a big dance call (like that seen in the movie *A Chorus Line*). Many will wear brightly coloured vests, jazz bottoms, tights or leotards to stand out from the crowd, and will be referred to as 'The girl in light blue' etc. This is a good thing, making life easier for those on the panel, and should be continually adhered to, especially as an increasing number are reverting to the dreaded black. Wearing the same outfit if you are recalled will help to remind the panel of you, so make sure it is clean and well pressed after your first audition, just in case.

Think seriously about your type and playing range and invest in several interchangeable looks, including formal, informal, smart-casual and casual, using your own interpretation for each and asking the advice of others where necessary. As I've already mentioned, this need not cost you a fortune, especially as you won't wear these often, so designer labels are unnecessary. Always keep an eye out and think of the potential of a certain garment for your professional life. Being unprepared when a deadline is short will cost you more financially and increase your stress levels, so the fuller your dressing up box can be, the better. Remember, though, that nobody wants, or needs to see you in the full regalia complete with accessories, as this can be considered patronising and induce broad grins and giggles from the panel, so just a hint of costume to fire the imagination will suffice – and can work wonders for your success.

So remember to . . .

✓   Keep a supply of useful clothes to create types and looks.
✓   Wear memorable accessories to inspire.
✓   Look out for bargains in charity shops and car boot sales.
✓   Wear something distinctive so you will be memorable.
✓   Give a hint of costume, but don't go over the top.

CHAPTER 7

Perceptions

We have talked about dressing for the part and creating an audition wardrobe, but it is also valuable to consider others' perceptions. How work-givers perceive us is important, especially during the first meeting. There is nothing truer than the old adage 'You never get a second chance to make a first impression.' That impression may be when making your entrance into the building or room, near the venue (perhaps at the station or in the car park), it may even be ages before the event in some totally unrelated place. It is worth remembering that, as a performer, you publicise yourself photographically and therefore can be recognised by those you have contacted and are going to meet. Many directors, producers and casting directors shun such publicity – there are many members of my profession that I wouldn't recognise if I walked past them in the street, but all of us will recognise some performers from the photographs they have sent us, by seeing their work or from having met or auditioned them. It is therefore important to be on your best behaviour at all times, especially when en route to an audition. I remember a director with whom I was working coming into a room in high dudgeon. He had been lost and had asked someone the way to the audition venue. The person – who was booked in to see us half an hour later – told him the way, facetiously adding 'But I hardly think you're right for anything they'll be seeing people for.' The look on the poor actor's face when I introduced them was a picture, and his embarrassment undermined his confidence, weakening his audition.

I recognise many actors who live in my neighbourhood when passing them in the street, having seen their work in theatre, television or film. Most are not aware of me, even though I may have met some of them in a different context or place. There was one well-known actor who regularly walked down my street and we always nodded or said hello to each other whenever we met. I knew full well who he was, but he had not a clue about me. One night, when seeing a show at a drama school on the other side of London, I met my neighbour in the bar and he came over to say hello. I could tell he was surprised to see me there, 'Are you a student here?' he asked. 'No, I am just here to see the show,' I replied. 'Well I hope you enjoy it,' he said, and walked off. As far as he was concerned, I was an enthusiastic theatregoer who had travelled across London to see drama students in a show.

There is also a very well-respected director who lives locally. I, like all of you, know who he is as his name and photograph regularly appears in the newspapers. I see this man frequently in the supermarket, the street or at opening nights and he always says hello to me. He knows that he knows me but doesn't know who I am or what I do for a living. If I were pushier, I would have given him my CV years ago and asked for a job; however, shyness prevails in my case, though perhaps one day we may be formally introduced and work together.

So should we all be more pushy and will doing this get us further up the career ladder? The answers to these questions depend on several factors, such as the person concerned and the way the situation is judged and handled. There is a time and place for everything and people's privacy should be observed (the same goes with stars and fans). If I am at the theatre or an industry party, then I am more than happy to talk shop (like an actor being asked for autographs at a stage door or while making a personal appearance). However, if I am doing my shopping, enjoying a quiet meal or am on holiday, I would prefer not to have CVs or showreels thrust into my hands, be regaled with tales of woe about someone's career, or the lack of it, be asked why I never get them in for castings or to recommend a good new agent.

All these happen on a fairly regular basis, I always respond politely, but those who behave in this way rarely endear themselves to me. There are some who are pushy to the point of obsession (one of my colleagues had to call the police when an abusive drunken actor persistently rang her doorbell at 3am), but if you think matters through and approach somebody politely in an appropriate situation, you will be perceived as likeable and thus receive a more positive response.

When you arrive at an audition venue, always take an interest in everyone you meet, finding out their names and what they do (remembering these facts will earn you extra brownie points). An extremely well-known actor endeared himself to staff at film studios by not only recognising them when he returned, sometimes after a gap of many years, but remembering their names and other information which had come up in conversation, such as their children, wives or husbands and the area in which they lived. This was no ploy, as he was a genuinely nice man and believed in treating people with the respect they deserved – it didn't matter to him that he was the star on that set, he was first and foremost a human being. This is a lesson from which we could all learn at times. Be nice to absolutely *everyone*, as you never know who they are, or might become in the future (many a casting director has been brushed aside as a mere tea boy or lady by arrogant, ill-informed actors).

For the human memory to work and our minds to process things, everything must be given a label. Therefore, a performer's name is by far the most important feature about them. People only become famous, or even recognisable, because we remember their names – rather than 'That tall chap' or 'The blonde girl' – so if no one can remember your name, you will not be remembered, no matter how well you are perceived as a human being. The importance of names will be looked at in depth in Chapter 25, but, in the meantime, think about your own name – whether it is the one you were born with, or have chosen to work under – how it will be remembered and the image it projects.

As well as being perceived as someone who is pleasant, well behaved and worth employing, it is vital to show people what they want to see from the moment you walk into the building. This might mean 'acting' – looking or behaving in a way you wouldn't normally, or speaking with a regional dialect that isn't the one you use in everyday life. Start the pretence way before you reach the audition venue, making everyone believe that you are what you say you are. Keep it up until way after you leave the venue, just in case your cover is blown. There is nothing more gratifying on the first day of a job than seeing the look of surprise on the director's face when they discover that you are actually ten years younger, or naturally talk in a different accent or dialect instead of the one they wanted to hear and assumed was your own. Be prepared, however, to reassure them that it is really you and that you can repeat and sustain what you did at the audition.

Another differing perception might be the outcome of an audition. How you feel you have done and the panel's thoughts on the situation could be two different matters entirely. Sometimes you will feel the job is yours and in the bag (perhaps because you have been given that impression by the creative team). Indeed, this may have been the case at that time, until someone who came in later changed their point of view and pipped you to the post. This often happens, with minds sometimes changing as every new person walks through the door, so that everyone who auditions believes they are first choice and the last person in gets the job. They may, however, be letting you down gently by making you feel you have done a better audition than you have, so do your best to forget about it and don't be surprised if you hear nothing. On the other hand, you might come out of the room and feel you have not fulfilled your potential but the panel may have thought very differently, liking you enough to recall or offer you the job. You could have been second or third choice – you will never know if the first choice accepts, and it is not something you will be told if others have declined and an offer is made to you. Who cares how far down the list you are? A job is a job and you have got it. Whatever the case, keep records of thoughts and feelings about your meetings using your audition log, be aware of your weaker points, noting areas that need improvement and work on putting these improvements into practice for future occasions.

Always look at your appearance objectively, as others will. We might like to believe that we're something we're not, or different from how we are and while acting comes into play here, physicality cannot often be disguised. Be truthful about your current look and size – do not, for instance, try to convince people that you are a size 10 when, in fact, you are a 14 or 16 – trust me, they will know the difference. There's nothing wrong with being you, or whatever size you are – and if you are really not happy, then take sensible action to change what you can and work at accepting what you cannot. Lying – either to your agent, who will sell you according to the information you have given them, or in person at a casting – will gain you nothing but mistrust.

So remember to . . .

✓ Make a good first impression – you never get a second chance.
✓ Be on your best behaviour at all times, not just in the audition room.
✓ Be totally believable – show them what they want to see at all times.
✓ Be nice to *everyone* – you never know who they are, or will become.
✓ Stay confident, but never assume the job is yours.
✓ Use your audition log to record feelings and areas for improvement.
✓ Ensure your name is memorable and think what it says about you.
✓ Be truthful and proud to be yourself.

CHAPTER 8

The Power of Positive Thinking

As an aid to confidence, it is important to maintain as positive a mental attitude as you can when you have an audition. This can be especially hard when you have not worked in a while, not had many auditions or those you have been to have not resulted in offers. Positivity is vital when projecting yourself to others – in person, on the telephone and even when writing – but no matter how you are feeling that day, there is always hope, so smile and go for it. Keeping motivated and having a sense of purpose will also help you greatly. If you are having a quiet time, remember that auditions can be like buses – nothing for ages and then several may come along at once. The same sometimes also applies to jobs, and often when you least expect it.

The first point to remember as you enter the room is that you are over the greatest hurdle, having been selected and invited to audition. You obviously stand a pretty good chance of getting the job and no matter how it may seem in your mind, everyone in that room is willing you to do well and help them in their quest to find the perfect cast. This thought alone should help you feel more positive about your situation. Coupled with research, knowledge and preparation, you really are in a strong position. When you are on your way to an audition, instead of thinking 'I'm going to fail', or 'I don't stand a hope in hell's chance of getting this job', use the 'I Can' theory. This involves repeating positive statements in your head, such as 'I can do it', or 'I can get this job'. Repeat them frequently, and whenever you feel the need throughout your audition – or life – it really works for anything, trust me.

There are many books written on mental powers and strategy for success, which you might find useful. The two authors I heartily recommend are the American mind guru Marc Salem (www. marcsalem.com), whose techniques will empower you with skills in relaxation, positivity and thought processes, and Peter Thomson – not the talented theatre writer, director and teacher, who has written some excellent books himself, but the renowned business and personal growth strategist. Further information on Peter and his theories can be found at www.peterthomson.com. The books of both these experts are brilliantly motivational and their powerful words, thoughts and theories will help you to gain the right mindset when auditioning.

As you stand a better chance of achieving the desired outcome by positive thinking, unsurprisingly, the reverse can also be true as a result of negative thinking. I was always told throughout my schooldays, if you feel inferior you are inferior, and in many respects this is true. If you program your mind into believing 'I will never get this part', the chances are that your prophecy will come to fruition. Painting negative pictures of scenarios in your mind will not improve your chances. When preparing to go into an audition, think only that you stand a far greater chance of getting the job than you did when you applied, think of all the positive attributes that you could give to the job concerned, as well as of all your past successes. Remember the best auditions you have ever done – the ones that resulted in positive feedback, recalls or offers of employment – and how you felt before you went into the room, during the audition and after you had left. Think of the elation you felt upon receiving that phone call telling you that the job was yours if you wanted it (this is often the best part of getting any job and arguably the greatest feeling in the world). Use these memories to reinforce your confidence. Visualise yourself entering the audition room totally calm and confident, delivering exactly what the creative team needs to see and being exactly what they envisaged that part to be. Keep thinking 'I can do this', 'I am right for this part', 'Everyone in the room knows this, and is willing me to do well and get this job', 'I will succeed!' Keep repeating these or similar positive statements in your mind – you can adapt them to suit your own needs or to words with which you feel more comfortable, but whatever you do keep it positive and do not let any form of negativity creep in.

Keep these visualisations and positive statements going round in your mind on your journey to the audition and when you enter the building. Remember that by being invited to audition, you have already overcome many barriers and are 70 per cent of the way towards getting the job you desire. While you are waiting to go in, as well as reading the script, think of all your successes to ensure that everything you say is positive. When you walk into the room, smile and appear happy to be there, ensuring that the corners of your mouth are turned up, rather than down, throughout the meeting. This will help you to appear more confident than you may be feeling at that time – everybody prefers happy people to miserable ones. If you have not done something that the panel asks you about (like a commercial or television work, for instance), be honest and confident, demonstrating your enthusiasm to do so in the future and eagerness to learn (something we are never too old to do – 'The day we stop learning is the day we stop earning'). How many times have we all wished that the ground would swallow us up when we have said the wrong thing? Avoid doing this, and especially making comments of a negative nature about yourself or others, by thinking before you speak. If you really need to, you can always play the time by repeating the question that you have been asked (a tactic often used by stand-up comedians when confronted by hecklers).

It may be that the people interviewing you make negative comments to see how you react. Think of potential negativities that might be mentioned and work out positive responses to counteract them in advance. Positive thinking can manifest itself in many ways, often when you do not realise or expect it, and to a degree you can practise positive thinking over anything. I have often thought of someone because I have seen or heard something that reminded me of them, only to see them or hear from them shortly afterwards. I'm sure this is something that has happened to us all at one time or another. I sometimes know that someone is going to end up playing a part, even before I have checked their availability and they've come in to meet the creatives – don't ask me how, it is just instinct. Another instance of positive thinking paying dividends was that of an actress who was told by a creative whom she knew that if she got herself an audition for a show on which he was working, the job would be hers. Made confident by this knowledge, she phoned the production office and said she was told that she had to be seen, but was given the brush off. After three phone calls she was given an appointment, and when she went into the room, she realised that her contact was not there, as he had since withdrawn from the project. His prediction, however, came true, as after going through the audition process, she was indeed offered the job.

Solid self-belief is essential. You have to always believe that you are the best at what you do in order to keep going – especially if you have received more rejection than success. I firmly believe that I am the best casting director in the industry and, luckily, many people agree with my way of thinking. I do, however, have enormous respect for all my colleagues, some of whom have different areas of knowledge from me and cast outstanding productions. That said, I believe that I am better, and know that I always give my best and commit myself wholeheartedly to everything I do – if I feel that this will not, or cannot be the case, I politely decline the project.

So remember to . . .

✓ Think positive – by auditioning, you are 70 per cent of the way towards the job.
✓ Visualise the outcome of the audition.
✓ Ensure that everything you say is positive.
✓ Turn potential negatives to positives.
✓ Focus your mind and practise with your own mental energy.
✓ Always believe that you are the best at whatever you do.

CHAPTER 9

Gatecrashing

We are doubtless all familiar with the process of gatecrashing (trying to gain access to an event to which we have not been invited) from teenage parties and the like. The same can apply to auditions, though rather than trying to blag your way in on the off chance – brandishing a cheap bottle of alcohol at the door and tentatively announcing yourself 'Oh hi! I'm a friend of . . . ermmm John's' – an audition crasher not only has to have just as much confidence and nerve, but far more advance knowledge and preparation. The practice of actors gatecrashing auditions is actually quite rare in the UK and mainly works for those in the theatre, as television castings often take place in the company's studios or offices, making access difficult to achieve without an appointment, and commercials are usually very specific, happening at fairly short notice, so are harder to hear about and track down.

As I've mentioned before, knowledge is power, so keep your ear to the ground and apply for every suitable job that you could feasibly do, and with any luck you will be offered the chance to audition. If, however, that doesn't happen and you are so right for a part that you (and others) feel vehemently that you should be seen, try to find out where and when the auditions will be. You can do this in several ways. First, one of your networking circle might be being seen (hopefully for a different part) and will let you know the details. Second, some people get chatting and make friends with those who work in the reception of casting venues, which can sometimes yield results, but these relationships, like any others, take time to form. Lastly, you could try to wheedle the information out of one of the staff in the casting or production office, though most are wise to this ploy and are very guarded as a result. However, if you are nice about it and humorously admit your cheek, they might divulge the information, or give you an appointment if there is a last minute cancellation, so, while a long shot, it's worth a try.

Assuming you know where and when it's all happening, what do you do now? Find out as much background information as you can about the piece and production concerned (though you will have some information from when you applied anyway) and anticipate what sort of preparation will be required, working on every possibility, just to be sure. Keep your diary clear for the day concerned and go to the venue in the middle of the morning, armed with all you could possibly need, as well as two or three stapled sets of résumé and photograph in case you are asked. It is also a good idea to pack sandwiches and drinks in case you have to wait for hours on end and cannot leave the venue to get sustenance for fear of missing your opportunity.

When you arrive at the venue, ask at reception where the waiting area or room for the project is and who's running the casting session (looking after the auditionees while they are waiting and taking them in when the time comes). The person at reception may tell you their name and might even introduce you to them. This person might be a casting or production assistant, stage manager, or even someone who has merely been roped in to help for the day and consequently knows very little about what is going on, so please be tolerant if this is the case. Sometimes, there will be nobody running it and the director or another creative will come to the door to fetch the next candidate when they are ready, so you may have to wait patiently for a while before you can ask, which can be even more nerve-racking. Whatever the case, keep your confidence and ask politely, saying something to the effect of 'Hello, I wonder if you can help me please? I don't have an appointment today, but I know that you are here casting for (production name) and was wondering if I could please audition for the part of (character name) if you have space or anyone drops out?' You should also mention that you are happy to wait, or return at a more suitable time (which may be just before they break for lunch, near the end of the session or on another day). If you are friendly and pleasant, the person you ask, whoever that may be, will warm to you, as they will appreciate the courage and tenacity that it has taken for you to ask, and this will reflect on their decision, or how they put the question to the panel. I have had many an assistant or stage manager pleading somebody's case as they have chatted with and liked the gatecrasher concerned. Even if you have to wait for hours, keep mentally stimulated so you are ready and focused to wow the panel whenever you are called.

There may be some times when it's not possible to see you, when they are running late or the list is over subscribed, for instance. The director might see the character differently from how you look or are perceived; perhaps they need to match a family with other actors who are already cast. If a negative response is given, for whatever reason, accept it, thanking them before departing – no pouting, sarcasm, tears or emotional blackmail are necessary – just thank them and ask to be kept in mind for the future, offering them your résumé and photograph, if they have not already requested it. Nothing ventured, nothing gained, better luck next time!

The most famous gatecrasher was the late, great actress Beryl Reid, who in the early days of her career, in 1936, walked from her bed-sit in Kilburn, north-west London, to Leicester Square every day for three weeks to sit outside the office of legendary impresario Tom Arnold for eight hours each day in the hope of getting an audition. In the end, Arnold grew bored of seeing her in his reception and relented, giving her an audition, and subsequently her first break. Nowadays this level of obsession would be considered stalking rather than commendable, with security or police soon called, so don't do this.

However, it pays to keep an eye out when walking around, especially in major cities, for signs for auditions on venues and stage doors. In the 1980s various friends and I used to take our flasks of tea and sandwiches to spend the day at the Abbey Community Centre in Westminster, the most popular venue at the time, as many of the repertory theatres would hold their auditions there, sometimes up to five on the same day. The Abbey no longer offers space, but there are now many more audition venues for producers to choose from, so if you keep prepared, who knows what opportunities for gate-crashing you might come across.

Occasionally you might be in a venue, such as the Actors Centre or a rehearsal space, when somebody comes up to you and asks if you are someone else or are there for the audition. Tempting though it may be to lie, always be honest, as you will surely be found out – though you could always ask if you were suitable for whatever was being cast and if they might fit you in should someone not turn up. Several times when I was asked if I was there for the audition and I replied that I wasn't, the person has followed it up with 'Well, would you like to be?' I once auditioned for something in this way in the lunch-break of rehearsals for another production and was offered a job as a result. You never know when this might happen, so, as always, be prepared.

So remember to . . .

✓ Research the part and ensure that you are absolutely perfect for it.
✓ Keep your ear to the ground for the dates and venue of the auditions.
✓ Prepare everything that you might be asked to do if auditioned.
✓ Have enough time to wait or return – all day, if necessary.
✓ Be confident and polite when asking if it is possible for you to be seen.
✓ Always carry at least one résumé and photo and everything you will need.
✓ Take no for an answer graciously, asking them to keep you in mind.
✓ Keep an eye out for auditions wherever you are.

PART 2

During

CHAPTER 10

Entrances and Exits

We've all heard about someone 'making an entrance' at an event or party, and the phrase can be equally applicable at auditions. You might have to wait far longer for your moment of glory than you expect or would ideally like, as a casting may be overrunning, sometimes for hours, and you might be left waiting in an overly cold or hot room or corridor. Conversely, a session may be running early, especially if there have been several cancellations before your allotted time, so despite arriving with plenty of time to spare, you may be thrust into the limelight far sooner than you expect, sometimes just as you have walked in through the door. In both these instances and indeed when a session is running perfectly to time, it is important to keep your focus and enthusiasm, being ready to make that entrance at any point.

By making an entrance, I don't mean go in all guns blazing as if you are taking the stage as the top of the bill at The London Palladium. When you are greeted or your name is announced, walk confidently into the room, smiling and say a cheery 'Hello', outstretching your hand, if appropriate, to offer a handshake to those you are meeting. Make sure you offer a firm handshake with a dry hand, however, as some can be put off by a limp 'wet fish' handshake or painful vice-like grip, and beware of sweaty palms (which can be a symptom of nerves, so it may be worth washing and thoroughly drying them, or perhaps wiping them on a handkerchief shortly before you are due to make that all-important entrance). Regularly practise your handshake on friends and family to ensure the firmness is just right and comes naturally to you.

Ensure you are focused, dressed and prepared to start your audition as soon as you enter the room. It can be easy to be overloaded with clothes and bags, especially when the weather is colder. Check if it is safe to leave coats and bags outside the actual room (perhaps with a friend) or, if not, take them in and put them down by the door. Try not to take too much with you in the first place, and make sure you have music and anything you need for your audition out and ready to use.

Equally, when you have finished, say your goodbyes and make a speedy exit. There is nothing so irritating as someone who gets completely dressed again – often very slowly – or chats at length to someone they know, when the panel are waiting to discuss them and move on to the next person, especially if the session is running late, and that person is not going to be offered a recall or job. If you find you have left something in the room afterwards, such as sheet music or possessions, ask the person outside the door, wherever possible, to go in and retrieve these for you as soon as there's a suitable break, rather than going back in yourself, as this will weaken any impact you have made. If there is no alternative but to return yourself, do so with confidence when nobody else is auditioning, knocking on the door, explaining the situation, picking up the item and exiting smartly.

As I have mentioned, try to be as confident as you can be when entering a room and don't let nerves hamper you. I remember going to see a renowned television casting director some years ago. I was very nervous when I arrived at her office, and as she was auditioning someone else, she pointed to a door and told me to 'wait in there'. There were two doorways next to each other and, in my haste,

I plumped for the left-hand one. What I didn't see was an electric heater across the doorway, which I tripped over, landing headlong at the desk of another casting director with whom she shared offices. The other lady looked up from her papers and austerely said 'The other door!' I was mortified and it totally put me off my audition, increasing my nerves. Needless to say, I didn't get the job.

So remember to . . .

✓ Take a deep breath, smile and exude confidence.
✓ Shake hands and remember names if you are introduced.
✓ Be focused, ready to start and not overburdened with bags and clothes.
✓ Leave promptly when you have finished – don't outstay your welcome.
✓ Avoid re-entering a room once you have left it, unless asked to do so.

CHAPTER 11

Nerves

Nerves can affect everyone in many ways, to different degrees and for a variety of reasons. Some people feel nauseous, others quake with fear, lose sleep, or even the power of speech. None of these is a problem unless it affects your ability to perform at your best. So we will now explore why we are prone to attacks of nerves at auditions. The primary reason has to be the fear of the unknown and lack of control over the situation we are in. How will we perform? What will the panel be like? Will they like us? Will their reaction and the outcome be positive and profitable to us? All these are valid questions, but ones we cannot predict or correctly answer until after the event – when it is *all over*.

As with many things, confidence is the key. Daring to be yourself and believing that you can succeed, or at least do your best with whatever is thrown at you is a very healthy attitude. Remembering the words of the advertising campaign for the soft drink Dr Pepper, 'What's the worst that can happen?' can be helpful too. In the case of auditions, it is simply that you will not get the job on this occasion, so what's the point of letting nerves hamper your chances even further? If you have the skill to do what's required, or at least have a go at it, what is the problem? I've never met a builder, plumber, bank cashier or sales assistant who gets nervous before they start work, or even when pitching for a job, as they know their skills and limitations and whether they can or cannot do what is required. Easier said than done for actors, but embrace the challenges and who cares if you fail, the world won't come to an end. If the job is yours, you'll get it; if it is not going to go your way, then it wasn't meant for you, so go for it and do your best.

With this in mind, find your own way to control your nerves and positively channel that nervous energy to help you do better in auditions, and other potentially nerve-racking situations, rather than worse. Think back on past experiences and work out how you could have improved what you did – and what was the worst incident that actually did happen? Looking back, were those nerves justified and would you have performed any better without them? As in most cases, perfection cannot be achieved without practice (not that there is such a thing as an always perfect audition, as I've already said) but the more you do, the more you will improve and banish those nerves, or at least learn to control them.

You can rest assured that you will rarely, if ever, come across a panel that will give you the treatment that Simon Cowell gives to those auditioning on *The X Factor*, bluntly speaking their minds with little regard for the feelings of the auditionees. In reality, most panels will try to relax you, if they see it's necessary, and, if after seeing you, they know you're not for them or the project on this occasion, will use the phrase 'Thank you, that's all we need to hear today' or something similar. While this phrase usually means that it has not gone your way this time and you will not be recalled, with some people it can simply mean that they have seen enough as they know you are for them, so try not to get too disheartened. I can only think of one occasion when I was treated badly at an audition. Luckily I had been warned by my agent that the gentleman concerned was notorious and had been known to leave people in tears, so I was well prepared. After he had asked me about my past theatre work, and told me that I was 'Far too inexperienced for his company' (something he also told a friend who went in after me, and who had just finished a two-year contract playing good parts with the Royal Shakespeare Company), I was told I 'might as well read anyway, as

I was there'. I duly did, and was begrudgingly told 'Well, you're about the best we've seen all day – but that doesn't say much for you.' I smiled, thanked him very much and made a speedy exit. It was, therefore, something of a relief not to be offered the job, as I heard his manner didn't improve to those who were employed.

As well as attacks of nerves before you enter the room, they can sometimes creep in as you start to perform. These can affect you in several different ways. One of the most common is knee trembling, which used to affect me the further I got through a speech or song, as I feared that I was going to be stopped before the end. One way to counteract this is by standing firm with your legs slightly apart and weight evenly balanced or, if it is appropriate, move around, which will take your mind off trembly limbs. Alternatively, if you suffer regularly and are concerned that the panel may notice (which they probably won't), wear loose-fitting trousers instead of tighter ones. Another common symptom of nervousness is forgetting the words ('drying') or getting them wrong. Should this happen to you, you can improvise your way out of the situation until you get back on track. I know an actor who regularly practises improvising in blank verse to ensure he is always confident should he dry (he never does the really well-known speeches though, to avoid being rumbled!). In the case of a musical audition, the pianist will normally help you out, especially if the lyrics are written underneath the notes they are playing, but if they do not, improvising can come into its own here too. The more natural, unflustered and in control you can be when doing this the better, as it is a great skill to fool the panel – and indeed an audience – into thinking that you are absolutely right when in fact you're not. If this does happen, don't beat yourself up about it – if you mess up, you mess up. Learn from the experience for next time and, who knows, you might still get a recall or the job anyway.

As with thinking about the next line while you are saying the current one in a speech or play, the same tactic applies with lyrics in a song. Nerves can sometimes get the better of you, making you sing the wrong lyrics for the verse concerned (especially when several are similar) or sing different lyrics from those written by the lyricist. They may only be little changes, but can be funny and therefore break the ice: 'And though he may not be the man some *guys* think of as handsome' was sung by one embarrassed lady, as was 'Summertime and the livin' is easy, Fish are jumpin' and your mother is high', and the lyrics of 'That's Amoré' were once changed from 'When the world seems to shine, Like you've had too much wine' to 'When the world starts to spin, Like you've . . . had too much gin', which met with gales of laughter – not least from the person concerned – and earned her a recall, as the panel thought she would be fun to work with.

If you dry severely and literally cannot go on, calmly ask if you can begin again – take a little time to mull through the words or lyrics in your head, take a deep breath and start again. If they say no, realise it is because they have heard all they need to.

Ensure your pace and performance is sustained all the way through an audition. An amazing number of people start magnificently then peter out into nothing. Have enough breath for everything, including the completion of sentences should the panel ask you questions, especially after you have finished projecting a song, speech or reading. With so much to think about, coupled with nerves, it can be easy to lose concentration. Think of every audition as the performance of your life – albeit a very short one – and totally focus on that performance until after the curtain falls, or rather the door closes.

So remember to . . .

✓ Analyse your nerves, channelling that nervous energy positively.
✓ Sustain your performance throughout – don't start well then fizzle out.
✓ Ask to start again if you dry and accept if they have heard enough.
✓ Ensure you have enough breath for everything, including chatting.
✓ Be confident and be yourself – what's the worst that can happen?

CHAPTER 12

Drama and Theatre Schools

In order to obtain the tools and knowledge necessary to become a solid and employable performer, a good specialist training is strongly recommended. Every year, many thousands of people are inspired to try to gain a place at one of the UK's many drama, musical theatre, dance and performing arts colleges. This will be the first real audition they will have to face, but preparation is paramount, even at this early stage, as auditioning can be an expensive process and the competition fierce, especially for the better-known and respected schools.

Before applying, it is worth thinking seriously about whether you actually want or need to train and the reasons why. Write down your reasons, together with the positives and negatives and discuss them with your family and friends. Think long and hard about what you ultimately want to achieve and what you are looking to get from the training and explore the various schools on offer. Are you ready to undertake a course of up to three years, or would waiting another year or two be advantageous in order to give you time to experience more of life (and perhaps raise more of the necessary finance)? If you're looking to train later in life to achieve a long, deep-seated ambition, are you financially stable enough to afford tuition fees and the associated costs? Degree or not degree? That is the question.

If you have been encouraged to take further training by your drama teacher or youth theatre leader, talk it through at length with them. If you are a theatregoer (something you really should be if considering this path), don't be afraid to approach actors at stage doors to ask for any nuggets of advice or their views on where they trained. I know many people who have kept in touch with some very well-known performers prior to and during training and even after graduation, so do try and network with others wherever you can.

You may already have your mind well and truly made up, which is great, but I urge you to think seriously about the following facts before making your final decision. First, you will be required to pay to audition. These fees cost anywhere from £10 to £40 per school . . . just for the opportunity to audition. This may seem harsh, but these charges cover administrative costs and the employment of the assessment panel. It also allows more, if not all, applicants to be seen in any given year. Some may make another charge if they recall you, so this should also be taken into account, as should travel and accommodation costs (recalls are sometimes workshops over two days) if the school is far from your home. Should you be offered a place without a scholarship or bursary, there is then the cost of tuition fees (in excess of £10,000 per year) as well as the expenses of living a student life, perhaps far away from home. Lastly, it is worth noting that the vast majority of graduates rarely remain in the business, some never even enter it, while others do not achieve the distinction of ever being paid to work in the profession they have spent huge amounts of time and money to join. If I've put you off, thanks for reading and good luck in whatever else you decide to do. If not, let's talk auditions!

Having done your research on what you want from a course or school, set about getting prospectuses from those you feel appropriate – all schools are listed in *Contacts* and many advertise weekly in *The Stage*. The following organisations will also provide you with useful information: The National Council for Drama Training (www. ncdt.co.uk); The Conference of Drama Schools (www.drama.ac.uk);

and The Council for Dance Education and Training (www.cdet. org.uk). Compare and contrast these, asking for advice where possible, and apply for auditions for those you choose. When you receive the letters confirming your appointments, check carefully what you will be required to do, so that you can prepare for as long as possible. An average first round audition will usually consist of two speeches of two minutes each, one Shakespeare or classical and one modern, with possibly one song. If you are auditioning for a musical theatre course, the order will usually be reversed – two songs (one ballad and one up-tempo) and a speech. Both will probably also include a short interview for the panel to meet you the person, rather than you the performer. If you can research what the specific school will like, always try to tailor your speeches accordingly and avoid doing the same old pieces time and time again as they will get stale (don't be afraid to call the admissions officer for advice if you need to – it's their job to help you). Try to be as original as you can and always choose material with parts you can feasibly play at the time – Shylock or Medea at the age of eighteen will not go down well, no matter how versatile you think you are. Always avoid overacting and if you can pick characters that are as near to you as possible, all the better. Don't be afraid of typecasting at this early stage, as it will show you off to your advantage.

Don't try to work on your pieces alone. As well as asking your friends and family to provide feedback and to be sounding boards, you could also ask your drama or youth theatre tutor for extra help or there may be a local actor or tutor in your area who can work with you (these are listed in *Contacts*, on www.dramaclasses.biz or you could ask at your local library, school or college). This will cost you for each session, but is well worth it, as is a good singing coach in the case of musical theatre auditions. When preparing speeches, always think carefully about who you are interacting with – are there other characters on stage with you? If you are talking to an imaginary person or people, where are they in relation to you? You may want to set two chairs on the diagonal so you can sit and focus on the other chair as your imaginary counterpart. It's never a good idea to play your pieces directly to the panel, as this can be daunting or off-putting for them. If you are going to play a piece, or song, standing in front of them, avoid eye contact whenever possible, focusing instead on a point slightly above their heads. If you are moving in a piece, please make sure you know the purpose of your movements and don't wander around aimlessly for the sake of it (the adjudicator may ask about your motives, so have a plausible explanation ready). Avoid pacing up and down from one side of the room to the other – known as 'corridor acting' – and keep props to a minimum (most items can, and should be mimed). I still smile when remembering the boy who brought a candle and box of matches into the room, and before lighting it, proclaimed 'This candle represents Juliet to my Romeo, and when I blow it out, it means she is dead.'

Do not learn your pieces so well that they become completely regimented in your head and body. If a panel member were to ask you to perform a monologue or song in a different way (mood, accent, style, etc.) to assess your comprehension or versatility, can you do this? Many people get totally foxed by this seemingly simple request, so make sure you are not one of them by asking your sounding boards to ask you to do things differently. This could be excitedly, melancholic, angst-ridden, striding or jumping around the room, sitting cross-legged on the floor – the choice is endless. As I've mentioned before, be prepared for absolutely anything.

Prior to the big day, work out how you are going to get to the venue. Some auditions are held at weekends, so will trains be running properly or will engineering works hamper your journey? Road works or extra traffic at rush hours, football matches, etc.? Will you have to stay over the night before if your appointment is in the morning and will rail and coach tickets and accommodation be substantially cheaper if booked way in advance, or as close to the day as possible? Check www.thetrainline.com, www.nationalexpress.com/funfares, www.megabus.com and www.laterooms.com for the best deals. Perhaps parents, relatives or friends might drive you and be there to give you moral support (there's nothing like a hug when things have gone well – or not so well). Maybe several of your friends from college or youth theatre will also be auditioning for the same schools. Try to make the auditions on the same day, so you can travel together and give each other that all-important mutual support, as well as possibly saving money travelling as a group with www.groupsave. com or another travel company's deal.

Keep yourself fit and healthy as the day itself approaches to ensure you are at your best, but should illness strike, here is what to do. If you find you are really too ill to attend by mid-afternoon of the day before, try to reschedule your appointment with the admissions officer within a reasonable amount of time. As most schools see applicants over several months of the year, this may well be possible. If it is not, go and audition anyway, taking special care, but rather than going into the room melodramatically wailing 'Ohhhh I'm dyyyyying!' or words to that effect, let 'Doctor Theatre' take over. For the uninitiated, this is a phenomenon, some say a miraculous one at that, which kicks in as you are about to walk into a room to perform and makes most ailments (a hangover is not an ailment!) somehow disappear until the end of your performance or audition. Don't ask me how it works, as I really couldn't tell you, but it has magically helped me on many occasions and with a variety of problems, so I am a firm believer. Whatever happens, do your best and don't *ever* make excuses – the panel will either pick up on the fact you are not 100 per cent without you telling them, or else not notice – after all, you would not come to the front of the stage and impart this information to an audience during a performance, would you?!

The audition

On the day itself, arrive at the venue – which will usually be one of the school's buildings – around 15 to 30 minutes before your scheduled time, as this will give you time to relax and refresh yourself before your appointment and to look around. There may also be further forms to complete and current students will usually be acting as ushers on the day with whom you can talk and get to know more about the school from their perspective (it'll be easier to ask them any questions that come to mind than the panellists in the room). These students often ask the panel how an auditionee they liked and got on with fared and the panellists may conversely ask for their viewpoint on a candidate about whom they aren't sure. As with any audition, it starts before you have entered the building and finishes way after you have left, as you never know who may be overhearing what you have to say, so be on your guard.

It is always a good idea to carry a bottle of water with you, even into the room in case nerves suddenly turn your mouth to sandpaper. When your name is announced, think a positive thought and smile (this will help relax you) before following your guardian usher to the allotted room. You may have to wait outside the door while the previous contender is auditioning inside. *Don't be daunted by what you hear – everyone* sounds better than you think you will, and that's a fact. When it's your turn, take a deep breath in through your mouth, as discussed before, hold it for a second and sharply exhale. Then smile and walk quickly into the room and up to the table (this may seem the longest walk of your life, but go for it). Even if you are terrified out of your wits, smile and appear happy to be there, which will help you to exude confidence. If you are introduced to the panellists (which you should be, and you should always ask your usher who will be adjudicating before going in), shake hands with each of them while smiling, and introducing yourself 'Hello, I'm (your name)'.

The initial panel may be either two or three people, usually with a male/female mix and containing teaching staff of the school concerned, even the principal, with perhaps an 'outside eye' (usually an experienced theatre professional who doesn't work there full time). How friendly they will be is up to your own interpretation. All should be courteous and civil towards you, though some may be overly friendly while others might be monosyllabic and po-faced by comparison. This may influence your decision on schools, although it is worth weighing up all the aspects before making your final decision – assuming all your chosen schools ask you to join them, of course. If you realise that a certain school is not the one for you, then don't waste your time, or theirs, by returning for a recall. Having said that, sometimes participating in the recall process might change your mind, so try to remain open.

It goes without saying, as mentioned earlier, that your speeches and songs should be well learnt with room for flexibility, and if you do 'dry' (forget your words), don't be afraid to ask to start again, accepting their decision if they have heard enough. You should be confident, though not overly so – I mean pushy or downright cocky, which a surprising number of people sadly are – but don't put yourself down either, just project your personality as well as you can. Do not try to be something you're not, as your sins will find you out, but do try to be as affable and 'get-on-able' as possible. Schools want someone who is going to be receptive, while building on the potential they have shown during the audition process, and a pleasure to teach. After all, nobody wants to be stuck with a downright pain for up to three years, no matter how talented they are. Think of as many pertinent questions as you can (again these can be practised beforehand) so that you have one or two up your sleeve when you are asked – there is nothing worse than responding 'Ummm . . . no' when asked 'Is there anything you'd like to ask us?' The panel want to see how your mind is working, so avoid asking questions about the financial and logistical aspects of the course, stick to the artistic and training sides. Be prepared, however, to be asked how you would fund the course fees and your living expenses if you were not to be granted a scholarship or government funding. A response demonstrating positive thought or action is essential, as a mere 'I don't know', or 'I'll face that bridge when it comes' will be off-putting and even balance tipping.

Knowledge is power, even at the competitive pre-training stage and when I have sat on panels as an outside eye, I am amazed how little people actually know about the profession they wish to enter – somewhat like an apprentice builder not knowing what cement is. Swot up on as much background information as you can, no matter how basic it may seem. I'll never forget the girl who twice told me she was doing a piece from William Shakespeare's 'The Tempits', or the boy who, after giving us a weedy English rendition of 'Oh What a Beautiful Mornin'' from *Oklahoma!* (exactly reprising the same performance when asked to try it again, relishing the new day as an American cowman) was asked who wrote the show. 'Oh I know this one,' he announced proudly, 'It was Cameron Mackintosh.' Sir Cameron had actually transferred the National Theatre's 1998 revival, which the candidate in question had seen – twice. The biscuit was taken for me, however, by the musical theatre hopeful who had come all the way from his native Norway to audition. After his two songs, which were adequate if uninspiring, delivered more in cabaret style than musical theatre, as they were written, our Norwegian friend proceeded to tell us that he would be doing his acting speech from *Chicago*, playing the role of Roxie Hart. 'So if I am talking about my husband,' he continued, 'It will not be *my* husband, because I am a man and of course I do not have a husband – it will be *Roxie's* husband.' At this point a broad grin broke out on my face and I dared not catch my fellow panellist's eye. Having given us his Mrs Hart, his explanation for his transgendered speech was simple: 'We do not have any people in Norway who write serious plays with good parts for men,' he earnestly stated. 'Have you heard of Henrik Ibsen?' I asked, somewhat shocked that one of the foremost European playwrights, and doubtless the most famous of his countrymen, had been overlooked. 'No, should I have?' was his response. These stories are just the tip of the iceberg, and while nerves may play some part in forgetfulness or gaffes, try to be as focused and prepared as you can, so you look and feel natural and knowledgeable when delivering facts, rather than as though they have been learnt by rote. Of course, along with the bad, there are also the good – very good in some cases. There have been two people who I have approached to come in for professional auditions on the spot, based on what I've seen for drama school. One got his first job in the theatre from that (and he is still working today without any formal training, so it can be done). 'What's his secret?' I hear you ask, 'And how can I be like him?' I wish I knew. He was a one in a million case and his, and others', magic has been so individualistic that it is virtually impossible to pin down. Besides, that is only my subjective viewpoint.

Another question often asked is 'Why do you want to be in this profession?' The two most common answers are very weak ones indeed: 'Well it is the only thing I am any good at/I'd ever be happy doing' and 'I am passionate about theatre' (often said with a dour expression and little hint of enthusiasm, let alone passion). How do you know it is the only thing you are any good at? As a teenager, what else have you done for any length of time to prove this theory? I often counteract these remarks with 'If you could never be a performer, what else would you do?' And 'If you do make it, how will you cope with the constant rejection and potential long periods of unemployment, *not* doing the thing you are passionate about?' Again, sensible, well-thought through responses are essential here to show your thought processes have found their way beyond the glitz and glamour aspect. If you are going to talk of passion, have reasons, facts and experiences to back this up and at least speak with some passion in your voice. Other questions that intrigue me about any potential actor are 'Do you go to theatre?' and 'Which theatres do you go to and to see what sort of productions?' We all know it is expensive, but if you are dedicated, you really should go to see a diversity of things as often as is possible. 'Which production did you enjoy the most or least and why?' Have opinions – saying you love everything equally will lose you credibility in the panel's eyes. 'Where do you see yourself fitting into the Industry in three, five or ten years' time?' 'Are you more classical, period or modern?' 'Theatre or television?' 'What part were you born to play or which famous person's career would you ideally like to emulate?' Please think realistically about all of these – we cannot all be leading players, but character parts can be far more interesting and challenging, and perhaps feasible to your type. A well-thought through answer could reap dividends galore.

However you think things have gone, always keep positive throughout the audition and after you have left the room, as there is no point in letting people know that you feel you've done badly. The people of influence may well have thought the opposite. Politely thank everyone concerned, from panellists to ushers, remembering names wherever possible (more brownie points here) and leave the room and building (it is worth waiting for your friends in a pre-agreed place away from the venue). Very occasionally, the panel may need to see more and you might be called back after you have left the room, or even the building, so it is worth being prepared for this eventuality and not switching off until a few minutes afterwards.

When you are away from the building, you can reflect on the experience. How did things go? What could you have improved? What would you do differently at other auditions? Were the school and people for you? Do you want and deserve a recall and place at this school? Write notes about how you feel and how it went in your audition log or diary as soon as you can after the event. Then it is back to life. You may have been told, in a few rare cases, whether or not you have been recalled, but if not, there is the agonising wait for that all important letter, which will usually take between seven and fourteen days to arrive, depending on the school. Try not to fret – easier said than done, I know, but be as relaxed as you can.

If you have been recalled, that is great and you can now prepare for the next stage. If you haven't this time, you will obviously be a little disappointed, though it's not the end of the world. As well as there being other schools, you can reapply to your chosen one next year, and some will give you feedback on your audition via the admissions officer, especially if you are unhappy about the result and feel it is unjust. Try not to whine, scream and shout, accepting their decision with dignity. Take criticism in your stride, remembering and using the experience in the future. Remember, also, that opinions are purely subjective and perhaps a different panel or school would have given you a place based on the audition you did – or what you will do next time.

Recalls

So you've got this far – well done! The recall day, or days, will vary from school to school, and so will what you'll be required to do, but here's an outline of what may be included. The letter of confirmation that you are recalled will give you full details of what they expect you to do on the day and prepare beforehand. If any preparation is required, start it as soon as you can after being notified, as you are far from home and dry yet. Don't forget in all the excitement to book your transport and accommodation at the best time to get the cheapest deal, especially if some of your friends have also been as lucky as you.

The day may well start with an informal meet and greet to get to know the other contenders and current students. You may have met some of these people at the first round, so do your best to remember them, as they might do with you. After this you may be asked to repeat your first-round audition for those staff members who were not present on that day (most or all the school's staff will be there at recall stage). At some point, you'll doubtless participate in group acting, singing and movement classes. These are revealing, as they show not only what you can do in these three important disciplines and how quickly you pick up and react to what you are taught, but also how you interact and behave with your fellow competitors, so be on your guard, if necessary. Having said this, these sessions are designed to be fun and should be enjoyed – as with all performing. There may well be additional one-to-one or group sessions on these and other subjects, but by now you should be prepared for anything, so just go with the flow. Also during this time, you will have at least one interview, perhaps with the principal, heads of department, etc., which will be far more in-depth than the brief chat of the first round, and will doubtless cover many more of the practicalities of you attending the course concerned as well as yourself in general and in relation to the Industry. Be prepared also for a medical examination, especially for courses concentrating on dance or physical theatre, as no school will risk legal action should you be injured or fall ill with an existing or underlying condition. You will certainly need a medical certificate before accepting a place, so please be totally honest and truthful on any form you complete at any stage of your application. One other word of warning, some schools may cut down the numbers at various points during the recall day. This can be common at professional auditions too, if the panel know who they want and who will not fit in to the group they are looking to create at that time. If this happens to you, again take matters on the chin, learn from your experiences (it is easier to ask for feedback in person at this point) and try again next year – or sooner elsewhere.

This may also happen to you when you have completed the whole recall, which is tougher in many ways, but the same scenario applies. A really useful factor when reapplying to a school in another year, having already done a previous first-round audition or recall, is that the panellists will generally be given your past notes for reference, so improvement can easily be monitored.

Should you, however, get the whole way through and be offered a place at the school of your choice, then the fun really starts – and before you know it, it'll then be time to start frantically reading the following chapters in preparation for all those auditions as a graduate out in the big wide world.

So remember to . . .

✓ Think seriously about why you want or need to train.
✓ Thoroughly research the best schools and courses for your needs.
✓ Budget the costs of auditions, travel, course fees and living expenses.
✓ Be focused, prepared and knowledgeable – even if nerves strike.
✓ Prepare speeches and songs that are original and parts you could play.
✓ Think carefully about motives for movement and the necessity of props.

✓ Enlist the help and advice of others when working on speeches.
✓ Never make excuses, put yourself down or be cocky and over-confident.
✓ Think positive, smile and introduce yourself while shaking hands.
✓ Prepare questions to ask and answers to questions in advance.
✓ Thank everyone concerned, including the student ushers.
✓ Leave the building afterwards, but be prepared to be called back in.
✓ Reflect on your audition afterwards and write notes or a diary.
✓ Take criticism and rejection in your stride and learn from your mistakes.
✓ Memorise everyone you met at the first round, if you are recalled.

CHAPTER 13

Theatre

During your career, the vast majority of auditions that you will be offered, or sent for by your agent, will doubtless be for theatre. The scale of productions will vary, from prestigious, lavishly produced plays to the most experimental of unpaid fringe pieces. As well as exploring the general techniques and dos and don'ts necessary for theatre auditions, we will look at the various genres of theatre and how requirements for each may differ.

As with everything in our business, working in theatre has become much more competitive over the years. Many years ago, when I was a young actor, I heard an old actor reminiscing about his father's experiences when he was an actor in the 1920s. He said that his father would come home to London on a Sunday morning, after finishing a play in an out of town repertory theatre the night before. On the Monday morning, he would go into central London and take a walk down Shaftesbury Avenue – as it was customary for actors who were out of work to do – and would invariably bump into a fellow actor, who would ask if he was looking for a job. When he replied that he was, his friend would tell him that the director at a certain theatre was looking for an actor, so he would go to the stage door and ask for an audition. He would be led to the stage, do his audition pieces and either leave with the promise of a job or be asked to start there and then. This concept sounded blissful to me and I was amazed how easy finding work seemed in those days. That said, the profession itself was a lot smaller back then – *Spotlight* consisted of just a single volume (containing both actors and actresses) as opposed to the current ten (five each for actors and actresses), as well as numerous other specialist directories – and the stigma attached to being an actor (it was not considered a respectable profession) kept lots of wannabes from attempting to break in. Times have changed radically; the pressure of numbers makes competition for jobs much fiercer, so we need to polish our audition skills to succeed in today's more crowded marketplace.

The first point to remember when auditioning for theatre work is that you will need to be able to project your voice and the panel will doubtless want to see some proof that you possess this skill. However, the one major mistake made by many actors, both new and experienced, is that when performing, they project to the level necessary to be heard in a 2,000-seat theatre, when the room in which they are auditioning is often substantially smaller. Spaces can differ radically. Sometimes you will be on the stage of a theatre, with the creative team sitting somewhere in the stalls, in or out of your view. Church halls, dance studios and rooms in arts centres are popular choices, as they are often reasonably priced and a suitable size. At other times, though, the room may be minute – about the size of a modest living room, which when filled with several people, chairs, table and possibly a piano is very tiny indeed, especially where sound is concerned. I have auditioned people in a multitude of different places from echoing churches to a photocopier cupboard (when a session overran and we had to quickly vacate our room which had been booked by another company). Wherever you are, the trick is to gauge the space when you walk in and tailor your sound level accordingly. If you boom throughout, because you have the skill to do so and want to show it off, it is not only monotonous and boring to listen to, but it can be downright scary in small rooms, especially if you are performing a piece of an angry or sexual nature. Varying the levels will help to retain the panel's interest.

It has been said that the less the job is being paid, the more the creative team have to prove, and in some instances this does seem to be the case. As I have mentioned before, there are some people who are on power trips, and this is sadly something that we all have to put up with from time to time, no matter how much we would like to tell them where to go. If you are treated with arrogance by a director, producer or even the person with the list on the door, this may be a sign of their inexperience and insecurity. To my mind this is inexcusable, and not something I have ever felt the need to do myself, but you should be prepared for it and rise above it, being utterly charming at all times. The opposite will be true of many experienced directors, who have a proven track record, know what they want and will be confident in their ability to recognise it when they see it.

I remember many years ago, I went with an actress friend to an audition for an unpaid fringe show one Saturday afternoon, as it was on the way to a party to which we were both going. The audition venue was a longish and quite expensive train journey out of London and a long walk from the nearest station. On the afternoon in question it was pouring with rain and so we were both drenched by the time we arrived. She went through the door and a man with a clipboard said 'Name?' She politely told him and was ticked off the list, before being told 'Wait in there.' What a charming man I thought to myself. He then looked at me and again asked 'Name?' By this time my hackles were rising fast, but I remained calm and explained that I did not have an appointment and was accompanying my friend, so would it please be possible to come in out of the rain and wait until she was finished. 'Well we don't really have the space for friends,' he replied, 'But I suppose you could sit and wait over there as long as you are very quiet and don't disturb the auditions.' I duly thanked him and was pointed in the direction of a long, empty bench, in the spacious foyer. I sat, quiet as a mouse, seeing a stream of people being treated exactly the same way by this tyrannical man, listening to each person auditioning and writing surreptitious notes on what they performed and my blind impressions. My friend was stopped half way through her song and given some script to look at. She went back in, was given no direction and read the piece with someone else. 'Thank you,' came the director's voice and she was ushered out. I was stunned, as despite having been to many hundreds of auditions in my acting career, I had never been treated as badly as that. My friend told me that the team inside the room were not much friendlier and she hoped she was not offered the part – a waste of time for everyone. Talking to actors about their experiences, I am disturbed to hear that instances like this seem to occur more frequently these days. It might be worth considering whether you actually want the part and if you want to put yourself through the experience of working with people who behave in this way. They may make the experience a less than happy one for you, especially if the job itself is paid badly, or unpaid.

Classical theatre

Classical theatre – regarded these days as the plays from Shakespeare's time up until restoration – has always been popular, and has never been so widely performed as it is now. In addition to the well-known mainstream companies who regularly produce major productions, such as The Royal Shakespeare Company, Propeller Theatre Company, Shakespeare's Globe, The Royal Exchange, Manchester and The New Shakespeare Company, there are an increasing number of festivals and touring productions in both the UK and internationally. The most widely known and performed classical playwright is, of course, William Shakespeare and his plays can be seen in a variety of settings. Many of these productions are staged outdoors and tour to Britain's parks, castles and stately homes by companies who often do not pay their actors vast amounts of money, if any.

So what will be required at an audition for a classical production? First, these are the one sort of audition where a speech or two will invariably be requested, so be prepared. If you are learning speeches by the Bard (Shakespeare), try to go for the less obvious plays – in the course of auditions, a company will see hundreds of Romeos and Juliets, Hamlets and Ophelias, Beatrices and Benedicks, Edmunds and Gonerils, and Malvolios and Violas. However, there will be far fewer pieces from the lesser-known plays in *The Complete Works* (if you read a speech and recognise it, or think you have heard it before, don't do it – be more original). There's also no law that says that a speech by Shakespeare has to be chosen – some of his contemporaries' work is just as effective yet forgotten by many auditioning actors (see the 'Playwrights to explore for speeches' section on page 117 for some inspiration). As I have mentioned before, make sure the speech you choose is feasible for you to perform, both age and type wise, have several up your sleeve, so you can offer a choice and ensure all are well rehearsed, yet able to be redirected if required.

If you are being seen for an outdoor production, make sure your vocal projection is up to scratch. You can do this by going to a park with a friend and delivering your speeches to them some distance away. This may sound silly, but having once seen a production featuring several well-respected actors, most of whom panicked and became inaudible when the radio microphones they were wearing suddenly failed, I cannot emphasise how much projection in the great outdoors is a skill worth perfecting.

Although we have covered 'dressing the part' for auditions at length, should this really apply to classical theatre? I would say no – donning a doublet and hose, or regal gown would doubtless be considered over the top and inappropriate. Instead, dress naturally, and perhaps neutrally (remembering to wear something memorable, albeit just an accessory). An ordinary shirt or T-shirt with black trousers for a man, maybe, and a blouse or T-shirt with a long, flowing (perhaps practise) skirt for a woman. In this instance, it is going to be your delivery of the text and not necessarily your look that will get you the job.

Work on your understanding, breathing and delivery of classical text, attending workshops with those who specialise in this kind of teaching and are able to guide you in the right direction, if you feel the need. It is also good to see productions of the classics performed well (or even badly), whenever you can, as watching others perform will inspire you, while increasing your knowledge of plays in which there could be suitable parts for you, now or in the future. While you might have a good instinct for this kind of theatre, you really cannot beat seeing truly great actors bringing the works of classical playwrights to life.

If you are fortunate enough to audition for one of the bigger companies, such as the RSC (Royal Shakespeare Company), bear in mind that most of their productions are through or cross cast – in other words, the same company of actors may have to fill, and understudy, the roles in several different plays in a season. You may, therefore be auditioning in front of several directors at once, who will all have a say in whether or not you are employed and what part(s) you will be playing (or spear you'll be carrying) in their individual productions. This can be quite daunting, as different directors will be looking for different things, with some arguing your suitability over others. Remember the adage 'You can't please all the people all the time', so keep your head and do your best, being prepared to demonstrate your skill at comedy, tragedy or whatever else is required, in the same audition.

Modern plays

At the opposite end of the spectrum to classical theatre are the plays of our time written in modern language. These are the type of plays that are set in the present day, but could probably be written up to thirty or forty years ago, and in which you would most likely be cast to play yourself as you are currently perceived. These plays might be gritty, hard-hitting or topical and current and will most likely contain characters that you can play easily and realistically. Auditioning for a part in a modern drama is somewhat like going in for a television soap opera. Think, therefore, about the kind of parts that you would play and avoid the temptation of being too versatile, as this can be a hindrance rather than a help.

If a play for which you are suggesting yourself, or have been invited to audition, is published, obtain a copy and read it thoroughly, knowing the plot and inner workings of the character for which you are right. You will then be better equipped to talk about this if asked to do so at an audition (though beware of knowing too much, which will be covered in Chapter 30). If you are asked to prepare a speech or two (or wanted to do so just in case), you could try looking up other works by the same playwright, which may be written in a similar style. Walk into the room as the character, which will not be far removed from you, and read accordingly. When you have time, go to see as many new plays as you can to discover which writers' works suit you best. This will help you to target the plays for which you are most likely to be seen and cast.

Comedy and farce

Comedy is a funny thing! What makes people laugh can differ greatly and really depends on a person's sense of humour. Playing comedy is a very serious business, especially where auditions are concerned as you will be required to make the panel laugh in order to make an impact – as a stand-up comic would in a comedy club. Some performers are born with natural comic timing, while others watch, learn and pick it up as time goes on. To gain a better insight into comedy, watch comedians at work, sitcoms (situation comedy programmes on television) and comic and farcical plays in the theatre. Pay careful attention to where the laughs come and how they are played and timed by the performers. Normally scenes and laugh lines will be played very straight, rather than with a giggle or a wink – if you read theories written by comedy writers and performers, they will all tell you that comedy is far more serious than tragedy. Good comedy will look effortless but its structure and timing are meticulously judged, in both the writing and the delivery, and rehearsed to maximise the impact on the audience and increase the laughs. Doing workshops on stand-up comedy or comedy acting will help you to perfect your technique and give you a greater insight into playing this genre.

If you have an audition, avoid walking into the room and immediately acting the fool and thinking how funny you are, as this will rarely work. Play your reading or speech for truth rather than laughs and let the humour in the script work for itself. If the play for which you are being seen is published and you can obtain a copy of the script beforehand, read it aloud with a group of friends so you can see where the laughs come and get a better idea of how to play them. In the case of farce, you can be slightly more frenetic (if the audition situation will allow), though be careful not to go too far over the top and always play the lines and your reactions to the situations that ensue with total truth. If you can make the panel laugh with your reading or speech, or while chatting with them, that is all well and good, but do not go out of your way to do this, or try too hard as it may backfire. It is also a good idea to have a clean and non-offensive joke up your sleeve in case you're asked to tell one.

Physical theatre

As the name implies, physical theatre is performed using the body's physicality, incorporating movement, mime, mask work and clowning in conjunction with, or in place of, words and text. This is a very specialised art form, and one that is not for everyone, but if you enjoy working with your body and feel this type of work would suit you, there are various avenues to explore. Numerous work-shops, masterclasses and courses (both short and long term) are regularly offered by drama schools, theatre companies and leading practitioners of physical theatre, which will introduce you to new ways of working, using your body more effectively and expressively, as well as sharpening and improving your existing skills. See the work of these companies and take as many workshops as you can with a variety of different practitioners if you are interested and serious about working in this medium. Two award-winning companies have brought physical theatre into a wider public consciousness: Complicite and The Right Size have been seen worldwide and their style of working is praised and often emulated. Inspired by their success, many more companies have sprung up over the years to produce their own innovative work.

Auditions for physical theatre productions usually take the form of workshops, which can then lead to further workshops, for which you may be paid. These secondary workshops could last for several days or weeks and may, in turn, form the basis of a production, as many pieces are devised using the skills and ideas of artists within the company. The important factor for performers in this genre is physical fitness, as your body really is your tool. Ensure therefore that you are in good enough shape to rise to the challenges that you will face throughout an audition workshop of this nature and be aware of your body's own traits and limitations. Ensure that your muscles are thoroughly warmed up (even before any organised company warm up) to avoid injury.

When you go to see performances by companies, look at the composition of the Company and evaluate if you could fit in with them and where your place would be. Use this information to target the companies you wish to work with and keep in touch with them whenever possible, especially if you have participated in auditions or workshops for which you have paid, or been paid to take part, in the past.

Repertory theatre

Repertory theatre, in its original sense, comes from the word repertoire (the practice of performing several plays in one season, and often playing two or three productions in the course of each week instead of just one play at a time). Up until the 1960s, actors would learn their craft by being employed in 'weekly rep', in other words rehearsing one play in the day for a week while performing another in the evening. This was an everlasting cycle, with each production lasting for a week and meaning that actors had to learn each play quickly and got to play a huge variety of roles. Many well-known older actors started their careers this way, learning on the job instead of studying at drama school. Sadly, this tradition has largely died out, though the Manor Pavilion Theatre in Sidmouth, Devon, still produces a season of weekly plays every summer. These days, the term repertory theatre, or rep, is used to mean those theatres outside London that produce their own shows (rather than taking in commercial tours) and employ actors. Usually, actors will be hired on a show-by-show basis, with each contract lasting around six to twelve weeks, but sometimes theatres will employ actors to perform throughout a whole season, consisting of several plays and musicals, which will usually be cross or through cast (in the same way as large classical companies sometimes do).

Casting may be dealt with by the theatre's artistic director, their secretary, a production assistant or a freelance casting director may be brought in for specific projects. A few of the larger repertory theatres have their own in-house casting directors or departments, this information can be found in the repertory section of *Contacts*. *PCR* (www.pcrnewsletter.com) publishes *Theatre Report*, a monthly bulletin containing information on the production plans of the rep theatres, which you may find a useful source of information. You may be at an advantage if you or your family live within commuting distance of the theatre, as you can then be booked as a local actor, meaning the company will not have to pay you subsistence and therefore save over £100 a week. This could be very welcome to them, as many such theatres survive on very tight budgets, with some even threatened with closure in these days of arts funding cutbacks.

When auditioning for a single play produced by a repertory theatre, read the script, if it is available, and prepare what they ask you to, having done as much research as you can. If you are invited to audition for a season, you will be seen for a variety of roles in productions of different genre and you should be prepared for this. If you suggested yourself for this job, the breakdown may have included specific 'tracks' (lists of parts for each actor, and the skills needed for each role), so you will have a good idea of what is required and be able to brush up on those skills that you will probably be asked to demonstrate at your audition. Keep in mind that you may be asked to read a number of very different characters in quick succession, perhaps using a variety of accent or dialects. Make sure you also have some speeches and songs ready, in case you are asked for them.

Working in rep can be great fun, and you might make some good friends, which is easy to do if you are all away from home. One final thought: if you are a parent, think about whether or not to mention that you have children when auditioning for a job that involves going away from home, perhaps for long periods of time. I know many people in this situation who have excellent support networks for childcare within their family, and are therefore fine about leaving home. However, they do not mention their circumstances for fear of losing the job or being treated differently. While not necessarily a major issue, it is something to keep in the back of your mind, should this apply to you.

Children's theatre and TIE

Theatre for children is of the utmost importance as they are the audience and ticket buyers of the future. Many performers start their careers by doing children's theatre and TIE (Theatre In Education) and it is indeed a great way of learning your craft while teaching the audience of tomorrow. Some actors return to this field regularly as they enjoy it and it can be a good source of work. There are many companies that produce this kind of work: several are building based, with their own theatres, such as the brilliant Unicorn and Polka Theatres in London, while others tour in their local area or countrywide. The styles of shows produced vary greatly, from specially commissioned plays on educational themes from the national curriculum, which are taken round schools, to adaptations of best-selling children's books, written by the likes of Roald Dahl and Jacqueline Wilson, which tour nationally to large theatres.

When auditioning for children's shows, you should be upbeat, yet always play the script for truth (children are the most severe critics and can spot a fake a mile off). You may be required to read, do a speech, improvise or participate in a full workshop (workshops will be covered at length in Chapter 16). If you are playing a character from an animated book or cartoon series, you could also be required to work in a 'skin' (character costume that covers your whole face and body and can be heavy and hot to wear), so be prepared to do your audition in one, if required. These days many shows for young audiences are spin offs from children's television programmes and books, so before going in to audition it is important to research the subject and characters thoroughly, by watching or reading the originals, and ensuring that you are knowledgeable about the project concerned if and when you are questioned. Always speak positively and enthusiastically about what you have seen or read, as the writer or creators may be present at your audition. You could also make a point of watching children's television shows, which are shown on CBBC, CITV and Cbeebies channels, to see if there are any characters that you could realistically recreate in a stage version, if one were to be produced. Watching these programmes may also give you ideas for people to contact regarding future casting. Do not forget to keep abreast of the latest best-selling children's books, for as well as being adapted for the stage, these can sometimes be made into films – the Harry Potter series being a prime example.

If you are being seen for theatre in education projects, the audition will usually be in the form of a workshop, to see how you interact with your fellow performers. There are additional skills that may be advantageous and should be mentioned at the audition, especially if they have been requested in the job advertisement from which you applied. Experience and aptitude for leading workshops with children in schools could make you a very interesting proposition to the company, as workshops that are based on the play that you are performing are sometimes offered as a follow up and can be led by the performers. Stage management skills are also considered useful, as you will most likely be getting the set, props and costumes in and out of each venue. Lastly, a full, clean driving licence, with experience of van driving may help too. General affability, tolerance and enthusiasm for the work are also essential, as you will usually be touring as a company in a small van and living in the same place. Keep in mind that you will be working in the day, usually starting early in the morning, so don't express a dislike for early starts and tell the panel that you're not a morning person, as you enjoy wild partying way into the night! If the production involves working with children and going into schools, you will need to have a satisfactory CRB (Criminal Records Bureau) check. The company should make sure that this is in place before offering you employment, but if you are interested in working regularly in this field, you could always look into having the check done for yourself, so you have the necessary paperwork ready to show future employers. Performing for children can be great fun and very rewarding and is something that every performer should do at least once in their career.

Pantomime

Pantomime is a traditional British art form intended for family audiences and performed at the Christmas season. It is often the first theatre to which a child will be taken and is mainly confined to the UK, although it has been exported abroad and has been seen by audiences in other countries such as Canada and South Africa. If you are reading this book outside the UK, you may never have even heard of pantomime and it is a unique concept, and not an easy one to explain. Although some male roles are played by women, and some female roles by men, this is not a drag show, and the emphasis is always on the force of good overcoming evil. You really have to see it to understand it (and even then some people still find themselves bemused). It was originally based on the harlequinade and these days many classic fairy stories are turned into pantomime, such as Cinderella, Peter Pan, Snow White and the Seven Dwarfs and Dick Whittington.

While you may be auditioned for pantomime – such as a commercial production, which may feature popular celebrities and comedians, an actor-led repertory style show or a smaller touring production, with several actors in a van playing single performances in community centres and working men's clubs – it is not an art form that's really taught in any great depth at drama school, and very few workshops exist to teach the very specific skills that are required. The best way of learning is by going to see as many pantomimes as you can and carefully watching the performances. Think when you are watching which parts you would naturally be cast in. Are you more the comic lad or pantomime dame, good fairy or wicked queen, principal boy or principal girl? The best way to become a good pantomime performer is to learn on the job, as many of the older artists are keen to pass on their skill, knowledge and routines to younger generations to keep the art form going. There are many cases of ensemble members having been promoted to a principal role in subsequent years, as a result of watching and learning.

So, how do you get your first pantomime and what do you do for the audition? First, are you being seen for ensemble or a role? For a job in the ensemble you will need to sing and dance, but if you are being seen for a role, find out which part you are being considered for and get in the right mindset. Will you be good or evil? Comic or more serious? You could try obtaining a script of the pantomime concerned (though the production you are up for will doubtless be radically different, as nothing is set in stone as far as pantomime is concerned, sometimes just the bare bones of the story is used). Scripts written by Chris Denys and Chris Harris, and John Morley are published, which are excellent examples of good traditional pantomime.

Whichever part you are auditioning for, keep your audition upbeat with lots of energy, perhaps dressing in brighter colours than you would normally, or according to the role. If you are required to sing, choose a light-hearted song (Stephen Sondheim and Kurt Weill are not for pantomime) – a pop song, of the light and cheesy kind, will probably stand you in good stead as recent chart hits are often incorporated. If your character is an evil baddie, ask before you read how evil they want you to make it (I have seen some extremely scary King Rats and Abanazers who have reduced the children in the audience to screaming wrecks). An outstanding actor was once asked to read a character as evilly as he could, which he duly did and was promptly rejected with the phrase 'There's evil and there's pantomime evil.' Keep this in mind and strike the right balance so this doesn't happen to you. If you have to be funny, try to work out when reading the script where the laughs come and play them for all they're worth – performances in pantomime are obvious and over the top, rather than subtle, so go for it and do not be afraid to make a fool of yourself. Be aware that every character will talk directly to the audience at some point in the show, usually asking for an energetic response ('Whenever I come on and say "Hello boys and girls", I want you to shout back "Hello Dame Dotty" . . . now let's have a practise . . . "Hello boys and girls!"'). You will usually be asked to read this sort of scene in your audition, so keep your energy right up, whipping the (imaginary) audience of 2,000 children into an absolute frenzy.

Probably the best online resource for pantomime is www.itsbehind you.com, which contains details of current and past productions (and the companies that produce them, to whom you could write regarding future casting) as well as other useful information. The renowned pantomime performer, writer and director Chris Harris leads workshops on the genre and has written a useful book entitled *The Alphabet of Pantomime*, available from www.chrisharris productions.co.uk. Panto is great fun and, while hard work with sometimes three shows a day, is an amazing art form to learn and break into, which can be a good source of annual employment.

Playwrights to explore for speeches

As I have mentioned before, speeches are rarely requested at auditions these days, but worth learning and having at the back of your mind, just in case. It pays to be original when choosing them, as many are vastly overdone and this can not only be boring to the panel, potentially making them switch off mentally, but also lead to comparisons with other renditions they have seen. By being as original as possible, this scenario will be avoided, and the panel will hopefully sit up and listen. Make sure that you have read the whole play, rather than skimming through it for speeches of a decent length, before adding a speech to your repertoire, so you will be able to talk lucidly about the piece and context of your speech if asked to by the panel. The playwrights listed overleaf are often overlooked when it comes to selecting pieces for audition. Many are not well known, some undiscovered or neglected, while others may be famous for one or a few works, but have written many more. If the latter is the case, explore their catalogue more thoroughly, steering clear of the plays and speeches you have heard of before. Most will have other plays in their cannon that are virtually unknown so search for these on the internet and in your local library. *Samuel French's Guide to Selecting Plays for Performance*, widely available in bookshops or directly from www.samuelfrench-london.co.uk, is another excellent source of research, as is Simon Dunmore's website (www.simon.dunmore.btinternet.co.uk). Detailed information on many playwrights and their works can also be found on the online databases www.doollee.com and www.playregistry.com, where you may be able to find the contact details of playwrights whose work is unpublished and who are unrepresented, enabling you to approach them directly to obtain scripts. The writers have been categorised by those genres for which they are best known, but many cross over into other styles. Notice a few appear twice and keep an eye out for these. You may also find some interesting adaptations or reworkings of the classics by modern day playwrights, as well as screenplays.

American drama

Edward Albee, Jeff Baron, TS Eliot, John Guare, AR Gurney, Beth Henley, Ken Kesey, Harper Lee, Ira Levin, Terrence McNally, David Mamet, Arthur Miller, Eugene O'Neill, Joe Penhall, Reginald Rose, Murray Schisgal, John Patrick Shanley, Sam Shepard, Aaron Sorkin, John Steinbeck, Thornton Wilder, Tennessee Williams, Lanford Wilson.

Black and Asian drama

Oladipo Agboluaje, Rukhsana Ahmad, Tariq Ali, James Baldwin, Biyi Bandele, Sudha Buchar, Trish Cooke, Athol Fugard, Tanika Gupta, Tunde Ikoli, John Kani, Jackie Kay, Ayub Khan-Din, Hanif Kureshi, Kwame Kwei-Armah, Kristine Landon Smith, Earl Lovelace, Mustapha Matura, Caryl Phillips, Winsome Pinnock, Rebecca Pritchard, Paulette Randall, Barney Simon, Meera Syal, Deepak Verma, Jatinda Verma, Derek Walcott, Roy Williams, August Wilson, Benjamin Zephaniah.

British and Irish drama

Brian Abbott, Rodney Ackland, Howard Barker, Peter Barnes, Richard Bean, Alistair Beaton, Brendan Behan, Peter Benedict, Steven Berkoff, Alan Bleasdale, Alecky Blythe, Robert Bolt, Howard Brenton, Fiona Buffini, Moira Buffini, Jez Butterworth, John Byrne, Ken Campbell, Jim Cartwright, James Martin Charlton, Chris Chibnall, Agatha Christie, Caryl Churchill, Brian Clark, Catherine Cookson, Martin Crimp,

NJ Crisp, Leslie Darbon, Andrew Davies, Sheila Dewey, Keith Dewhurst, Ellen Dryden, Daphne Du Maurier, Francis Durbridge, Bob Eaton, David Edgar, Georgia Fitch, Michael Frayn, Brian Friel, Christopher Fry, Anna Furse, Tudor Gates, Pam Gems, Peter Gill, Robin Glendinning, John Godber, William Golding, Steve Gooch, Simon Gray, David Greig, Trevor Griffiths, Lee Hall, Patrick Hamilton, Christopher Hampton, David Hare, Tony Harrison, David Harrower, Ronald Harwood, Carl Heap, Ray Herman, David Hines, Kevin Hood, William Humble, Ron Hutchinson, Stephen Jeffreys, Catherine Johnson, Terry Johnson, Charlotte Jones, Sarah Kane, Barrie Keefe, Dennis Kelly, Tom Kempinski, Frederick Knott, Bernard Kops, Mike Leigh, Rebecca Lenkiewicz, Doug Lucie, Stephen Lowe, Robert David McDonald, Frank McGuinness, Malcolm McKay, Stephen Malatratt, Patrick Marber, W Somerset Maugham, Glyn Maxwell, Anthony Minghella, Adrian Mitchell, Julian Mitchell, Gerald Moon, John Mortimer, Joanna Murray-Smith, Phyllis Nagy, Anthony Neilson, David Nobbs, Sean O'Casey, John Osborne, Gary Owen, Michael Packer, Stuart Permutt, Harold Pinter, Alan Plater, Gillian Plowman, Stephen Poliakoff, Bernard Pomerance, Dennis Potter, David Pownall, Terry Pratchett, Paul Prescott, JB Priestley, Philip Prowse, Terrence Rattigan, Mark Ravenhill, Arnold Ridley, Philip Ridley, Jeremy Sams, James Saunders, Anthony Shaffer, Peter Shaffer, George Bernard Shaw, Jack Shepherd, RC Sherriff, Christopher Shinn, NF Simpson, Robin Soans, Muriel Sparks, Dean Stalham, Simon Stephens, Shelagh Stephenson, Tom Stoppard, David Storey, CP Taylor, Don Taylor, Peter Terson, Dylan Thomas, Laura Wade, Colin Welland, Timberlake Wertenbaker, Arnold Wesker, Peter Whelan, Hugh Whitemore, Oscar Wilde, Emlyn Williams, Phil Wilmott, Polly Wiseman, Virginia Woolf, Nicholas Wright, Toby Young.

Classical and restoration

Aeschylus, Francis Beaumont and John Fletcher, Aphra Behn, Fanny Burney, Charles Dickens, Euripides, Oliver Goldsmith, Ben Jonson, Pierre Mariveaux, Christopher Marlowe, Middleton and Rowley, Thomas Otway, Richard Brinsley Sheridan, Catharine Trotter, John Vanburgh.

Comedy and farce

John Antrobus, Alan Ayckbourn, Patrick Barlow, Derek Benfield, Alan Bennett, Colin Bostock-Smith, Harold Brighouse, Marc Camoletti, Patrick Cargill, John Chapman, Donald Churchill, Michael Cooney, Ray Cooney, Noël Coward, Denise Deegan, William Douglas Home, Ben Elton, Chris England, Georges Feydeau, Alistair Foot, Dave Freeman, Terrence Frisby, Ray Galton, Willis Hall, Mike Harding, Richard Harris, Ken Hill, Marie Jones, Peter Jones, George Kaufmann (and Moss Hart), Philip King (and Falkland L Carey), Bob Larbey, Charles Laurence, Ken Ludwig, Anthony Marriott, Bill Naughton, Mary O'Malley, Michael Pertwee, Leslie Randall, Brian Rix, Laurence Roman, Willy Russell, Royce Ryton, James Sherman, Larry Shue, Neil Simon, Alan Simpson, Bernard Slade, Roy Smiles, Arthur Smith, Brandon Thomas, Sue Townsend, Ben Travers, Dick Vosburgh, Keith Waterhouse, John Wells, Hugh and Margaret Williams, Simon Williams, Arthur Wing Pinero, Victoria Wood.

European drama

Jean Anouilh, Bertolt Brecht, Georg Büchner, Albert Camus, Anton Chekhov, Jean Cocteau, Ariel Dorfman, Eduardo De Filippo, Dario Fo, Johann Wolfgang von Goethe, Nikoli Gogol, Carlo Goldoni, Vladimir Gubaryev, Václav Havel, Ödön Von Horvath, Henrik Ibsen, Eugene Ionesco, Federico Garcia Lorca, Molière, Franca Rame, Jean-Paul Sartre, Arthur Schnitzler, Joshua Sobol, Botho Strauss, August Strindberg, Ivan Turgenev, Lope De Vega, Frank Weidekind, Karol Wojtyla, Emile Zola.

Lesbian and gay

Luis Alfaro, Andrew Alty, Neil Bartlett, Scott Capurro, Jimmie Chinn, Grae Cleugh, Barcy Cogdale, Mart Crowley, Steven Dawson, Joe DiPietro, Claire Dowie, Rod Dungate, Kevin Elyot, Harvey Fierstein, Tim Fountain, Brad Fraser, Noel Grieg, Jonathan Harvey, Michael Kearns, Wendy Kesselman, Larry Kramer, Tony Kushner, Russell Labey, Gary Lyons, Claudio Macor, Terrence McNally, Joe Orton, Philip Osment, Mark Ravenhill, Peggy Shaw, Nona Shepphard, Martin Sherman, Bayla Travis, Michel Tremblay, Frank Vickery, Michael Wilcox, Tennessee Williams, Chay Yew.

Women's and feminist

Aphra Behn, Fanny Burney, Caryl Churchill, Sarah Daniels, April De Angelis, Joan Dugdale, Nell Dunn, Carolyn Gage, Pam Gems, Susan Glaspell, Bryony Lavery, Sharman Macdonald,

Clare McIntyre, Louise Page, Winsome Pinnock, Timberlake Wertenbaker, Olwen Wymark.

Young people's theatre

JM Barrie, Michael Bogdanov, Alfred Bradley, Lewis Carroll, Denise Coffey, Roald Dahl, Mary Elliott-Nelson, John Gardiner, Andrew Haynes, Peter Howard, Vicky Ireland, Roy Kift, Michael Mulpurgo, AA Milne, Adrian Mitchell, Stuart Paterson, Philip Pullman, Glyn Robbins, Hugh Steadman Williams, Roman Stefanski, Melly Still, Brian Way, Charles Way, Jacqueline Wilson, David Wood.

So remember to . . .

✓ Project your voice, at a level appropriate for the size of the room.
✓ Keep your head and be charming to arrogant people on power trips.
✓ Be as original as you can when selecting speeches.
✓ Make sure all speeches are feasible for you in age and type.
✓ Practise your projection ready for performing in the great outdoors.
✓ Dress neutrally for classical auditions, but wear something memorable.
✓ Ensure you understand the text you are speaking.
✓ Stay calm if auditioning for several directors for a cross-cast season.
✓ Not stray too far from yourself when auditioning for modern plays.
✓ Watch and learn timing and technique from established comedy actors.

- ✓ Not act the fool in comedy auditions, or go too far over the top.
- ✓ Warm up thoroughly before physical theatre auditions to avoid injury.
- ✓ Be aware of your body's limitations and do not overstretch them.
- ✓ Offer to be booked as local at nearby rep theatres as it may be an advantage.
- ✓ Be prepared to read for several contrasting roles in quick succession.
- ✓ Do your research if a children's play is based on a book or TV series.
- ✓ Mention appropriate skills at TIE auditions.
- ✓ Be prepared for a CRB check, or get one done yourself.
- ✓ Keep your energy upbeat at pantomime auditions.
- ✓ Gauge performance levels – 'There's evil and there's pantomime evil.'
- ✓ Search through playwrights' entire catalogues for original speeches.

CHAPTER 14

Musical Theatre

Over the years, musicals have overtaken straight drama as the biggest employer of performers in theatre. Apart from possibly panto-mimes, a musical might have been your first introduction to theatre as a child – it may even have been the reason you are reading this book now. While there is work in musicals, the competition is still phenomenally fierce, with many people competing for the same role or place in the ensemble. As well as acting skills, you will, of course, also need to sing and dance to a high standard. You may have trained specifically in the genre, in which case your tutors will have appraised your skill and suitability for the different types of musical. If you have not trained, it is worth thinking about regular classes in singing technique, performance and repertoire, as well as dance classes. While most start dancing from an early age – often as young as three or four – some still make it on the West End stage who have not started until their late teens, or even later, so don't despair as with the right natural talent and aptitude it is never too late.

Many more people will have been inspired to try their luck in musicals by watching the immensely popular TV shows *How do you Solve a Problem Like Maria?*, *Grease is the Word*, *I'd Do Anything* and *Any Dream Will Do* and on a broader scale, other talent shows such as *The X Factor*, *Fame Academy* and *Pop Idol*. Interestingly, most of the winners of the musical theatre-orientated shows had benefited from some training and/or previous experience in the field, which many would say is essential in order to be able to consistently perform a leading role in front of a paying West End audience eight times every week. Indeed, the first winner of *Pop Idol*, Will Young, entered the competition as he was coming to the end of a three-year musical theatre course at the well respected Arts Educational School in London, and therefore had the training, knowledge and skill to sustain his performance. It is, perhaps, no surprise that he is the only finalist from that contest still up there at the top of the tree, despite probably greater initial interest in Gareth Gates. If you look around, you will be surprised to discover how many people in the pop world actually started out training for, or appearing in musicals, and who still continue classes with legitimate singing teachers. That said, while training is an excellent choice and should be thought about deeply before entering the world of musical theatre, Will Young possesses a rare talent and had a very lucky break, so training for several years cannot turn every graduate into the next Will Young.

A more in-depth look into the requirements of auditioning for musicals was shown in Channel 4's 2004 series, *Musicality*. Many of you who watched this fascinating insight into the casting process will have been amazed to see how rigorous the selection process was and how the contestants – often with little, or no experience whatsoever – had to fight for their survival to achieve their goal and dream. The three judges, all renowned creatives in their respective fields, pushed those competing to the limit, which mirrored the audition process for many professional shows. This will have been off-putting for some and inspiring for others, showing exactly how difficult and demanding this medium actually is, with many thousands of established and experienced artists continually honing their craft and going through the process to get that all-important job. Auditioning for a big musical is either all or nothing, with one song (if you're lucky) followed by 'Thank you, that's all we need to hear today' on the one side, or recall after recall, being put through every possible pace and discipline, on the other.

Auditioning on the stage of a large theatre can be a daunting experience. What looks relatively small from far back or way above, can actually be a vast expanse, especially when making the long walk from the wings to the centre and back again. Spotlights may dazzle and half blind you and the creative team may be sitting deep in the dark at the back of the stalls, seemingly miles from you, either watching your every move like hawks or talking through what you are doing. This is all part of the process and something you should be prepared for and get used to. The best focal point, when your eyes adjust to the lights, is the dress (first) circle rail, as this will enable the team to see your face to its best advantage, as would an audience if you were performing a solo directly out front. Often the creatives will stay put and may talk to you or ask you questions from out of the gloom, which can be disconcerting. Unless you can clearly see the face of the person who is speaking to you, just respond in the general direction from which the voice is coming, remembering to project clearly. Occasionally, however, one or more may walk down the aisle to talk to, or work further with you. This is usually a positive sign. If the people concerned join you onstage, all well and good, but if they remain in the stalls, it helps to get nearer their level by coming to the front of the stage and crouching (keeping your balance) or kneeling to speak to them. They may ask you about yourself, what other songs you have with you or to look at something from the show. They might be telling you that you are being recalled or that on this occasion you're not right, but to keep trying, or stay in touch in the future.

Delivering a song

While it is lovely to hear a well-sung song, the music and lyrics are not really enough. We all know that it can be difficult to be expressive when you are concentrating on hitting the right notes, but acting a number – especially using your eyes, like in auditions on camera – is another way to make or break an audition. It is all well and good to look at a focal point above the heads of the panel, when being seen in a room, or at the back of the auditorium or dress circle rail if onstage in a theatre, but in many cases, there is nothing whatsoever going on behind the eyes when people sing. Now I am not suggesting going overboard and doing the actions, like a children's song, far from it, but there is a huge difference between seeing real emotion in someone's eyes when singing, and a stock still, stunned rabbit that has been caught in the headlights of a car (especially if bright spotlights are blaring down on to the stage). Acting really is the key here. Try to feel the lyrics you are singing and react accordingly. Real tears are not a bad thing if a song is particularly sad and they are controlled. As I've mentioned before, how you achieve them is up to you, but imagining yourself in the situation about which you're singing might help.

There are many schools of thought about the perfect delivery of a song but the more I see, the less I believe there is such a thing. However, there are several rules that should be obeyed. Many people stand stock still and sing the lyrics. This is fair enough and if your voice is beautiful enough, the panel might sit up and listen. However, if you did that in an actual musical, the audience probably wouldn't be so generous, especially if every number were similarly performed. A song needs to be brought alive to grab the panel's attention: breathe, take your moment and put over the number with boundless energy (and not just the physical type). Know what the song is about and *feel it*. Many people look self-conscious while singing, especially if they are attempting a song outside their vocal and physical range. Avoid this feeling by ensuring your song is right for you and your vocal style and in the correct key (ask your singing teacher's advice when choosing your repertoire). While delivering the number, lose yourself in the lyrics and meaning, but be aware of what is going on around you. As I have already mentioned, there should always be lots going on behind the eyes, so never sing with your eyes closed and always engage with your focal point (remember this should not be the panel, as it can be scary, though little moments of eye contact are permissible).

Repertoire

A well-chosen repertoire will be an asset to your musical theatre career. Interestingly, I can think of three experienced and gifted artists, who, through much of their careers, used a single song at auditions. While these numbers were perfected, having been frequently sung over many decades, their auditions were somewhat predictable and less interesting than others at which a choice was offered, as one could always mouth the song title slightly before the singer announced it. A repertoire of at least ten plus suitable songs which you know well will serve you well. Don't forget that musicals were written before the 1980s and having a wide selection of not only shows but also styles will pay dividends, especially with older creatives. Explore the full catalogues of these composers for imaginative and underused material:

Richard Adler, Benny Anderson, Harold Arlen, Burt Bacharach, John Barry, Lionel Bart, Irving Berlin, Leonard Bernstein, Jerry Bock, Anthony Bowles, Jacques Brel, Leslie Bricusse, John Bucchino, Roy Civil, Cy Coleman, Noël Coward, John Du Prez, Vivian Ellis, William Finn, Stephen Flaherty, Noel Gay, Gary Geld, George and Ira Gershwin, Howard Goodall, Hubert Gregg, Joyce Grenfell, Larry Grossman, Albert Hague, Marvin Hamlisch, James F Hanley, EY Harburg, Tony Hatch, David Heneker, Jerry Herman, Rupert Holmes, Billy Joel, Elton John, Paul Joseph, John Kander, Jerome Kern, Denis King, Russell Labey, Marvin Laird, Michel Legrand, Tom Lehrer, Jerry Leiber, Mitch Leigh, Andrew Lippa, Frank Loesser, Frederick Loewe, Hugh Martin, Alan Menkin, Johnny Mercer, Bob Merrell, Charles Miller, Connor Mitchell, Lionel Monckton, Randy Newman, Monty Norman, Ivor Novello, Laurence O'Keefe, Stephen Oliver, Cyril Ornadel, Jim Parker,

Cole Porter, AR Rahman, Richard Rodgers, Betty Roe, Sigmund Romberg, Jerry Ross, Dana P Rowe, Stephen Schwartz, Julian Slade, Charlie Smalls, Stephen Sondheim, George Stiles, Keith Strachan, Matthew Strachan, Charles Strouse, Jule Styne, Sir Arthur Sullivan, Donald Swann, Paul Todd, Pete Townsend, Björn Ulvaeus, Kurt Weill, Sandy Wilson, David Yazbek, Maurey Yeston.

A musical director once advised me not to sing a song from shows that are currently running, or anything that had been produced in the West End in the last fifteen years. I don't necessarily agree with his sentiment, but when you have heard the twelfth 'Memory', 'I Dreamed a Dream' or the often aptly titled 'Why God? Why?' of the day, imagination and originality are a godsend and more likely to make the panel sit up and take notice. If you hear the person in the room before you singing the song that you were going to perform, please don't be tempted to sing it again – no matter how different you think it will be. Always carry enough songs with you, up-tempo and ballads, to offer a suitable and interesting alternative.

So what's the difference between an up-tempo number and a ballad? The simple answer is that a ballad is generally slower in pace and more lyrical, while up-tempo, as the name implies, is faster and brighter. Some good, if well-used, examples of ballads could be 'I Dreamed a Dream' from *Les Misérables*, 'Hopelessly Devoted to You' from *Grease*, and 'Mr Cellophane' from *Chicago*, while up-tempo numbers would include 'Take Me or Leave Me' from *Rent*, 'Somebody to Love' from *We Will Rock You* and 'Consider Yourself' from *Oliver!* There are plenty of others to choose from, as while all of these are good songs, they are heard on a regular basis.

As well as songs by the composers listed, look for works by undiscovered composers or from shows that have not yet been produced in the UK and therefore not seen or heard by all and sundry. That said, unless you are accomplished at song writing, please don't perform your own works, no matter how good you think they are. Instead, see as many shows or cabarets as you can, buying a programme or subtly asking for the names of composers and lyricists. Also keep an eye on the Broadway and European theatre websites, such as www.playbill online.com and www.stage-entertainment.de for news of up and coming shows. Google and amazon.com will be able to help you with finding composer details and to order sheet music or scores. The staff at the London showbiz shop Dress Circle (www.dresscircle. co.uk) and Chappell's music store (www.chappellofbondstreet.co.uk) are also extremely helpful and knowledgeable on this subject. Sheet music for over 20,000 popular songs can be downloaded from www.sheetmusicdirect.com. Each number costs just a few pounds and songs can be previewed for how they will sound and transposed into your key before you print them and pay.

Every song you sing should have a 'wow factor', but unless you can perform them with the kind of Broadway panache that will blow the minds of the toughest creative team, repetitive songs should be avoided at all costs. By repetitive, I mean songs with several straight verses that have little or no change in tune, just different, sometimes witty, lyrics. Sung ordinarily and without the said sparkle and panache, these songs can sound mundane and will often soon bore the panel, who will stop you, perhaps before your big finish. Two immediately come to mind which are done repeatedly: 'Man Wanted' from Barry Manilow's musical *Copacabana*, has several similar verses with a key change leading to a biggish finish, and is often done very tediously indeed; the other is Cole Porter's classic number 'Always True to You (In My Fashion)' from *Kiss Me, Kate*, which has some very clever lyrics fitted to the same tune throughout. I have only ever seen this song performed amazingly once – by the American Nancy Anderson in Michael Blakemore's multi award-winning 2001 production. You can see and hear this outstanding rendition as this revival is available on DVD and CD, which I would strongly recommend doing before thinking about attempting the song yourself. There is also a school of thought that says you should only ever choose songs that are for people of your correct age and sex. I personally disagree, especially about the age criteria (though not if you have to play it elderly in order to make sense, and therefore give a caricatured or hammy performance as a result). If a song can be naturally performed and the lyrics safely changed to the opposite sex, then go for it, though ask the advice of your singing teacher and others first.

Sometimes, the team who are auditioning you will not need to hear all the song you have prepared, especially if it's long or repetitive, with the same phrases sung over. They may have heard enough to either ascertain that you possess the vocal (and perhaps physical, or other) attributes to play the part, or, on this occasion, you're not the one for them, so don't want to use up any more time. If you sing songs that are quite long, you should consider cutting them down with your singing coach, especially if the 'money notes' or more effective parts, happen nearer the end. Sometimes if you do not fit the bill this time, you may be allowed to sing all your song, as they want to let you down gently. However it goes, accept what is said – after all, the job may already be yours. Don't take it personally if you are not asked to sing a second song, or do anything else which you have been asked to prepare. The casting director may well have included these as a precaution and they either may not be needed, or will be requested if you are recalled, so keep practising these until you know the definite outcome.

While not that common these days, if a casting session is running very late, or especially in the case of an open audition, where anyone can come along and queue to be seen, you may be asked to give the panel your best eight, twelve or sixteen bars of music, instead of a whole song. As well as saving time it also shows the best part of the number. Think ahead and work out which bars show you off to the best effect – you should also ask your singing teacher for their advice and get them to mark the music of the songs you sing regularly, just in case.

As irritating as this may seem, especially as you will be rehearsed thoroughly should you get the job, the panel will often want to see much of the finished product and performance at your audition. If you know the piece for which you are auditioning, prepare as much as possible in every aspect, including the libretto and songs from the show. However, when you are up for a new show of which you know nothing, do not learn anything new or perform material with which you are not totally confident, as you may be brushed aside as a result. Instead, offer the two songs that you do best and which you feel have your personal wow factor. If they then see that you sing amazingly, and have potential for the show and role they are casting (regardless of the styles in which you have sung), they may ask you to look at a song from the show with the pianist, or give you the music to learn for the recall to see if you can bring the same wow factor to their piece and will fit into their company. If you are given or sent music to learn, do learn it thoroughly no matter how short the time frame, getting it as perfect as you can. If you know you have a musical audition, check the availability of your singing teacher or other pianist and ask them if they could fit you in at short notice should this eventuality arise. Really work on both the notes and the presentation of the number(s) as much as you can in whatever time you have – after all, you will stand more chance of getting the job the more prepared you are, and, as I have mentioned before, there is nothing so weakening as a prelude of excuses before a bad rendition. You may have only received the call and music a matter of hours before and had a very important dog walking appointment that took up most of your available time – the panel really don't care and will go for someone else who just gets on with it and delivers what they need to see. Remember your priorities here – if you want the job, and to be a working performer, rather than a resting one, then be prepared to drop everything, if needs be, and convince the panel that you are the one for the job.

Dance calls

Having practised the three disciplines of musical theatre – singing, dancing and acting – you will be aware of your strengths and weaknesses in each. You may be a hot dancer who can hold a tune and competently read the words off the script, or else a wonderful singer and actor but not as strong in dance. If you are a 'triple threat' (equally fantastic in all three) that's great, but regardless of how strong a dancer you are, you will usually be asked to demonstrate some movement or dance, so be prepared. If the panel asks you about the standard of your movement skills, be honest, and again avoid facetiousness. You may feel you have two left feet, or that someone has to be kidding when asking, as a great many do, but admitting you are not a trained dancer is fine.

Always ensure your body is thoroughly warmed up before the call, as you don't want to risk injury while you are dancing (don't forget to allow extra time in order to do this). Dress in clothes that allow movement and that you don't mind getting dirty, should you be asked to roll around on a grimy floor. You will also need comfortable, soft-soled shoes, trainers will usually suffice if you don't possess the proper equipment, as many studios will not permit the use of hard street shoes on their expensively sprung wooden floors. Should you be asked to bring specific dance shoes, such as tap, ballet or pointe, make sure you have them with you, as choreographers are a strict breed and you could be sent home and lose the job as a result. Also carry a hand towel to wipe yourself down, as you will perspire while working hard, a large bottle of still water to rehydrate during breaks and your résumé and photograph in case they are requested. As I've mentioned before, it helps if you avoid wearing too much black and are dressed in something distinctive or a more noticeable colour to grab the panel's attention and stay in their memories. If you don't know the studio concerned, call them in advance to check on the facilities that are available to you. Will there be changing rooms, enough space to warm up beforehand and working hot showers to clean up afterwards? These are especially essential if you have to return to your day job, or have another audition later in the day. Don't despair if the studio has no working shower facilities, as they can be found next to the toilets at most major railway stations and are useable for a fee.

If you are asked to dance (which you invariably will be if they are seriously considering you for the job) always do the very best you can and don't feel daunted if those around you are far more experienced and seemingly better than you – after all, in most instances you won't know which qualities the team are looking for and they may see potential in you for the part they have in mind. The show's dance captain, resident director or choreographer will take you through a routine of moves and steps, taught slowly in short sections which are eventually brought up to speed and put together to form the finished routine (which may seem to last forever, but actually will be only a few bars of music long). While the audition will usually take place in a dance studio, with the routine demonstrated in front of a mirror, it may happen on the show's actual set on a raked (sloping) theatre stage, or even in a carpeted room, where movement can be constricted, so be prepared for both. While the routine is being taught, you might want to stay near the back of the room following quietly until you feel confident enough to move forward. Don't be afraid to ask questions if you are unsure of a step, timing or what comes next (the person demonstrating will usually make sure everyone is happy with everything at the end of each section, but if they don't, raise your hand and ask, however simple it may seem). The choreographer will usually be looking for precision in the steps or movements, so do your best to emulate, or mimic, exactly what has been demonstrated to you.

After everyone has gone through the routine several times with the music (either recorded or played by a pianist), you will be split into smaller groups and asked to perform it in front of the creative team to enable them to evaluate your performance. Your group will often comprise four or six people, depending on the size of the call (the minimum will always be two, the maximum perhaps fifty or sixty) and if there are only a few dancers at a time, you will often be staggered with one at the back then one at the front and so on, in a zig-zag formation, with people changing to the front or rear on the repeat. It is usually performed twice with each group, maybe more if the team cannot decide about one or more members, and you may be shuffled around into other groups (which could be the yes, no and reserve lists). If you are not in the first performing group, stand at the side and watch what the others do, quietly running through the steps you need to work on or feel unsure about until it is your turn. It is customary to applaud the other groups after each rendition, no matter how well or badly they have done. Although you may be thinking about where your feet and arms are meant to go, try not to look down, or at others. Smile and sell the routine to the panel, doing it as best you can. If you forget a step or two, stop and rejoin at the next section of the routine, but whatever happens, try to make it look as though you are enjoying what you are doing and finish with a smile and in the correct ending position. There may be times you feel out of your depth and want the ground to swallow you up – we've all been there at some time or other, believe me. Tempting though it is to lose your nerve and run out of the room sobbing, please *do not give up*. Keep going, no matter how badly you think you are doing and how nervous or wretched you are feeling about it all. The worst comment I can ever hear is an auditionee saying 'I'm really not up to this, so I am going. Sorry.' It really does not make me look upon that person in as good a light in the future – and on several occasions, by bottling out and leaving the room, the person concerned has missed out on a recall, without even knowing it. Take solace in the fact that often the hardest moves or most difficult routine of the entire show is used in dance calls to test the skill and prowess of those auditioning and therefore much of the actual choreography may well not be half as harrowing. As I've mentioned before, if you mess up, do it with aplomb and a big smile. You can always make a joke about it afterwards if anyone says anything (which they probably won't).

If you are not trained in dance, or need to brush up your skills, it is best to find a weekly modern jazz or aerobics class, where routines are taught over the weeks. This will help you to follow routines set by the choreographer or dance captain at auditions. Such classes are regularly held at the major London studios, such as Pineapple, Dance Attic and Danceworks, which are excellent, but filled with highly skilled, often professional, dancers and can be daunting and demoralising if you are a beginner, or not at their standard. It may boost your ego, or make you feel stronger about your own ability – whatever that may be – to go to a more local class where the standard will be not as high. It is often easier to be a big fish in a small pond, rather than vice versa. Once your confidence and ability has grown, head down to a professional studio and take a beginners class (no matter how good you feel, please do not attempt an advanced class until you know you are at the standard to cope with it). When you have done quite a few classes and feel you are at a sufficient standard, it is a good idea to attend as many open dance calls as you can (which you will often find advertised in *The Stage*) to gain experience, learn how the audition system works and gauge the standard of the competition on the audition circuit. The experience might be a shock to you, or you could be offered a job.

Pianists

Being an audition pianist is a very special skill indeed, and one not every pianist is suited to, no matter how good they are. Someone able to read, play and interpret any song that is put in front of them, regardless how hard or badly written, without practise or rehearsal, is an absolute godsend for everyone concerned. While the producers of big shows will invest in one of these great human beings, some companies just will not spend the money and you may have the production's musical director, a pit pianist or even someone who can neither play the piano nor read music (as I was faced with on more than one occasion). If this is the case, be prepared to sing a song of the pianist's choosing that they know well and can play – 'Happy Birthday to You' and 'Somewhere over the Rainbow' are firm favourites – and to even sing acapella (without accompaniment), only being given your starting note. All the above should therefore be practised rigorously and regularly, in case of such eventualities.

When invited to give your music to the pianist, make sure it is clearly copied and easy to read, the pages are firmly stuck together in the correct order, and the paper is stiff enough to stay upright on the music stand. You should always tell them at which tempo you would like it played (which you can describe by softly singing the first line or two at the speed you normally perform them), as well as drawing their attention to any repeats or little quirks your music has. Sometimes you will not be asked to explain this, so it's up to you to take the initiative (it might be a test to see if you actually ask). The pianist will play your music exactly as it is written on the page, so *always* ensure you rehearse with the sheets you are presenting and check it has been played all the way through by your singing teacher or another pianist before using it. I'm still bemused at how many people have only bought the sheet music or songbook on their way to the audition and are surprised when it bears little resemblance to the song they know or have rehearsed with a recording. The musical director might ask the pianist to transpose the key of your song higher or lower if they want to check that you can adequately reach and deliver the upper or lower notes demanded by the role, so be prepared. Whether you are asked to do so or not, always take a song (or several) that you know well, are totally comfortable with, and can sing on demand, you never know when it may be requested, so it is better to be safe than sorry. I have known many cases of someone being employed after putting their heart and soul into a number they know well rather than the shaky rendition of one they have learnt especially for the occasion.

You may also be asked to go through scales, and possibly be taught part of a song from the show concerned by the MD or pianist, which you will then be asked to perform to the panel. No matter how high, low or impossibly outside your range this may seem, do your best, as you never know what they require – this may be merely done to test your prowess and nerve. You will be frequently asked about your vocal range, as well as where your 'break' is (the highest note you can comfortably hit in your chest voice, before it turns into your head voice for women, or falsetto for men). Check these out with your singing teacher and have the facts ready in your mind for when they are requested, re-evaluating at regular intervals, as you progress and your voice grows.

Very occasionally, and usually well into the recall stage, some artists will bring their own pianist with them, to whom they pay a fee and expenses to play just for their audition. This may be their singing coach or someone who accompanies them regularly, who will play their song exactly the way they want it, thus avoiding the risk of the pianist booked to play for the session messing it up. Happily, this practice seems to be rapidly dying out, and rightly so, as it shouldn't be necessary to use anyone else but the pianist provided by the company concerned, no matter how difficult the songs you have brought. In most cases, the MD will realise that the accompaniment is not correct and as long as you keep going as best you can, will not hold it against you. On no account should the pianist be blamed for messing up your audition, shouted and sworn at, or, as in one memorable case, showered with sheet music when an auditionee's fist landed hard on top of the piano, sending everything flying. You should always politely thank the pianist when collecting your music after singing, no matter how you feel they have played for you. They are often consulted and may be a member of the panel.

Backing tracks

In these days of karaoke culture, it is an easy and tempting option to use backing tracks. While they may sound nicer with orchestral arrangements and backing vocals, they should be avoided at all cost when auditioning for musicals. Many directors and musical directors with whom I have worked loathe the use of backing tracks – some even preferring to send a candidate away unseen than hear them sing to recorded music. If you really have nothing else but a CD, explain the situation to the person outside the room, who can then speak to the panel on your behalf and ask if they object. If there is nobody that can help you, politely ask the panel yourself and see what they say. If there is a good pianist, they may be able to busk a song you both know, though it is helpful if you know the key in which you normally sing it. If sheet music has been clearly requested, then this should be adhered to. If you sing a song or repertoire regularly, you could have both sheet music and backing track (in the right key for you) to be prepared for any eventuality.

So remember to . . .

✓ Be focused and don't be daunted by bright lights and big stages.
✓ Act and feel the song, bringing it alive with energy – the eyes say it all.
✓ Avoid repetitive and overdone songs. Give every song the 'wow factor'.
✓ Explore less well-known songs and composers.
✓ Mark your best eight, twelve or sixteen bars on your music, just in case.
✓ Smile and do your best. Keep going and *never* give up!
✓ Ensure your music is stuck together, legible and in the correct key.
✓ Be prepared in case the pianist cannot play the music you have brought.
✓ Practise concisely explaining the tempo of your songs to the pianist.
✓ Be nice to the pianist and thank them as you collect your music.
✓ Avoid backing tracks unless they are specifically requested.

CHAPTER 15

Actor/Musicians

The use of multi-skilled actors, who are not only able to act, sing and dance roles in a play or musical production, but also play one or more musical instruments as part of the orchestra, is greatly on the increase. Shows in this genre range from West End blockbusters, such as *Buddy* and *Return to the Forbidden Planet*, to smaller shows staged by repertory companies – The Watermill, Newbury, London Bubble Theatre Company and the New Wolsey Theatre, Ipswich, are leading exponents in this field. Several of John Doyle and Sarah Travis' innovative Watermill productions have transferred to the West End and Broadway, winning numerous awards. It therefore stands to reason, that the more skilled you are in these fields, the greater your chance of being employed – some would say that a triple threat has turned into quadruple. If you learned an instrument at school or during childhood, no matter how simple, take it up again and you could be surprised how quickly your aptitude returns. Playing the recorder could be a springboard to learning the clarinet, saxophone or bassoon; the piano may form the basis for the organ, harpsichord or accordion; and the acoustic guitar might give you the impetus to progress to the banjo, ukulele or electric bass. Many local authorities run adult education classes teaching musical instruments to beginners or those more advanced; details of these, and other tutors in your area, can usually be found at the library or by searching the internet.

Keeping those musical skills fresh, improving and being ready for auditions is important. You could regularly get together with a group of friends to jam, improvise or learn new pieces. If you are good enough, join or start your own local band for more regimented practise – you might even earn some extra money with paid gigs or even chart success. Whenever you can, learn to play new instruments, taking classes or teaching yourself if you know the basics. Don't forget the less ordinary ones that not many other performers play – the saw played between the knees with a violin bow always raises a laugh, the spoons (played expertly, rather than half-heartedly), harmonica, stylophone or even the washboard and thimbles – the weirder the better. Keep an eye out for reasonably priced instruments in sales or second-hand shops. If you use them as part of your performance skills, they will be tax deductible against your earnings, as will lessons and other associated expenses.

When you hear about a potential job, ensure that your skills are correct for the brief and up to the required standard before applying. As with everything, be realistic about your abilities, re-evaluating them as you improve, and always be truthful about your grades when asked (you will invariably be found out if you fib). When you are offered an audition, ascertain which instruments will be required and if there will be larger items in the room, such as a piano, drum kit, etc., which you can use. Ask if there is any music you should be learning prior to the day and get as clear a picture as possible of what you will be required to do. The first-round auditions might not be very structured, and you might just be given a few minutes and told to show the panel everything you can do. Be prepared for this and formulate and rehearse your own audition just in case. Take every instrument that you claim you can play with you to auditions – one actor I know always carries his trumpet with him to every audition he attends, whether it is required or not. He sometimes uses it to spice up the song he is singing, other times, he just takes it in with him and asks if the panel would like to hear a solo. This breaks the ice, even if he doesn't get to play it, and gets him remembered as 'The guy with the trumpet'. Like this man, you might want to punctuate a song with some music in an appropriate place, such as a dance break, or you might even choose to accompany yourself on the piano while singing. This should probably be avoided, as you will be static and seated throughout, so generally not fully projecting the number, or your personality.

If you have the right level of skill, you could always offer your services as an audition pianist, which will not only provide income while you are not acting, but may result in you being auditioned yourself if there is a suitable part. You will have a unique advantage here, as you will not only have got to know the panel and what they are looking for, but you can also gauge where others have gone wrong and improve upon it. If you are going to employ this tactic, leave asking (politely) until late into the day, or a couple of days in, be prepared for a negative response and, if they do agree to consider you, don't expect an automatic recall or to be offered the part. Be aware that you might jeopardise future work as an audition pianist if you are too pushy. In other words, don't make getting yourself an audition your primary reason for accepting the job as pianist.

If you are recalled, be sure to take everything that you took for the first audition back with you, as other creatives may now be meeting you for the first time and will not have heard you before. You might have been sent music to learn, be asked to improvise a piece on the day and play it with a band of fellow auditionees, or need to learn something from the show concerned and perform it, perhaps as part of a scene. Again, try to get as clear an idea of requirements and structure prior to the day as you can and be prepared for anything. One production I cast some years ago recalled a different team of performers each day and asked them to improvise a scene and songs from the piece using just a skeleton script and some pre-written tunes. They worked with the creatives and each other throughout the course of the day and presented the finished product to us all at the end. The results were phenomenal to watch, with all the groups bonding and pulling together to create some outstanding work, with everyone's appetite whetted and eager to be part of the finished production. As you can imagine, this made the final decisions of who to employ all the harder, but the company we ended up with was truly amazing.

One final thought. If you play several instruments to a high standard and are auditioning and working regularly as both actor and musician, you should consider joining the Musicians' Union (www.musicians union.com) as well as Equity, as you then can ask employers if you can be issued with an MU contract, as their rates of pay are often higher than those paid to actors.

So remember to . . .

- ✓ Relearn musical instruments from childhood and schooldays.
- ✓ Practise regularly, always keeping your musical skills honed and ready.
- ✓ Be realistic about your ability and grades when applying for jobs.
- ✓ Learn new instruments, both mainstream and uncommon.
- ✓ Take every instrument you claim you can play with you to auditions.
- ✓ Be prepared to demonstrate your skills.
- ✓ Take necessary instruments back with you if you are recalled.
- ✓ Join the Musicians' Union if you regularly work as an actor/ musician.

CHAPTER 16

Recalls and Workshop Auditions

If you are recalled (called back) for a part, it means that you are one step closer to getting the job and it is a great boost for your confidence. It reassures you that not only did you do well in the first round and were liked enough to merit another look but you also have potential to play the part or parts concerned. While your confidence may be boosted, you may feel under more pressure to do well. Strange though it may sound, some people do brilliantly at first-round auditions, and then go to pieces when recalled. Who knows why this should be, and it doesn't happen to everyone by any means, but what should you do if this happens to you at any point? First, remember that your chances are phenomenally increased, and the audition panel are now willing you to get the job more than ever. You are obviously right for the part and could play it – the job could even be yours already, but they just need reassurance, perhaps other creatives or production staff who may not have been at the first-round auditions need to meet you before a final decision can be made, or they want to see how well you pair up, or match with the other cast members they have in mind.

When being recalled, it is important to remember those you have met, as you will doubtless be remembered by them. Use the notes that you made after your original audition to remind you of the names of the various panel members, their job within the team and what they looked like. Remember as much about them as you can, though it may be difficult as you may have been in and out in a flurry, with more pressing matters going through your head than remembering the people behind the table. If you can, walk in and confidently shake each of them by the hand whilst using their name, this will earn you brownie points. No matter how grand they may seem, everyone likes to be remembered and feel valued by others. If you are unsure, ask whoever is running the recall session the names and functions of those in the room (or in the darkness at the back of the stalls) and to describe them, if they can, which is especially useful in the case of the people whom you did not meet at the first round. Conversely, it is important that they remember you too, so always ensure that you wear exactly the same clothes as you did in the first round (washing them as soon as you get back, if necessary), and are looking as you did when they met you before.

You may be given, sent or emailed pages of script (sides) and/or music to look over or learn before your recall. Make sure you do this in whatever time you have, to the absolute best of your ability, fully learning the piece concerned, even if they give you permission to keep the papers in your hand. Whatever you do, don't make excuses about your lack of preparation or the shortness of time that you have had the information. It won't wash with many creatives, and an unprepared or under-prepared artist will usually not be given the benefit of the doubt and lose the job – especially if the material was actually sent well before the day. As casting director, my heart always sinks when this happens, as I may not be able to push for another chance for that artist, even if they happen to be the panel's number one choice or there are limited other choices to bring in for the part in question. This makes the casting director look bad as well as the performer – my reputation is hard earned and important to me, so I will certainly think twice about getting that artist back in for future projects. Prepare as much as you can and do your best, asking if you can refer to the material if you really feel it necessary to do so. Remember, if you don't prepare, there will always be someone else who will – there is a job in the balance, so if you want it, work hard and do everything in your power to get it. I cannot stress this enough, as the amount of outstanding artists who have lost work in this way – without obviously knowing it – is disturbingly high.

Depending on the project, you may be asked back again and again before the creatives come to a final decision, so be prepared for this. You may not get through to the final round – however many meetings that may be – but if you are recalled, try to build the necessary time into your schedule and other work commitments. I was once recalled for a show seven times over ten days, and was asked to prepare different material each time. I duly did so, to the best of my ability and, on that occasion, got down to the final two, only for the other actor to get the job. This may be harder to take, having been right through the process, but that is part of the excitement and a better job will soon come your way.

Workshops

Some recalls (or indeed first round auditions) may take the form of a workshop lasting several hours and requiring the participation of a group of actors. The purpose of these is primarily for the director and other members of the creative team to see how artists interact with each other, usually using improvisation, movement, dance, mime and other skills, so be sure to wear comfortable shoes and loose fitting clothing, which you don't mind getting dirty. These may be skills in which you excel, but if not, do your best as you never know what they are actually looking for. The kinds of companies that find the recalls of this nature especially useful are those specialising in physical and children's theatre. The real trick with workshops is not to worry about shining or trying to be better than the next person, a mistake made by many, which does them no favours as it hampers their performance. Remember, interaction is the key here, not competition, so if you are invited to participate, just go in, be yourself, do whatever is asked of you (taking whatever that may be and any direction offered in your stride) and, above all, enjoy yourself. The panel may be looking for very specific attributes, and a company who are going to work well together, perhaps enjoying a process of devising work, so there really is no point in worrying or trying to overcompensate. If you're for them, you're for them.

You will usually start by introducing yourself to the group and may then continue by playing theatre games, or games of trust, similar to those you have probably played in drama classes, youth theatre or at drama school. Play along wholeheartedly with these, as they help to show your company spirit with your fellow performers. You may then be put into smaller groups and asked to work together improvising scenes, perhaps based on the text or subject matter of the piece they are casting (which you will have researched beforehand). These groups may be changed, with some people being moved from one to another. It may be that some groups contain people that they wish to explore and keep an eye on and others those that do not interest them on this occasion. You will rarely be aware of this until the end, so don't waste time fretting about the calibre of your group, just throw yourself into what you are doing, enjoy it and let the outcome take care of itself. If the job is meant for you, then you will get it, and if not, you might make some useful contacts for the future, or even friends, so you may as well have fun.

So remember to . . .

- ✓ Think positive – your chances of the job increase with every recall.
- ✓ Remember who you have met before and check who will be in the room.
- ✓ Be remembered by looking the same at each audition.
- ✓ Thoroughly prepare everything they request – a job is in the balance!
- ✓ Keep your time flexible in case you are recalled again and again.

✓ Wear loose-fitting clothes and comfortable shoes to workshops.
✓ Interact rather than compete in workshop situations.
✓ Throw yourself into what you are doing and enjoy it.

CHAPTER 17

Television

Many people enter the acting profession as a result of watching television. As actors, how often have we watched a TV soap opera or other series and thought that we should be doing that instead of the actors on the screens in our living rooms? Along with the general public, most actors have wished they were a TV star, at one point or another; indeed, the concept of stardom is now pushed to the fore in the minds of the viewing public, thanks to reality television competitions, where fame is guaranteed to the winner (and often some of the losers too). While fame and fortune sound very nice, especially to a struggling actor, it is a rare commodity and there is more to life than playing leading roles and being recognised and photographed wherever you go. It can be far more satisfying in the long run to be a 'jobbing actor', who works regularly playing the smaller and often more exciting character roles, possibly working your way up to those that are more prominently featured or recurring in a series, than to begin your career playing starring roles – 'If you start at the top, you're certain to drop', to quote an old song. That said, as with everything in this industry, the competition is extremely tough. I regularly meet very experienced actors, who may have been well known in the past, who tell me that they went up for a three-line part in whatever television series and, despite their experience, didn't get it.

Television is the one medium in which you will always be cast as what you are or feasibly could be and as how you come across, rather than what you are plainly not. In other words, you will be playing you, or the you that you have projected to the panel at the casting concerned. It's not worth your while telling television casting directors that although you are a Londoner, you could play a Geordie. If they want a Geordie, nine times out of ten they will cast someone who was born and bred in Newcastle-upon-Tyne, unless you can walk into the room with the accent and convince everyone concerned that you are exactly what they are looking for. The downside of doing this, bearing in mind that the human memory believes what it is told and especially takes notice of the first impression that a person has given it, is that you risk being always remembered as a Geordie, so will never be seen for those London parts that you were born to play. Beware of being too versatile – work out the most useful type that you can realistically play and stick to it. Save playing character roles that are against your type for when you are working in the theatre. Most 'stars' do nothing but play themselves, or a close variant of themselves, as they know their niche (where they fit into the jigsaw puzzle) and earn a very good living from it. The majority of them are more than happy to do this, and only when they have really made it will a well-known TV actor suggest demon-strating their versatility by playing a role significantly different from those that they are known for. This only happens very occasionally, with most high-profile screen actors sticking firmly to their typecasting throughout their careers – as should you.

Dressing to give an idea of the part is also of great importance where television castings are concerned. As I've mentioned before, avoid going over the top at all costs, but giving all those who see, or watch your performance an indication that you can look the part may bring you nearer to getting it. Take another look at the script examples in Chapter 2 and write down ideas for what you would wear if you were being seen for every part (including the police officers, lawyers, children, etc.).

So what will happen in a television audition? Well, for a start it is most unlikely to be called an audition. When calling you with an appointment, your agent or the casting director may use the term 'casting', or else you may be invited to 'go in for . . .' or to 'meet and read' or to 'meet and chat'. Whichever term is used, it all basically means that you have an audition for a part in a television production. The meeting will rarely be in a television studio itself, more likely taking place in the offices of the production company, or any other available venue (some of these can be quite unconventional) if they need to see people far away from where the company is based, for instance in the town or city where the production concerned is set, or to be filmed, and local talent or accents are required. The casting session will usually be taken by the casting director, who may be joined by the director and/or producer, and what you do will always be filmed for future reference. There are many other people who will also have a say in which actor is cast in each role (right up to the head of drama, or even the controller of the channel, if the character is a regular or very significant), but you will probably never meet these people, as they will only see you on film, the footage of which will usually be unedited, so keep your eyes and face focused throughout the casting and be careful what you say and do in between readings.

You will never be asked to perform a speech in a casting for television – you will always read from the script of the production concerned (unless you are just invited to meet and chat, in which case you will do just that, though be prepared and don't refuse to read if they ask you to). Always ensure your sight-reading skills are up to scratch. Go back and reread the advice and sample TV scripts, which will remind you of what is required and inspire you to get your skills ready for your next appointment.

Camera technique

Your reading may be filmed with you seated, or standing on a mark on the floor, which you may be required to walk to and 'hit' (accurately stop at, without looking down at your feet). They will want to see proof that you will be able to do this on the actual set, where all positions are marked for the correctness of camera angles, so this is an important skill to practise in advance. When you read the pieces of script on camera, bring your performance right down and avoid over projecting with both your voice and your face. Less is most definitely more in this case – and far less is even more! The camera and microphone see and hear every little movement you make, so keep this firmly in your mind. The following pictures will give you a good idea of the length of camera shots and the importance of keeping your eyes and face focused throughout.

This is a long shot

This is a mid-shot

And this is a close-up

The actor pictured is Tom Bennett, who is already very experienced. In the five years since leaving drama school (where he was offered representation by several agents and chose excellently), he has filmed around twenty-five good character roles in television plays and series. This has happened because his agent got him to the right place at the right time, he has a castable look and has studied his craft, both during training and on set, so can show creatives what they need to see.

Learn the dialogue as much as you can, especially if you are sent the pages before the day of the casting. This will help you to avoid staring more at the words on the page than showing the camera your eyes, which are the most expressive part of your face or body, as far as the camera is concerned. When learning the script, either at home or in the waiting room before your meeting, be sure to learn it accurately, word for word (Dead Letter Perfect, as it is known in the trade), as the sense may be distorted if words or phrases are changed around. The script will have been meticulously timed using a stopwatch to fit the exact episode slot and the addition and subtraction of words will affect these timings. The writer of the series or episode may also be in the room as part of the panel and might not react favourably towards you if you cut or change their precious words, so precision really is the key here. If no script pages (sides) are available in advance, ensure that you can get to the venue as early as possible to familiarise yourself with the lines.

Reacting

If someone else is reading in with you, always respond and react to what they are saying – this is one of the great secrets of acting, yet one that many actors, even those with years of experience, sometimes forget in the heat of a casting – your reactions may often be more important than the lines you actually say. Even if you are reading solo, reacting to what you are saying is equally important. If the reader's face is in the shot, or just off the camera, play the scene to their eyes whenever possible. If this is difficult to do, pick a focal point somewhere between their eyes and chin and use that. If the person reading in with you is beside the camera lens, look at them, but if they are nowhere near it, or you are doing a solo reading, fix a focal point either just to the left or right of the lens, or just above it and play the scene to that. Whatever you do, never look directly into the lens unless specifically directed to do so. If you are unsure where to play something, or how close or wide the shot is, don't be afraid to quietly ask. Always ensure that your eyes are focused on whatever you are meant to be looking at and don't let your eyes wander aimlessly. If your eyes look unsure, the camera will pick up on it. If one of the people in the room who is off camera asks you questions during the interview time, direct your answers to the camera, if it is still rolling, rather than to the person who is asking. This will look far better on the tape when it is played back. In short, the director and the rest of the team need to see from this casting that you can come onto the set, play the scene(s) after whatever rehearsal is available (which may be minimal), understand any direction that is given and alter your performance accordingly, and leave again as quickly and quietly as you came, having been a pleasure to work with. Do not waste people's time by visibly acting and pretending to be what you're not – just be the character, and a great human being with it. If the character has any moments of vulnerability and you can convey these in your reading, it will stand you in good stead. Show the panel, and camera, exactly what they want to see, first time. In all filmed media, time is money and in short supply, many scenes will be scheduled for each day of filming, so actors who can come on set delivering the goods (preferably in one or two takes), with the minimum of fuss, are a godsend and will be re-employed time and time again. I have even heard of actors like this who have initially played small parts being thought of for, and offered, regular characters in the same series for the simple reason that they got on with the job in hand and were good to work with.

There have been many books written on television acting, all of which offer in-depth advice on working in the medium. My favourite is

Acting On Television, by the actor, TV producer, director and writer, Colin Bennett (www.actingontv.com), in which he shares his knowledge and experiences from many years on both sides of the camera. He also occasionally leads short courses on television acting technique at RADA in London (www.rada.org), at which I sometimes join him for an afternoon to watch the final presentation and talk about the casting process and audition technique. Colin is an 'old pro' in the greatest sense and a brilliant teacher. Both his book and courses are excellent tools to learn more about the craft of acting for the small screen and come highly recommended.

Finally, if you are up for a part in a series, soap or other long-running TV show, *always* make sure you have thoroughly researched the production, storylines and regular characters. This is absolutely essential, even if the show concerned is not being transmitted at the time – beg, steal, borrow or rent some episodes on DVD or video and watch them several times. The newer the episodes are, the better, as there is a greater chance of the structure of regular characters being the same. An actress I know once got to the final recall to be a new regular in a long-running, prime-time television series. The job was hers – until she revealed, when chatting to the entire team at the final meeting, that she had never seen even one episode of any of the show's five previous series. The room fell silent and she was quickly ushered out. The second choice was fine – and stayed for a further three series.

So remember to . . .

✓ Aim to be a good jobbing actor, rather than a star.
✓ Avoid being too versatile – know your typecasting and stick to it.
✓ Dress to give an indication of the part, without going over the top.
✓ Keep your eyes and face focused throughout the casting.
✓ Ensure that your sight-reading skills are polished in readiness.
✓ Practise 'hitting your mark'.
✓ Learn the script as much as possible, always Dead Letter Perfect.

✓   Not act and pretend to be what you're not – be the character.
✓   React and respond to those reading in and know where you are looking.
✓   Never look directly into the camera lens, or far away from it.
✓   Check how close the shot is set, if you need to.
✓   Show them exactly what they need to see, first time.
✓   Always thoroughly research any series for which you are seen.

CHAPTER 18

Films and Screen Tests

There can be few actors who haven't dreamed about starring on the big screen and film is indeed a great medium in which to work. Whether or not you are ever one of the lucky few that end up as an internationally famous, Academy Award-winning star, there are numerous ways of practising your craft in movies.

Thanks to the advanced technology that is widely and inexpensively available, short films are now made, and sometimes entered into competitions, by aspiring filmmakers using basic camcorders or the video mode on digital cameras and even mobile phones. While this may sound primitive, the digital quality is usually good and this work can act as a springboard for their future careers, showing their talent and creativity to potential funders and audience alike, without it costing a fortune – this can also be the case for the actors in these films. Keep your ear to the ground as this is a great way to practise your camera technique and you never know when an opportunity might arise through a friend of a friend or someone in your social network.

Film schools often require actors for their students' graduation projects, in exchange for expenses and a DVD copy of the movie, which you can then include on your showreel. Casting breakdowns for these films are usually advertised on *Shooting People*, Mandy.com, *PCR*, Castweb or other information services, but if this type of work interests you, contact the schools (which are listed in *Contacts*) to ask how and when they cast and whether they keep general files of actors' details. Send them yours, especially if a particular school is based near you. The interesting thing about working with student directors is that you never know how their careers will progress. I remember talking to an elderly American actor some years ago who told me he was in the graduation production of a young film student back in the 1950s. The director worked his way up, becoming a legendary name in Hollywood and he remembered the actor throughout his illustrious career, giving him good character roles in seventeen major movies.

The casting may well take place at the school itself and you will be asked to read from the script and put on camera. The technique and sound levels required for this, and all film castings, are the same as those needed for television – remember, *less is more*. As the students may not be that experienced in auditioning actors, this might be a situation where it will be necessary for you to take the lead, so be mentally prepared for this scenario. Conversely, you might be treated with a little arrogance, so remember to smile and rise above it. If you are offered the part, enjoy the experience and learn from all those around you. Ensure that everything is agreed and confirmed when the offer is made (negotiation will be covered in Chapter 36). I mention this, as students are notoriously bad about actually sending DVD copies of their films to the actors who have given their time and skill to appear in them. While some are great, sending the disc and a letter of thanks within a few weeks, others can take many months or years to do this (if they do at all), despite the actors regularly phoning and emailing. This is unfair, especially if you are having a showreel made and need to include your scenes on it, so if this happens to you, do not be afraid to pester the student, taking your complaint to the principal of the film school concerned, if you have no success, to ensure that you receive what has been agreed and promised.

There are many excellent British and international short and feature films made every year, the casting of which is not usually widely publicised, but, in the case of most feature productions, will be handled by a casting director. Keep your ear to the ground for advance news of films that will soon go into production, which can be found in numerous publications, including *Advance Production News UK*, *PCR*, *Screen International* and *Variety* (as mentioned in Chapter 1). If a film is based on a book, make sure you read the original novel to gauge whether there are suitable parts for you (remembering that some may be cut from the final screenplay). If you know who the casting director will be for the project, you can send them your details with a letter expressing your interest and asking to be kept in mind for whichever parts, if you know the storyline, or any suitable parts in the case of a new and unpublished script. If the name of the casting director is not available, write to the producer at the production office, asking for your letter to be passed on to whoever is dealing with casting, when the time is right.

While the casts of some short or feature-length films, made by recent graduates or more established directors and producers, may be paid in accordance with union rates, others may be offered on a low budget or deferred payment basis. Low budget means exactly that – you will be paid a small fee, usually far less than the minimum stipulated by Equity. If a film is offered on deferred payment, this means that a percentage, or the whole of an artist's agreed fee, will not be payable until that production has been sold and distributed to cinemas, rather than guaranteed and paid after you have finished filming. This is basically a way for producers to minimise their risk, by not having to pay the cast and crew before they have made any money themselves. Some performers are wary of working in this way, as even if a movie in which they have appeared is a huge success at the box office, it can be a difficult and lengthy process to obtain the payment that is due to them from the producers, despite their contracts often stating otherwise. Some of these movies will never make it to the cinema so the cast will remain unpaid. You may find that your agent advises you against taking such a project, especially if they have encountered problems in the past.

The Indian Bollywood film market has gone through rapid expansion over the years and an increasing number of Anglo-Asian actors are making the long journey to Mumbai to try their luck in these Hindi language films. Such is the interest in the UK that movie star Anhupam Kher has opened Britain's first Bollywood acting school (www.actorprepares.co.uk). Based in Ealing, West London, the school is open to anyone keen to learn this style of acting, regardless of their race.

The majority of big-screen blockbusters are still made by the Americans and are shot in Hollywood, and many other locations around the world. Because of this, I have known many non-American artists to obtain visas, pack their bags and head out to Los Angeles to try their luck in finding fame and fortune on the other side of the Atlantic. While agents and casting directors there are reputedly easier to meet than their UK counterparts, and happier to introduce and refer artists to others who may be in a better position to help them, the amount of actors in the USA is even greater than in the UK so the competition is extremely intense. The majority of those people I've known who have tried this route have returned home some weeks or months later, with no money and their dreams shattered – the Americans may think the British accent cute and elegant, but this is not enough to make a career out there, as many discover to their cost every year. The only actors I've known to reach their goal in this way are those who have already achieved significant success in their own country, and their name, reputation and work has filtered through across the Atlantic, creating interest and demand. That said, even some of these actors soon return home to continue their careers, having had a much harder time making inroads over there than they had originally anticipated. If the thought of conquering the American market has crossed your mind, wait for a while and concentrate on becoming successful in your home territory first. Go to LA for a holiday, do the studio tours, research their working practices, even take an acting class or two to acquaint yourself with the competition that you would be up against, before coming home and knuckling down to your career, storing the knowledge ready for (if and) when the time comes.

Sometimes, big American movies will be shot abroad and thus require local talent. In which case, the director and other creatives will fly over to meet and screen test (a term for seeing an artist acting or reading the script on camera) suitable artists, who will have usually been brought in by a local casting director. These meetings will often take place in centrally located hotels, in which they will hire a suite and invite artists (perhaps stars or those with some profile in the country concerned, who are not necessarily known by the Americans) to come in for a chat and maybe a read. Both of these will usually be filmed or put on webcam to enable their colleagues back at home to see and help in the decision-making process, so don't ignore the camera. Don't be surprised if a meeting of this nature happens outside normal working hours – evenings and early mornings, even weekends, are not uncommon, so be at your best regardless of the time. You may be asked to meet at a certain hotel and instead of being directed to a suite by reception, you could find yourself in the ballroom or conference facility, where you will wait together with what seems like half of Equity. Don't let this daunt you (especially as you will have budgeted more than enough waiting time), just wait your turn, enter the room (either by yourself or as part of a group) and do whatever is asked of you as best you can, bearing in mind that it will be filmed. As there are so many actors in America, directors often see what they want as soon as someone walks in through the door and will usually only spend time working with someone who they feel is right for the job. You may therefore be in and out of the room very quickly, having read very little, if at all. Don't take this personally, it's no reflection on you, your talent or ability, it is just the way they work, especially if they have many actors to get through in a limited amount of time. Conversely, British directors working in America for the first time, spend time with each audi-tionee, politely sitting through entire readings, songs, etc., sometimes redirecting them or asking for other pieces, as is their way, so each American actor leaves the room convinced that the job is theirs.

Occasionally, the meeting might take place in a house that has been rented by the director or producer. I remember a friend being summoned to a posh London address to meet for a small but significant role in a major American movie. He walked up the long drive, rang the doorbell and was rendered a quivering wreck when the door was opened by the film's star (who was also one of its producers, and of whom my friend had been a huge fan for many years). The star was extremely gracious, ushering him into a room to wait and calming his nervous babblings, before taking him through to meet the rest of the team. They were all charmed by him and he was delighted to get the job, though he never quite knew what he did to make it happen. If you are ever faced with a major Hollywood star or legendary director at a casting, keep your cool and don't gush or ask for autographs. A one sentence compliment about a piece of their work (the obscurer the better) that you have seen and enjoyed is enough and then get on with the meeting, remembering that you are both professionals and you want their job.

So remember to . . .

- ✓ Always look out for opportunities and pre-production news.
- ✓ Work with film students – you never know where it may lead.
- ✓ Keep in touch with film schools, especially those based near you.
- ✓ Ensure you get DVD copies that have been promised.
- ✓ Read books on which upcoming films are based to find suitable roles.
- ✓ Be wary of deferred payment and respect your agent's advice.
- ✓ Be prepared to meet Americans outside normal working hours.
- ✓ Not take it personally if you are in and out of the room quickly.
- ✓ Not gush if you meet a star or legendary director – you are both professionals.

CHAPTER 19

Commercial Castings

Whereas with theatre auditions there's often a formula and you can gauge roughly how you have done, commercial castings are not so structured and the outcome can be far from easy, if not impossible to predict. Commercials and photographic stills shoots are in the main about your look and while acting and improvisational skill and style come into the equation, the look of the artists and balance of a cast (in the case of a family, for instance) are paramount. Increasingly, these days, commercials are cast initially, or even totally from photographs, with the casting director showing a selection of artists' pictures to the creatives instead of live actors coming in for a casting. It therefore pays to have good quality photographs with a selection of 'looks' ready for this eventuality.

The ever-repeated motto, 'Be prepared for anything', really comes into its own here. For some commercials you will merely say your name, height and agent's name into the camera, while for others you'll read from the script, eat imaginary food, inspect an imaginary fridge in the imaginary showroom, apply imaginary spot cream to an imaginary spot on your face – the list is endless, and you may well not be given warning of what is required before you enter the room. I still remember seeing the tape of an ice cream commercial casting session some years ago where the girls were asked to pretend to eat an ice cream and then recreate the orgasm scene from the film *When Harry Met Sally*. It was hilarious, with renditions varying from embarrassedly contained to downright over the top, not to mention one lady who froze after taking an imaginary spoonful and said 'I'm sorry, I couldn't possibly', before hurrying out of the room! Was she right to do this? I would say no. First, I know that all the selected artists' agents were fully primed of the requirements and so had the lady concerned been unhappy with this, she should have asked her agent to withdraw her from the session, giving as much notice as possible, so that the spare space could be filled by another artist who was more comfortable with the brief and wanted the job. Second, no matter how she felt, the actress concerned should have *gone for it*! I was once summoned to a casting for a cornflakes campaign. 'What could be easier?' I thought, little knowing what lay ahead. I entered the room and met the director – an esteemed choreographer. The assistant gave me the brief – 'You're lying asleep, you wake up bleary eyed, stretch, rub your eyes and stagger out of bed. You go across to the window, open the curtains and are shocked to see this massive great beanstalk growing outside your house and blocking out the light. You look shocked, go back over to the bed, put on your dressing gown and slippers and head towards the door. Then put your hand on the handle, open the door and look stunned when you see the thick green forest outside your door. You hack your way through the branches and down the stairs, you find the kitchen door, hack your way to opening it, open it and see your mum and dad sitting at the kitchen table. You join them, pour a bowl of cornflakes, take a spoonful, crunch and smile – and we need all of that done stationary on that spot there,' he said, pointing to a small white spot on the floor. I gulped mentally. Could I even remember all of that in the correct order, never mind mime it convincingly for the director and rolling camera? I thought for a moment, took a deep breath and went for it. 'Nothing ventured, nothing gained,' I said to myself, launching into it, giving my all. The job didn't go my way, but at least I tried.

More dauntingly, you might have to work with the actual product concerned, while reading the script, which requires double the concentration as well as the dexterity to convincingly show off the product in its best light. Getting a grass stain out of a piece of white cotton may be easy enough, but doing it on camera while describing what you're doing can be an entirely different matter.

All these scenarios are looking for a reaction and sometimes it is up to you to figure out which one is required, as often in this case the creatives don't know what they are looking for until that person walks in through the door and shows them. An actor I know was booked for a yoghurt commercial, for the one reason that he not only looked at the mimed spoon and smiled after licking it, but noticed that he'd missed a bit, so licked it a second time. The director loved this and he was rewarded with a trip abroad and a very handsome fee as a result. Some artists who are regularly called in for commercial castings (and are perhaps represented by a specialist agency) introduce themselves slightly differently to the camera. They will make a speech to the effect of 'My name is Joe Bloggs, I am with XYZ Agency, I am 5 feet 8 inches tall, here is my left profile (turning sideways on to the camera), here is my right profile (turning the other way), and these are my hands' (showing the backs of their hands and nails to the camera, then turning their palms uppermost, before turning their hands back to their original position and holding it for a couple of seconds). This is a tactic which is really only used by established artists in the medium, especially models, but might be one that is worth perfecting and remembering for the future, especially if you are a good commercial 'type'.

So what is a type? Extremes work well in commercials. As well as those with stunningly good looks, such as models and supermodels etc., those who are very ordinary (boy or girl next door), quirky, fat, thin, as well as archetypal mums, dads, grandmothers, grandfathers, teenagers or children are all very useful. We can probably all think of campaigns past and present where these and other definite types have featured, and maybe even remember the artists concerned more than the product they were advertising. Look regularly at the commercials that appear daily on our television and cinema screens and the sort of artists and faces that appear in them. You will find the type of commercials varies on the different channels and depending on the time of day (for instance, commercial breaks on weekday afternoons on Channel 4 or Five are tailored to a radically different audience than those between prime-time programmes on ITV1). Ask your family, friends, colleagues and, wherever possible, agents and casting directors how they see you and what type they feel you are. It may or may not be glaringly obvious and you may receive many conflicting and confusing answers, or you may be surprised by home truths that had not occurred to you. Take these perceptions on board. If you are a definite type, then don't be afraid to market yourself and play to that – it will pay dividends. If, however, you don't fit into a particular category, do not despair as not everybody is that specific and you can be seen for a wider selection than someone in a niche or pigeon hole.

So how should you dress for a casting? Again, there are no hard and fast rules, but you will usually be given a rough idea with the brief when you are called with the appointment. If not, ask your agent or whoever has called you for as much information as possible. As with types, there are also various looks including casual, smart casual and executive. The way you interpret these is up to you, but you should always make it look as if you have made an effort, avoiding dirty or ripped clothing at all costs (unless it is specifically requested, of course!). Executives wear a smart suit, pressed shirt, tie and polished shoes. One commercial regular told me of a time when he had a call from his agent while away from home giving him an appointment for a casting a couple of hours later. He was to play a businessman and told to go looking smart. There was no way he could make it home and back in time, so headed for the nearest branch of Marks and Spencer. He bought a suit and the full accessories, went to the casting venue and changed in the toilets, taking good care not to damage or soil his new clothes. Once finished, he changed back, carefully putting the clothes back in their packages, went back to

M&S with the till receipt and obtained a full refund on everything. A clever, if somewhat cheeky ploy, and one that should only be used in a dire emergency.

Prior to the casting day, or perhaps when you arrive at the venue, you will be required to complete an artist declaration form, which contains questions about yourself in relation to the commercial concerned. When you get inside the room, you will be faced with a camera or two and anything from one to a whole team of people. You might be introduced to them, or probably just the main person who will be directing you, and you will usually be told what is required. It's important to judge when to look into the camera and when to avoid contact with the lens. Don't be afraid to ask this if you are unsure, though the usual simple rule is if you are merely saying your name, height, agent's name, etc., look straight into the lens, but if you are delivering script on your own, then choose a point slightly off camera, perhaps to one side or slightly above. If you are with other artists, then look at them or the product, etc., and if the director or cameraman is asking you questions, answer into the lens rather than to them.

One of the most common reasons that artists are unsuccessful when auditioning for commercials has nothing to do with them. It is intriguing when actually seeing the finished product on screen to notice that the character brief has totally changed. Many a time numerous middle-aged ladies have auditioned, only to have been replaced by someone in her late twenties when the commercial is actually made. So why does this happen? Well, as I've mentioned before, the director often doesn't know what they want until that person walks through the door, though in the commercial world, the decision rarely lies solely with the director. They will have some say, as will their colleagues at the production company who have been employed to produce it. Creatives from the advertising agency, whose job it is to create the campaign and place it on screens or billboards, will also give opinions, and the casting director, employed for their skill and knowledge to bring the best people in, may also be asked for input. However, the majority of decisions usually rest with

'The Client'. These mysterious people work for the group or company responsible for manufacturing and marketing the actual products being advertised; in other words, the people ultimately responsible for footing the six or seven figure bill for the entire campaign. They are therefore keen to know that everything about it is right and exactly to their liking before proceeding, and that includes the artists.

I have known many artists come out of castings absolutely positive that the job is theirs, as the director and others in the room (who can include those from any of the groups listed above) have made all the right noises, yet frustratingly they hear nothing more. Agents frequently ring for feedback, there is often very little to give on commercial castings, but the same reason is the case again and again, 'The Client decided to go with someone different.' It's sadly the luck of the draw. The rule of thumb especially applies to commercial castings: prepare as much as possible, do your best and then *forget it!* It is rare for performers to have a high strike rate in this medium, though you never know, you may get lucky, and so it's always worth going for it, as some campaigns are very lucrative indeed. A word about fees, while we are on the subject; some commercials run for years and offer a daily fee for the shoot followed by a 'repeat' fee every time it is shown, based on the daily fee, which gives you an income for the life of that campaign. However, while my fellow Casting Directors' Guild members always encourage employers to offer repeats, they are becoming less common and some advertisers now offer a 'buyout', often a cheaper option, which means you get an agreed fee – usually a percentage of your daily shoot fee – which allows them to use the commercial(s) in certain regions without paying each time. Buyouts usually apply as standard for all foreign commercials, with different percentages for different countries or territories. Nowadays, another common offer is an all-in fee, with everything included, some of which can be very low. I heard recently of £400 all-in being offered for a major national campaign, which may sound good, especially if times are hard, but considering that it not only buys your services for the shoot, but potentially puts you out of the running for similar future campaigns, as your face may be plastered on our TV and cinema screens, as well as perhaps internet virals, websites, billboards and in-store or on pack promotions for up to a year, it's really not much at all. It is up to you and your agent to decide whether to take such deals, especially as fees for commercials are as offered and not usually negotiable.

Casting and even shoot dates (which may be outside the UK) can often come up at short notice. Therefore if you have other commitments outside your acting life, make your agent aware of the situation and perhaps ask them to check that you will be around before suggesting you, thus avoiding letting down the casting director and blemishing your good name.

Sometimes you will be recalled and be asked to do more in front of the camera, perhaps in a pairing or group (or several different combinations) to play husbands, wives, families, etc. and as with the first round casting, you may be required to improvise or perform the script to the camera, interacting with those in your group(s). A small fee should be payable if you are called back for commercials, so check when you are given the appointment, or ask your agent if this is so. The current Equity recall fee is included on their website (www.equity.org) or you can call the Commercials Department at their London office (the direct number will be in the Equity diary, sent annually to members, or under organisations in *Contacts*).

You may then be offered the job outright, being told the shoot dates and wardrobe calls, etc. Have your measurements and sizes up to date and written down (many agents will also give you a form to complete containing this information when you join them). Details that could be required are included in the list opposite, from top to bottom; keep them all on hand, in centimetres and inches, just in case.

Some of these measurements you will know (or think you do, so please make sure you are correct), others you may never need and in most cases you will get measured by wardrobe staff to double check before costumes are bought, hired or made for you. For the awkward ones, such as elbow to cuff or waist to heel (used in the

Men	Women
Men	*Women*
Height	Height
Hat	Hat
Collar	Neck to heel
Shoulder to elbow	Shoulder to elbow
Chest	Bust/cup (bra size)
Elbow to cuff	Elbow to cuff
Waist	Waist
Glove	Waist to heel
Inside leg	Glove
Shoe	Hips
	Inside leg
	Shoe
	Dress size

making of period-style skirts), get a friend to measure you, and for the obscure ones, such as hat and glove, go to a department store with specialist departments and get accurately measured – rather than putting small or medium, as most do. A staggering statistic is that 85 per cent of women are wearing the wrong-sized bra, so visit Marks and Spencer or any other large store that has a dedicated lingerie fitter and department to be properly measured. It's a good idea to properly measure yourself regularly, as ill-fitting costumes are a wardrobe person's nightmare, and won't make you feel good either.

Another vital point to remember is that the shoot may be abroad, so always ensure that your passport is current and not on the verge of expiry. Getting a passport renewed at short notice is a stressful experience – sometimes touch and go – and not being able to show valid documentation to your employers or at the airport could cost you a lucrative job, as well as being expensive and irritating to the production company concerned, especially if they have to recast or have applied for visas or work permits on your behalf.

However, more often than not, you will be what is known as 'pencilled'. This is a common practise whereby an employer may call on your services for certain dates if they desire, without actually officially offering you the job and booking you. It is their way of ensuring that you will be available when they want you and other potential jobs won't get in the way of their plans. It may sound good, and indeed it is promising, not to mention ego boosting, but there are various degrees of pencil, from light to heavy. If you have been lightly pencilled, you may be among up to fifteen other artists, all up for the same character and many agents will deal with it, without informing the client concerned so as not to falsely raise hopes, as they often come to nothing. At the other end of the scale, you might be put on 'heavy pencil', meaning you are the first and only choice for the part, or one of two or three. You may well be told by your agent at this stage, though, again, be prepared for events not to work out, in case the pencil is taken off (about which you may not even be informed). If you are pencilled, you will need to fill in a second artist declaration form, which is longer and more in depth. I only believe that a job is actually mine when everything is confirmed and the contract is signed and sealed – a philosophy I cannot recommend highly enough, especially where commercials are concerned.

Street castings

Although more applicable to models (or people with model-like looks), you could be approached while walking down the street by a talent scout, who is looking for 'real people' for a commercial or photographic campaign and invited to attend a casting. You may have seen this on the BBC Three series *Find Me A Face*, in which two model scouts compete to find a certain look that fits a brief. While it can be flattering to be 'scouted', always be sure to inform the person concerned about your circumstances (that you are a professional performer, have an agent or are a member of Equity, if this applies to you). Some of the campaigns that are cast on the street require people with little or no experience and therefore pay accordingly (far less than other commercials), if, indeed, they pay at all. Most people outside the industry would find it fun to go to a casting and be selected to be the face of a product, but bear in mind that, as a working performer, you are in this business to earn a living as well as to have fun. You may choose to go to the casting for experience, though be careful not to waste anyone's time if you do not intend to accept the job for whatever reason. If you don't accept their offer, find out if the scout works in a casting office, you can then tell them a little about yourself and ask if you can send them your details for other projects in the future.

So remember to . . .

✓ Be prepared for anything, especially improvisation – *go for it*!
✓ Gauge your 'type', or types you could play.
✓ Ensure you have a good selection of photographs with different looks.
✓ Keep your agent informed about your commitments and availability.
✓ Dress to give an idea of the part you are up for.
✓ Always have a valid passport and renew it well before it expires.
✓ Get regularly measured and record your measurements and sizes.
✓ Make it clear that you are a professional if scouted on the street.

CHAPTER 20

Roleplay

In recent years, roleplaying has become increasingly used in business to train staff to deal effectively with a variety of situations that they might encounter in their workplace. Actors are especially suited to this type of work as they are not only trained and used to creating characters and working from scripts, but also often have the skill of improvisation, enabling them to react immediately to whatever is said or done by the staff member being trained. Roleplay is most often used by two major industry sectors – corporate, legal and financial companies, and medical – and this training is given either as a face-to-face meeting or on the telephone, with the roleplayer and the person who is being trained or assessed in separate rooms, speaking on an internal phone line.

The premise involves an actor or group of actors going into a workplace where they are given a scenario by the trainer for their character to play repeatedly with numerous staff members who will be sent in to be assessed during the course of the day. The scenarios could include angry or complaining customers, business people trying to negotiate a better price for an item; patients who are trying to describe their symptoms to a doctor (sometimes actors may be required to have had genuine experience of these symptoms), or people to whom bad news has to be imparted by a doctor or other professional. The trainer will watch the interview (either from within the same room, or via CCTV) to study and analyse the responses and reactions given by the staff members being tested or assessed in order to evaluate their progress and discover any areas on which they need to work and improve. This can be a very interesting and useful process for the actors too, as participating in this type of training is brilliant for people watching and character study, looking and gauging how different people react under stress or when put in awkward situations.

Roleplay work is not really 'cast' that often, relying on experience and word of mouth – 'It's not what you know, it's who you know' comes into play here too. The majority of jobs or assignments in this field are allotted to actors who are already known to the companies concerned and have experience in the field(s) in which they work, or to those friends or colleagues whom they recommend, when asked if they know of anybody to fill a specific gap, usually at short notice. While many of the actors are booked directly by the training department of the company, medical school or hospital concerned, there are also some specialist companies (listed in *Contacts*) who recruit and provide actors for roleplay, matching the most suitable person to the brief – somewhat like casting. A few of these companies occasionally advertise general auditions, when they feel the need to increase the roster of artists available to them, so keep your eyes open for these. In these auditions, you will be asked to participate in several scenarios, with their established roleplayers, which will test your roleplaying and improvisation skills and how you react in given situations. You will also be interviewed, so ensure you have plenty of pertinent questions in your mind. Practising both face-to-face and telephone scenarios with your friends prior to the audition day itself will stand you in good stead.

Once you feel confident about your skills and have some experience, research if there are any specialist companies in your area – Interact (www.interact.eu.com) based in London is the biggest and best known of these – and contact them to ask about their policy for recruiting new artists. You could also call the training departments of larger locally based companies and medical schools to ask if they ever use roleplay, or have need of actors for staff training. You could ask your actor friends or agent if they have any contacts in the field, or even get a group of friends with suitable skills together and offer your services to companies. (Some actors also help or coach business people on effective use of the voice and conveying information when speaking in public, which may be another sideline to make money from your skills.)

An increasing amount of actors are earning money from roleplay work in between acting jobs, so polish your skills, research the market (especially if you have had experience working in other non-theatrical careers) and you too could be one of them. It could also lead to work in corporate training films.

So remember to . . .

✓ Practise your skills and possible scenarios with friends.
✓ Contact roleplay providers and companies, especially locally based.
✓ Mention areas of work and symptoms of which you have experience.
✓ Study the reactions of those being trained to use for future characters.
✓ Assemble a group of friends and offer your services to companies.

CHAPTER 21

Corporate Training Films

Corporate training films are commissioned by large and multinational companies to assist in the training of their staff. This is a fairly similar concept to roleplaying, only in recorded format which can be watched by many more employees time and time again. Actors performing in these films will be playing scenarios that commonly occur in the workplace to bring these to the viewers' attention and to equip them with the necessary skills to deal effectively with tricky or problematic situations, and to follow procedures or impart specialised information. These films therefore give the employees concerned the competitive edge in the workplace and a sense of personal development. This form of work, while not as highly paid as many television commercials, can provide a steady stream of employment for the right type of actors.

Your agent will probably hear about and suggest you for suitable parts in them, but you can make contact with casting directors and production companies yourself. Listings of companies can be found in *The Knowledge* (www.theknowledgeonline.com) and in the 'Film, radio, television & video production companies' section of *Contacts*.

There are two essential skills for corporate work: an excellent knowledge of roleplaying techniques and the ability to improvise. It is also important to research as much as possible about the field of business that the film will be set in, as well as the work of the client company who are commissioning it. You may be given a scenario by the director before or when you go in to the casting, and it will usually be up to you to decide how to play this, so quick thinking is needed. Practising various scenarios with friends or colleagues will give you a store of ideas to draw on when you need them in castings – perhaps some will be original and make you stand out from the competition. When you are called with an appointment, try to ascertain what type of character you would be playing – will you be the powerful boss, problem solver, inept or lazy office worker, or something in between? – and any technical knowledge that might be needed, such as the character's traits and the director's general perception. If you can get to watch some existing training films, you will have a better idea of their format and potential requirements (the star studded ones made by Video Arts in the 1980s are a great example, and immensely entertaining).

Being dressed for the part is especially important in the corporate world. If you want to try making a niche for yourself in this marketplace, or are regularly being seen for training films, it pays to invest in a smart, good quality business suit (probably dark), shirt or blouse, tie and black shoes, which should always be clean, pressed and polished. Also ensure that you are well groomed whenever you have this type of casting, with your hair tidy (and possibly well cut) and your nails manicured – as high-earning city workers will be. It is essential to have at least one corporate-type photograph in your portfolio for suggesting yourself for work, so remember to take smart clothes to the photographer.

We will now explore what may happen and be required if you are called in to audition. The casting will invariably take place in the production company or client company's offices, rather than a casting suite, and may be filmed if all the decision makers are not present, or as a memory aid. Be prepared for the scenario and character (as well as for changes they may make). Sometimes you may be asked to devise your own scenario, perhaps even on the spot, so don't be fazed if this is requested. Be on your toes and keep thinking in character at all times. If you can remember key facts about the industry and company concerned and drop them into the scenario or interview conversation, where possible, this may earn you extra brownie points. Think of how you would currently be perceived and cast. What type are you? Which character would you be most suited to play in the Ricky Gervais comedy series *The Office*, for instance? If you can be pigeonholed (type cast) as a definite business type, you will have an excellent advantage in the case of the corporate world and it will increase your chances of being employed on a regular basis.

Finally, after your audition, think back on what you did and what you said in the casting, writing down extensive notes in your log, as you could be asked to repeat or adapt some of these ideas if you are recalled or get the job. You can also think about how you could have improved and use all this information in future castings for corporate work. All these factors will most certainly give you the competitive edge over the other actors.

So remember to . . .

- ✓ Research the field of work and specific company thoroughly.
- ✓ Practise possible scenarios in advance for ideas.
- ✓ Dress appropriately and be well groomed.
- ✓ Think about the types of characters you are most suited to play.
- ✓ Be on your toes and think in character at all times.
- ✓ Make notes about what you said and did in the casting, just in case.

CHAPTER 22

Radio Drama

In these high-tech days of TV and movie stardom, the medium of radio drama is often overlooked by actors as a means of employment, and, while there are no multi-million pound fees on offer, radio can provide a steady stream of work. If this medium interests you, the first step is to tune in and listen to as many plays and serials as you can so that you can judge the types of actor and voices they need and use, which can vary from play to play. Details of these can be found in the *Radio Times* and other listings magazines and websites. If you have little or no microphone experience, you will need to work on this before auditioning for the more established companies and there are several options open to you. The various Actors Centres around the country, the City Lit (www.citylit.ac.uk) and some drama schools offer workshops and short courses led by experienced practitioners and often held in actual studios. You can also enquire if your local hospital radio does any drama (and if not, you could always suggest it, and get together a group of like-minded actors volunteering to record some programmes, which would be an excellent way to learn on the job while entertaining the patients). When you have some technique and experience behind you, make contact with your local radio stations to see if they ever make dramatic productions and ask about their casting policy. You will stand a better chance with the smaller stations where there will doubtless be fewer actors for them to choose from. When you feel confident enough, it is then time to contact the big boys in search of an audition.

By far the highest output of radio drama is made by the BBC, and broadcast on Radio 3, Radio 4 and the World Service – details of dates and times, together with lists of the casts and production teams, can be found in the *Radio Times*. They not only use actors on a freelance (production by production) basis, but also offer some longer-term contracts as part of the Radio Repertory Company. If you are soon to graduate from a recognised drama school, you will have been taught some radio technique and several of your year may be chosen to compete in the Carleton Hobbs Award. This annual competition is keenly contested by all the accredited schools and the prize is a contract with BBC Radio. Even if you don't win, some entrants are offered work on a freelance basis. If this is an area that interests you, be sure to make it known to your tutors.

Auditions for more established actors are in the form of workshops, which are held from time to time and encompass various aspects of radio technique. These are recorded and kept in archive for the future reference of their producers and directors when casting. Participation in a workshop does not, of course, guarantee employment, though it may be a foot in the door for you. Invitation to these workshops is given to actors who have previously written to the radio drama co-ordinator, requesting to be considered for future casting and enclosing a CV (which should feature any radio or voice experience and training at the top) and a CD of voice samples.

You can record your own sampler (showreel) on a computer, using a good quality external microphone, though be aware of two major factors of microphone technique. The first is to avoid rustling the pages from which you are reading, either turning them silently or picking them up and gently dropping them to the floor – both of these should be practised regularly. Second, be careful not to 'pop' into the microphone, in other words paying special attention to the pronunciation of the letter 'P', which, if said too violently or close to the microphone can create a popping noise. Be aware of this, and any other vocal traits you may have. Good sight-reading skills also come into play here, as while you will be able to thoroughly rehearse the pieces for your sampler, you may have very little time beforehand with the script when recording an actual play.

What should be included on your sampler? First and foremost, your own natural speaking voice reading a story or narrative from a script in your native accent. If you are able, do a second piece which demonstrates your versatility, incorporating any character voices, accents or dialects in which you are proficient to a native standard (ones that are so accurate that you can switch them on or off without thought and fool people into thinking that you actually come from the place in question). Keep both pieces short and convincing. Advice for compiling your sampler and information about the BBC's audition workshops can be found online at www.bbc.co.uk/soundstart.

Increasingly, radio stations are buying in plays and programmes which are made by independent radio production companies (a list of which can be found in *Contacts*). You can find out the name of the producer, director and which company made the show concerned by listening to the credits at the end of the broadcast and then either call the station's switchboard or search on the internet to find contact details to write to them and send your sampler CD. Acting on radio is a very specific art form and, as is often the case in this industry, there is a pool of actors who are used again and again because they are trusted to deliver the goods. Keep working on your technique and gaining experience and you could well be joining them.

So remember to . . .

✓   Listen to radio plays and serials regularly.
✓   Practise your technique and gain microphone experience.
✓   Research directors and companies by listening to the credits.
✓   Make a sampler CD and send it to companies requesting an audition.
✓   Create a separate CV for voice work.

CHAPTER 23

Voice Work

One of the greatest assets of any actor is their voice, so in this chapter we'll discuss ways to unlock its potential and use your voice to the full in various media. Performers with these skills can earn a good living.

Voice-overs

I've mentioned how competitive the profession of performing is, and it is a fact that cannot be stressed strongly enough. Well, now we come to *the* most competitive and closed off area of the business – that of voice-overs. Unless you live in a wilderness without television or radio, you will hear voice-overs every day of your life. You may not really pay that much attention to them or you may think how easy they sound. You've also doubtless heard talk of the staggeringly high fees reputedly earned by people in this medium and thought 'I could do that' and 'That's money for old rope.' Well, I'll dispel these myths and put the record straight. Like any form of acting, voicing is a very specialised skill, which can sometimes come naturally but is usually learnt over time, often taking years of practise and experience to perfect. When you hear a voice-over on a commercial – perhaps someone instantly recognisable, or maybe just 'the voice next door' – it *does* sound effortless, but that is down to the delivery and expertise that the particular artist brings to the job. 'But just how hard can it be to say a couple of lines extolling the virtues of a random product?' you may be asking. There is actually a huge amount of skill involved. Vocal versatility is a great asset, as is modulating the tones of your delivery. Some campaigns will need a harder, more urgent sell 'Sale must end Friday – *buy now!*', while others benefit from a softer stance 'Relax your cares away in a long, soothing bubbly bath.' These are the two extremes and most voices will be somewhere in between. Authentic accents and dialects (or the ability to do several) and character voices can be useful too. Listen to commercials whenever you can, see what sorts of voices campaigns need and are using and which best suits your vocal capabilities. Can you emulate them or even offer something completely different? As with everything mechanical, commercials are timed meticulously to fit into the advertising slots that are booked with the radio and television companies. Sometimes a script might be far longer than the slot – 37 seconds, for instance, when the slot lasts just 28. While the powers that be might decide to cut it down to size by those 9 seconds, they sometimes will not want to lose that much valuable information and so it will be down to the artist and director to speed up and make everything fit, without compromising vocal quality, enunciation and audibility. This is no mean feat and can be nerve-wracking to say the least, especially when time is of the essence to get it right. Practise all these skills as much as you can and keep your eye, and ear, on changing trends. While sessions can be quite highly paid, with buyouts or repeat fees on top, the really big money goes either to those famous voices that we all recognise instantly, or to the unknown people who voice major worldwide campaigns for years on end (sometimes appearing on several different ones simultaneously).

To stand a chance of breaking into this mostly closed market, you will first need a demo showreel of your voice to send out to prospective employers. Until you have amassed enough voice-overs that have been actually broadcast to include on a showreel (voice sampler), you can either make one yourself, showing your voice off to its best effect by delivering the sort of scripts you hear on television and radio advertising campaigns (make them up though, rather than using actual copyright ones), or go to a specialist company that makes showreels. For a fee, these companies will take you into a studio and record your voice with jingles as background, giving you a master disc and possibly some copies. While these demos can sound very good and far more professional than a home-made version, the jingles they use will be used again and again, appearing on the reels of other artists, many of whom, like you, will have never been paid to record a voice-over, so using this type of reel might make you look like a wannabe rather than an experienced voice. To get some experience and variation on your showreel, you could always see if your local hospital radio ever uses voices for its jingles and volunteer your services there, in exchange for a copy.

Research the names of those responsible for booking voice artists at advertising agencies, radio stations, commercial, video and audio visual production companies and send them your showreel with a covering letter. If you live far away from a big city, target those smaller companies which are based near where you live (try Googling them, or look in the Yellow Pages), as there may be less competition, especially for lower paid jobs that come in at very short notice. Ensure you have enough copies of your reel, which are easy to burn on a computer, as the majority of companies will not return your disc, even if you enclose an SAE (the postage for which will probably cost more than the actual CD). Present your CD well, printing your details (especially your name and mobile phone number) on a label or directly on the disc, and send it in a plastic sleeve or jewel case, which you can buy cheaply in bulk from most computer stores and websites. You could put your photograph on the sleeve, with your details. Once you have sent out your showreels, wait for a week or two and then perhaps phone the contacts and ask for an audition or meeting. You may strike lucky and be given an appointment, which is great, but if your request is declined, ask if you can keep in touch with the company from time to time in the future, in case the situation changes. If they say that you can, ask for the name of the person with whom you are speaking and make notes in your diary to call them in about three or four months' time.

So what will happen if you get an audition? You'll be invited down to the company's offices or radio station's studios and either just chat with the producer and creatives there, or be given some scripts and asked to deliver them. This may happen in an actual voice-over booth and be recorded for their future reference, or just where you are sitting in the office. Being sat in a booth can be daunting, especially when you're not used to it, or things are not going according to plan, as these are soundproofed with a thick panel of glass between you and the control room. The microphone you use is always switched on, so the people behind the glass can hear every word you utter (be careful what you say to yourself!), but their microphone is turned off and you cannot hear what they are saying about your performance until they choose to turn it on and talk to you. Before you start, get as much information as you can about the kind of delivery that the script requires and don't be afraid to ask for pointers and direction in between takes. Try to stay as relaxed as you can and don't lose your nerve, even when all is not going well. When the audition is over, thank them for seeing you and ask if it's worth you keeping in touch with them for future work, making sure you do so, if their response is positive.

If you are asked to do a voice test for an actual commercial, there could also be numerous executives to keep happy, especially if a campaign is international and will be used in several countries. Your work may be beamed live to clients around the world, who may all have differing opinions. Do your utmost to keep your head – and everyone happy – in these situations, as the actual job could be very lucrative.

Most established voices are not auditioned, they're just booked because the creatives at the advertising agencies know and love them and can make the booking safe in the knowledge that the artist will come in, deliver the goods and leave before the expensive studio time has expired with the track firmly in the can. This is the major reason that voicing is such a closed shop industry. I was lucky enough to do many voice-overs when I was an actor in the 1980s, which mostly came through my acting agent, thanks to a couple of voice casting directors who asked for me. Sometimes I would be called in to meet and audition for the creatives of the company concerned, often at just a couple of hours' notice (a touch and go business in the days before mobile phones and pagers) and other times I would be booked on their recommendation. These days, the vast majority of voice work comes through a growing number of specialist agents, most of whom represent a small and select list of established voices of the sort that are known and loved by advertising executives. An agent is an especially great asset in the voice-over world, but most take on only a handful of new clients each year out of the many hundreds of people who approach them. They want to be sure that whoever they do represent has the potential to earn a good living, especially as the competition is so fierce. There is a section devoted to voice-over agents in *Contacts* and most of them have websites so you can see and hear the artists they look after. You will stand a better chance if your voice fills a gap on their list, so think about this and mention it, if you feel you can offer something they don't already have, when writing.

The majority of voice-overs for mainstream national UK campaigns are recorded in studios located in the Soho district of Central London, and voice tests and sessions can take place very early in the morning (from around 6am). Be prepared for this and ensure that you are awake and your voice is fully warmed up before going in. If you are in sufficient demand as a voice artist, you could consider converting a room at home into your own soundproof studio and installing an ASDL connection to link with the creatives in the studio via a telephone line. This can be costly, but could pay dividends in saved travel time (and therefore extra sleep time) as your earnings from this field mount up.

Narration

The narrator is the person whose voice we hear describing or commenting on the action in a TV show. A good example of this is the distinctive Geordie voice which keeps us up to date with the goings on in the Big Brother house. In these days of reality television, narrators are being used more frequently and it can be a good source of work and income. Improvisation can be a useful skill when working in this medium. While some shows are scripted, or narration added later to programmes which have already been filmed and edited, others require the narrator to react spontaneously to the broadcast while it is live on air. Being live television, all this must be done precisely, without drying, talking rubbish or swearing. This can be nerve racking and requires a clear head and extremely quick thinking.

To be considered for this type of work, you should record a showreel, showing your voice narrating a fake programme and send it to producers at television channels or independent production companies (check the end credits of shows that use narrators to get the names of the companies and producers). If you are called in for an audition, it will probably take place in a voice-over studio and you will either be asked to read from a script or shown some footage on a monitor or screen and asked to provide a narrative commentary for what you see. Before starting, get as much information as you can about the piece you will be narrating and ask for pointers on the style of delivery that is most suitable – serious and factual, light hearted and jokey, or somewhere in between.

Another type of associated employment is that of continuity announcing (providing the links between programmes on a television channel). This is done live, in shifts, in the channel's studios, where announcers are on call in case of problems or breaks in transmission. During the programmes, the announcers write their own scripts for the next links from synopses of the programmes. This can be a regular source of work, in which you will not be recognisable, so listen out for the styles of announcers on different channels and look out for vacancies which may be advertised in trade publications, such as *The Stage* and *Broadcast*.

Dubbing

Another good source of income from the voice can be dubbing, which is usually used in films or television shows and is done for one of two reasons. The first involves dubbing American or English movies into foreign languages, or vice versa, to make them more accessible to local audiences in the international marketplace, increasing the film's potential worldwide sales. The artists who are normally considered for this type of work are native speakers of the languages concerned, to ensure authenticity. Second, productions may be in the same language, but dubbed into a different accent, for example from American to English, if it is felt necessary to change the nationality of the dialogue to increase popularity. These are both very specific skills and it can pay to practise the latter.

An audition or test for this type of job may take place at one of the major film studios on the outskirts of London, such as Pinewood, Shepperton or Twickenham, though they can be held in dubbing studios in Soho. When you get in the studio for your audition, one of two techniques will be used: either headphones or bar. If head-phones are used, you will read the script whilst listening to the voice you are dubbing through the headphones. You are then required to speak the lines at exactly the same time as the voice you are hearing, while watching the action on the screen and synchronising the two. If the bar technique is used, you will see the action on the top part of the screen, while at the bottom the written dialogue is scrolling from right to left through a vertical black bar, synchronised with the mouth movements on the screen. You must then read each syllable of every word the moment it passes through the black bar. This is very exacting work, but is a skill worth learning and perfecting, especially if you are native or fluent in foreign languages.

Animation

The animation market is expanding, with an increasing number of cartoons being created and made for both adults and children. While the majority of these are made and voiced in North America, there are some great UK exponents in this field, so it is a worthwhile avenue to explore.

Watch as many animated programmes as you can and listen carefully to the vocal qualities used by the artists. Do they fit the characters? How much are they over exaggerated compared to the voices of people in real life? Experiment with your own voice and see how many different characters you can create. For inspiration, you could look at a children's picture or comic books and explore how the characters might speak. Take another look at the scripts for *My Garden Gnomes Are Aliens* and work on voices for Joomflana and Neddareeg, to fit their descriptions. When I used the scripts in mock auditions with drama students, the person who metaphorically 'got the job' was the only one to give the character an alien-sounding voice – everyone else read them normally.

As with voice-overs and dubbing, providing voices for animation is a specialised market and not an easy one to break into. However, if you, and others, feel you have the aptitude and talent to give it your best shot, why not make a demo CD of examples of character voices and selectively send it out. As I have mentioned before, watch the credits of the animated series in which you feel your voice could fit and send your demo to the producer.

An audition or voice test will be similar to that for dubbing, as your voice will have to synchronise exactly with the character's mouth movements. Make sure you are not too rigid in the delivery of your created voices, and can adjust or alter their tone or pitch should the director ask.

You could always include a couple of short examples of animation voices and narration on your voice-over showreel. As with everything in this business, you never know where it may lead.

So remember to . . .

- ✓ Listen to current commercials and practise different styles of delivery.
- ✓ Keep your eye, and ear, on changing trends in advertising.
- ✓ Gain as much actual experience as you can get for your show-reel.
- ✓ Get as much information as you can about the style and delivery.
- ✓ Stay focused while in the voice booth.
- ✓ Be careful what you say as your microphone is always switched on.
- ✓ Keep your head and everybody happy.
- ✓ Ensure your voice is warmed up before early morning sessions.
- ✓ Be prepared to think on your feet for live narration.
- ✓ Watch animated programmes and study vocal qualities.
- ✓ Experiment with your voice to create animation characters.
- ✓ Allow for flexibility in tone and pitch of voice, if needed.

CHAPTER 24

Presenting

There are many different types and styles of presenting and the demand for presenters has steadily increased over the years, thanks to the rising number of channels on satellite, cable and digital television. So we'll now take a look at the various options to explore in this field.

First, the style of presenting can differ radically: would your personality and talents be better suited to delivering serious factual information such as news or current affairs; imparting scientific or technical information, making it interesting and comprehensible to a non-expert audience; inspiring people to buy from shopping or auction channels by demonstrating products; putting contestants at their ease in a game show; or are you more a crazy and wacky children's TV presenter? You could be versatile enough to fit into more than one of those categories, but do your research and watch as many channels as you can to see the kind of shows that are on air and the people who currently present them. Keep in mind that this is the only time you will ever be asked to look directly into the lens while working on camera, so enjoy it.

Presenting doesn't have to be limited to television though, as live events also often require this expertise. Some actors are employed at presentations, trade fairs and exhibitions to make facts and technical jargon – which they do not necessarily have to understand, but have learnt meticulously, like a script – sound interesting to the delegates. Live roadshows, product launches and promotions will often be fronted by a presenter, either to get a passing audience interested or to entice them on stage to participate in competitions (good people skills and a sense of humour are essential here). This type of work can be lucrative, and fitted around other performing commitments.

Routes into presenting

So how do you learn the necessary skills that will make you more employable in this market? There are numerous training courses for presenters that are advertised from time to time in publications such as *The Stage* and *PCR*, which will teach techniques such as working to camera, using microphones and reading off 'autocue' (a system whereby a script is scrolled on a TV screen which the presenter then reads). Actors, stand-up comedians, DJs and journalists already have excellent transferable skills which can be drawn upon when it comes to presenting. One of the best ways to learn though, is actually on the job – in another interesting opportunity for employment – while working as a 'coat' or entertainer at a holiday park or onboard a cruise ship (the latter is not only a good training ground, but also a great way to see the world, and be paid to do so). While there are many different holiday parks in the UK, the two major groups audition in the following ways. Butlins (www.butlins.com/redcoatrecruitment) normally audition new redcoats in London, Birmingham and Leeds each January, where candidates are put thoroughly through their paces in all aspects of performing in a six-hour audition. Pontins (www.careers-pontins.com/bluecoat_auditions.php) hold their auditions four times a year in Manchester, Birmingham, London and Blackpool, and there are three types of performers that they look for (though applicants can try out for more than one genre, if they wish). The general category involves artists talking about themselves on stage and performing a short sketch; dancers are asked to follow and present a routine, while singers are asked to sing a song of their choosing to a backing track. Cruise line auditions usually involve singing and dancing (with perhaps acting in some cases) and often take place in the early months of each year. You could also explore work opportunities at theme parks, many of which use presenters for their seasonal shows, such as Alton Towers (www.altontowers jobs.com), Legoland (www.legoland.co.uk/jobs), Blackpool Pleasure Beach (www.blackpoolpleasurebeach.com/jobs.php) or Disneyland Paris (www.disneylandparis-casting.com). Most audition calls are widely advertised, especially in *The Stage*, so keep a look out.

The experience to be gained from working as a coat, in a theme park or onboard a ship is invaluable, and it has been the starting ground for many hundreds of well-known presenters and entertainers.

Another possible way into presenting (and acting, in some cases) is by working as a stand-up comedian. It is a skill that comes naturally to some and can be learnt by others. There are two potentially terrifying factors to bear in mind: the first is that you are standing totally alone on a stage (unless you work as part of a double act or group) and, second, you have to make your audiences laugh, which can be a lot harder than it looks. If you are undeterred and wish to pursue this avenue, there are courses led by established comedians available in London and other major cities. The Actors Centres run them regularly and you could ask at your local comedy club if they know of any taking place near where you live. A course will teach you the basics of comedy and improvisation, and give you the skills you need to put together your own routine, or 'set' as it's known in comedy circles, of original material which you have written (using jokes and routines which are already performed by other comics is strictly off limits). As well as an excellent complement to your presenting and acting skills, comedy could also provide you with a secondary career, if you are lucky enough to get paid to make audiences laugh on the stand-up comedy circuit. Once your act is formed and polished, you can start asking comedy clubs for 'open spots' (a shorter unpaid slot, lasting between three and ten minutes, usually five) to practise working in front of an audience, judge and improve your material and be seen by potential bookers. Your performance will usually be assessed by talent scouts, casting directors and club promoters, who sit anonymously in audiences (and are usually the hardest people to make laugh). Another possibility is that you may be auditioned for a spot in a club or as part of a competition and these can be daunting. You will usually be asked for your best three minutes of material – and when they say three minutes, they mean exactly that. You will be timed with a stopwatch and a strip of lights which resemble traffic lights might be used. When the green light is on, you must make them laugh; when the yellow light appears, you have 30 seconds to wrap up your set; and when the red light goes on, your time is up, whether you have finished or not. Your audience might only be the club promoter or competition judges, who may be totally humourless and writing notes about you throughout your entire set. Another alternative is to have all the comedians sitting in, watching what everyone else does, invariably trying not to laugh, for fear of making someone else look better than themselves. When you have a comedy audition, always make sure your material is written and memorised, as making something up on your way there can be disastrous. The trick when performing stand up in any situation is to carry on regardless of whether you get laughs or not (waiting and not talking over any laughs you do get) and not to look desperate or flounder if the audience silently stares at you. Keep your confidence and belief in yourself and your material, noting what got laughs and what needs improving or rewriting. Many extremely well-known and well-loved comics took years to formulate their style and, in some cases, get audiences on their wavelength, so if comedy is something you are keen to pursue, keep working on your style and material and don't give up.

So once you have worked out what style(s) of presentation suit you best and have honed your skills, how should you go about getting work? As I've mentioned before, thoroughly research the current market and contact the companies or channels that you feel would be best for you to work with. Usually, before actually auditioning you in person, companies will want to see a showreel on DVD or video cassette. You could do one for each medium using a camcorder – selling goods on a shopping or auction channel is far removed from presenting a children's or schools' programme, and should thus be treated differently where showreels are concerned. Whatever the medium, however, always remember to keep your delivery real and not to over project on camera.

If you are invited to audition, or test, for a job, you will doubtless be asked to perform whatever a particular brief requires, either using a script, improvisation techniques or a mixture of the two. While you may be given plenty of information and guidance by the director or producer, before or during your interview, ensure you do as much research as you can on the actual project, or those of a similar type prior to the day itself. Study the delivery and energy levels used so that you can emulate them if required, but remaining flexible enough to take direction and adapt to their needs.

Like everything in this industry, good presenting should look effortless, but is actually much harder than it seems and is an extremely competitive market to break into. If you are serious about presenting as a career path and are getting regular work in the medium, you may want to approach some of the agents who specialise in this field with a view to them representing you. They will want to see your showreel, preferably with examples of work for which you've been paid, and there is a section devoted to these agents in *Contacts*. Many have websites, which will help you to gauge the type of artists they represent and any particular fields in which they may specialise. *Spotlight* also publishes a supplementary directory each year, *Spotlight On Presenters*, which is regularly consulted by employers and those responsible for casting.

So remember to . . .

✓   Research the style of presenting that suits your personality and skills.

✓ Study the delivery types and energy levels used in each medium.
✓ Learn your craft by taking a course or working as an entertainer.
✓ Research the market and target suitable employers accordingly.
✓ Make a separate showreel for each specific presentation style.
✓ Keep your delivery real and do not over project on camera.
✓ Investigate specialist agents and *Spotlight On Presenters*.

CHAPTER 25

Interview Technique

An interview is the talk or chat you have with the creative team before and/or after you have delivered whatever they have asked to see. Sometimes, the interview may be all they need and you will not be asked to do anything else to be judged for a part. So is there such a thing as a perfect interview? Yes there is – one that goes exactly the way you wanted it to and when you have responded to all the questions with what everybody wants to hear. But, as with every type of audition, there is no proven formula for this success 100 per cent of the time. How the interview goes is all dependent on how everyone, including you, is feeling at the time in question. There are, however, right and wrong things to say and do, as well as proven techniques that will ensure that the effect of your interview is maximised more of the time.

As with everything, preparation is the key. In advance of the audition day, think of questions you might be asked by the panel, perhaps those that you have been asked before in similar situations, and work out effective answers to them, rehearsing these if you feel the need (though not too thoroughly, as they should still look spontaneous and unrehearsed). Think of what you are going to say if the panel says 'And is there anything you'd like to ask us?' as you will sound more intelligent and committed if you have a question up your sleeve, rather than responding 'Ermmm . . . no I don't think so.' Try to think of imaginative, interesting and pertinent queries, as these will show you in a better light than those who asked the same old boring and mundane questions the panel hear time and time again – or committed the cardinal sin of having nothing to ask. If you are going to tell anecdotes, keep them short (30 seconds maximum) to the point and, where possible, witty – bearing in mind that not everyone's sense of humour is the same (some people don't have one at all), so what you think is roll on the floor hysterical may be met with blank stares from others.

I am always surprised how many people bring portfolios with them to auditions and proceed to bore the panel with lengthy displays of endless pages of production shots of themselves in costume, exam certificates, reviews and glowing testimonials from impressed tutors, fans and employers. This is the theatrical equivalent of showing endless video or slide shows of holiday snaps to dinner guests who you don't really know, and should be avoided, no matter how polite and interested the panel may seem. Also avoid the temptation to give out voice demos, showreels or handbills for your current show. A mention of any of these is enough, they should only be proffered if specifically requested and don't try to press gang members of the panel into coming as it will seldom work.

One of the major letdowns at interviews is the inability to answer the most often-asked question. I refer to those four little words that can strike fear into even the calmest of actors: 'Tell me about yourself.' The answer varies from person to person, and can be anything from 'Ermmm what sort of things do you want to know?' to a long ramble about life, love and career from birth to present day (the longest I have heard was 4 minutes and 18 seconds without stopping). Both of these are not good. When I was an actor, I was of the first group, and despite knowing that the question would more than likely be asked, would bumble my way through a rough spiel saying the first thought that came into my head. It was only when I switched to the other side of the table that I realised how bad it looked when actors failed to respond succinctly to this relatively simple question – sometimes being the lynchpin between success and failure.

So what is the ideal response for maximum effect? A well-prepared, succinctly delivered speech containing the five most important facts about you (the person and performer) that invites questions and interaction, yet is short enough to leave the panel wanting more, will improve your chances no end. What should these facts be? They can vary and be tailored accordingly depending on who you are meeting and the project concerned, though the first should always remain the same – the most important fact about you. I am not referring to the fact that you are the greatest actor since Laurence Olivier, are utterly unique or the most versatile performer ever seen on stage or screen. The most important fact about you, and the one that everyone must remember in order for you to succeed in this business is *your name*. It may sound obvious and simple, but I'm amazed how many performers throw this vital fact away when introducing themselves by not saying it clearly or even sounding embarrassed about it. The words of the song say it all: 'Remember my name – fame', which may be cheesy but is very true. Stars did not get where they are today by not getting their names into the heads of potential employers. Nobody has ever asked for 'The balding Scot who played James Bond', 'The Oscar-winning English actress who now gives James Bond his orders' or 'That posh bloke who was in all those movies and dated Elizabeth Hurley'. What these three people have successfully done is got their names into people's heads – and kept them there. It makes no difference if you want to be famous or just a working actor, if people don't know and remember your name, you may as well give up and find a new career where you can be anonymous.

So how do we get our names into people's heads? The first trick is to project it clearly, rather than swallowing it, whenever you are asked for it or to introduce yourself. If you have two or three names, separate the words rather than mixing them up into one. I am not

Richardevans, or Richaevn but Richard Evans, pronouncing every syllable and putting a slight pause between the two names. These are two words of which I am immensely proud and want people to remember, associating them with me. I would smile as I say it, shake the person's hand, if appropriate, make eye contact with them, and, if I knew they were meeting several people in quick succession, add to their memory by painting a picture of my name. By painting a picture I mean giving mental images to go with the words you are saying which act as a memory aide. For instance, I would say 'Hello, my name is Richard Evans – that's Richard as in Burton and Evans like the clothes shops for larger people.' Now the person has not only heard me say my name and repeat it, but also has two images to remember – that amazing actor Richard Burton and a clothes shop with my surname emblazoned in large letters on its shop front – which is far harder to forget than Richaevn.

If your name is less conventional or more exotic than mine, the better pictures you can paint. If nothing obvious comes to mind but your name contains several syllables, you can put a picture to each syllable and paint it that way – the more you dare to make a positive statement rather than apology out of it, the more memorable you will be. The worst thing you can do is tell people that your name is too complicated and they will never remember it (if that is what you believe it will come true, and if you really feel that's the case, then you should change it). It is far better to say my name takes a little more learning than some, but once you know it, you will never forget it. There are many actors who I'll never forget through having to learn their unusual names.

So that's the first and most important fact about you, but what about the other four? As I said before, you can tailor these to the audition concerned and where you are in your career, but they could include: your age (if you don't want to keep it to yourself, as many do), where you are from, how you came to become a performer, where you trained (especially pertinent if you are a recent graduate), your last job, the kind of work you have done or the direction you want to go in, your skills or strengths and anything else which could make you a more attractive and saleable proposition for the project concerned (you may have already mentioned some of these if your audition came as the result of writing a letter).

Now with your five points written in a list, work on formulating them into a short and interesting story lasting no longer than 30 seconds – think of it as the story, or commercial of you. Rehearse this story in front of a mirror regularly, making sure that it is not too rigid, as you may be interrupted with questions from the panel, or you may want to change some facts just before you go into the room, or even as you are saying it. Having the five facts in order and the rough story inside your head will enable you to do this easily.

Let's return to Robert who applied for *Song of Syracuse* in Chapter 3 'Submitting Yourself for Work' and see how he went about formulating his 'Tell me about yourself' speech for his audition. So starting with his name, which is Robert Bloggs – that could be Robert as in De Niro, or Redford, or Burns, or Downey Junior, or The Bruce ('if at first I don't succeed') and Bloggs like Joe or web diaries. He might then have chosen to mention his age or height, that he has a strong tenor singing voice, his six months living in New York, which gave him a good American accent, driving delivery vans and his musical skills, playing trumpet, saxophone and lead guitar in the jazz band. He could have also included other information, such as where he was born, family heritage, where he trained and how long ago he graduated and the kind of work he had since done. So how would he turn all of those important facts into the story? He would have presumably said 'Hello' when entering the room and shaking hands, so the next word most people would automatically use to open is 'Well . . .'. While this isn't necessarily bad, it's not the strongest of words, as it sounds a little vague. Some might merely use 'I am . . .' which is OK, but to maximise the effect, tell the panel exactly what you are saying by starting confidently with 'My name is . . .'. This is by far the strongest opening, especially when accompanied with eye contact, a smile and open body language.

So Robert thought initially about the five points he should mention and came up with:

1   I am Robert, but my friends call me Bob or Bobby.

2   I'm an actor.

3   I was born in Kent 26 years ago, where my father is a carpenter and mother a housewife.

4   I share a flat in London with three other people.

5   I had a pet dog as a child who was named George.

He showed it to his recruitment consultant flatmate, who was concerned about all the points. First, if he wanted to be known as Robert, he should call himself by his proper name and not abbreviations or nicknames, to give people a better chance of remembering it, and she advised him to try painting a picture with his name to increase those chances even further. She thought the second point was stating the obvious and the other three, with the exception of being born in Kent 26 years ago, were completely irrelevant to his career and had therefore weakened his speech further. She told him to go away and rethink them, trying to tailor them to the audition concerned. He wrote a list of everything he could include and whittled them down to these five points:

1   My name is Robert Bloggs, that is Robert as in Robert The Bruce (if at first I don't succeed, I try, try again!) and Bloggs like the diaries on the internet.

2   I trained at the ABC Academy of Drama, graduating four years ago.

3   I have spent time living in New York and van driving (which he sneakily joined together as one item).

4   I play three musical instruments to performance standard.

5   I will mention two of my jobs since leaving college that would be of interest for this project.

His flatmate thought these were all far more pertinent and loved the picture painting of his name, thinking that was memorable, giving the panel two mental images to remember him by, as well as dropping in a very positive statement about himself. Spurred on by her enthusiasm, he then set about turning them into a script, which read as follows:

My name is Robert Bloggs, that's Robert as in Robert The Bruce (if at first I don't succeed, I try, try again!) and Bloggs like the diaries on the internet. I trained at the ABC Academy of Drama, and graduated with a BA Honours degree four years ago. Between finishing my A levels and going to drama school, I spent six months living in New York, where I worked hard on perfecting my American accent, and since graduating I have driven vans to earn money while I'm not working as an actor. I've been interested in music from an early age and I play the trumpet, saxophone and lead guitar, which I keep honed by playing in a jazz band every week and my theatre work has been varied and has included a small scale tour of *Death of a Salesman* playing 'Biff' and *Return To The Forbidden Planet* as the Bosun on the London fringe, which was a brilliant show and used my musical skills.

He read it aloud a few times, and his flatmate timed it using the second hand on her watch – it took 47 seconds which was too long. He tried to speed it up by saying it more quickly, but it sounded like he was racing through it and there was no point in doing that. His flatmate told him to keep the important facts, cutting some of the embellishments while keeping the story worth listening to. He set about that and came up with:

My name is Robert Bloggs, that's Robert as in Robert The Bruce (if at first I don't succeed, I try, try again!) and Bloggs like the diaries on the internet. I graduated from the ABC

Academy of Drama four years ago and have since appeared in a small-scale tour of *Death of a Salesman* playing 'Biff' and *Return To The Forbidden Planet* as the Bosun on the London fringe, in which I also played the trumpet, saxophone and lead guitar. Before going to drama school, I spent six months living in New York, so have an authentic American accent, and since graduating have had experience of van driving when not working as an actor.

After going through it again out loud to get his mouth round the words in the new order, it was timed, and came in at 30 seconds exactly. Both he and his flatmate agreed that this new version is much stronger and more memorable, thanks to the cuts and rewrites. 'Leave them wanting more', is the adage here, rather than wanting less – so many performers do this, often without even realising.

They then imagined some possible questions that the panel might ask him, some of which could be potentially negative and deflating to him, so he should be prepared with pertinent answers, just in case. These are the ones they came up with: 'The ABC Academy of Drama? I've never heard of it. Why didn't you go to a good drama school like RADA then?' 'Tell me about the production of *Death of a Salesman*' 'What have you been up to lately?' 'How well do you play the guitar/saxophone/trumpet and in what styles?' 'Why did you go to New York and what did you do there?' and 'What sort of vans do you drive?' They thought through succinct answers to the questions, turning negatives into positives wherever possible, and wrote them down, as, in the case of Robert's career most of these things would not change and would probably be asked at many future auditions.

Another good form of preparation is to try to find out if anybody you know knows any of the panel you will be meeting, especially if you can pass on their regards and thus open up a conversation. Members of the panel might also (positively or negatively) mention directors on your CV who are known to them, or shows you were in that they saw, which can be another good talking point to keep the conversation flowing. If you have seen the company or director's past work, do try to introduce it into the conversation, but only if you have enjoyed it – never be negative about *anything*, no matter how tempting. Always be positive about everyone, no matter how you feel, or even if the creatives are being negative – they may be doing this to see how you react. Never forget, this is a small business (and gets smaller the longer you are in it) and it's surprising who knows who and reports it back (I regularly hear reports about myself, good and bad, true and untrue). You may have a negative opinion about somebody for whatever reason, just keep it to yourself and be positive about everyone at all times.

After you have told the panel about yourself (but only if you are asked to do so), they might ask you questions or expand on your past work or skills, what you think you can offer the company or role, and where you feel you would fit in. They might also test how you react to questions or situations (this happens in interviews for any kind of job). A common one is to call you by the wrong name. This happened to me at one of the first ever auditions I attended. In addition to a bad attack of nerves, I was absolutely mortified when the director called me Nigel, making me think that I couldn't be a very good actor if he couldn't even understand my name. I took all my courage in both hands and said 'Sorry, my name is Richard, not Nigel.' 'Oh OK, sorry,' he replied and carried on. I was stunned when I was offered the job and I quizzed him during filming as to why it had gone my way. He told me that, as well as being the best and most suitable actor they had seen for the part, I was the only person who had noticed and corrected him when he had got their name wrong, which he liked because I had the confidence to stand up to him and correct his mistake. If you are asked about a specific credit, or recent credits in general, don't rhapsodise for hours on end, or give the entire plot, cast list and your views on it all. Again be prepared and concise, thinking beforehand of any project about which you may be asked and précising the most important points into one or two short sentences. For example, if you played a doctor in an episode of *Coronation Street*, rather than risk boring the panel by speaking at length about your part of however many lines, the brilliant experience you had on the set in Manchester and the lovely/charming/stroppy/starry actors you worked with, you could merely say 'I played the hospital doctor who diagnosed Steve McDonald's sprained ankle, in an episode that was aired last July. It was a great experience and has whetted my appetite to do more TV work.'

Other obtuse-sounding questions may sometimes be asked. How many stairs are there where you live? This is a weird one, but there is good reason why it is asked. What would you answer? 'Now let me see . . .'? 'Ermmm, I dunno'? 'Twenty-seven'? To be honest, it doesn't matter what you answer, as the person asking probably doesn't know where you live, and even if they had been there, they wouldn't have spent their time counting the stairs. So why ask? It is purely to see how you would react. Imagine you were in a play where in the final scene you grab a gun from a table and shoot your enemy dead. Your stage manager, however, is inefficient and one night forgets to set the gun on the table. What do you do? There are three obvious ways out: first, you could make your index and middle fingers into the shape of a gun, pointing it at them and saying 'bang' very loudly; you could pick up the nearest heavy object and whack the poor unsuspecting actor over the head with it so they fall to the floor (perhaps not getting back up for the curtain call); or you might go to the front of the stage, break out of character, and explain the situation to the audience. The choice would be yours and you would have a split second to make that decision, so basically this supposedly simple yet irrelevant question, or others like it, are sometimes asked to check that you are able to think quickly on your feet. Whatever your opinion may be on this tactic, keep it to yourself and play along.

I was once asked if I had a girlfriend during an interview with a prospective agent, and when I replied that I did, was then asked 'What's your sex life like?' I was a little taken aback and asked for the question to be repeated to check that I'd heard it correctly. The question was repeated, as naturally as if it had been 'do you take sugar in your tea?' I replied that I didn't think that the state of my sex life had any relevance to my representation with their agency. 'Oh OK', they said, and the subject was promptly changed. After they had agreed to take me on, I was told that they always asked potential clients the question, to check how they would react if something similar was asked at an audition, and congratulated me for remaining calm and unflustered. Some people may also make personal remarks about you. 'Are you aware how badly you lisp?' one actor was asked by a forthright director. 'Badly?' he replied without hesitation, 'I always thought I did it rather well!' This may be considered facetious by some, but it shows the actor was aware of the situation and was not going to let it get him down or stand in his way. Acknowledge your own traits, change what you can, or want to, and accept what you cannot.

If there are several creatives on a panel, you might find that one person leads the interview, while the others say nothing. You should then direct the answers to the questioner, but try to give momentary eye contact to the other panel members while you are speaking, as it will involve them in the conversation and keep their attention. Alternatively, more than one panellist might ask you questions, seemingly firing them at you from all directions, which can be hard to cope with. Whatever you do, keep calm and answer their questions in order, taking time to think if your mind should go temporarily blank and including everyone in your answers. I often ask people what part, speech or song I saw them perform in a show or their drama school showcase, sometimes years before, which is not intended as a test of memory for the performer, but merely to remind me about them and thus enable me to sell their merits more lucidly afterwards to my fellow panellists. It is therefore worth keeping everything you have ever done at the back of your mind, as some casting directors or other creatives have very long memories.

It may be that the person or people interviewing you are inexperienced or shy and you have to take the lead, asking them questions in order to ascertain what they would like to know about you. This can be difficult, as you do not want to come over as too much in control or overly bossy, and possibly scare them, but if you try to read the signals you are being given and react to them accordingly, you should be able to strike an acceptable balance. This will hardly ever happen, but should it do, all your preparation will help you to keep relaxed in this awkward situation.

If a member of the panel were to get up and go to the toilet during your audition, or have a conversation on their mobile phone whilst you were reading or singing, you would perceive them to be rude, and rightly so. If it should happen to you, keep your head and try not to get upset or angry about the situation – rise above it and never respond to their rudeness in a like-minded way, as this will do you no favours. If it is appropriate, you could always ask to wait or start again when the person's attention is fully focused on you, but make sure that you ask politely and are not stroppy and insistent, as some people are.

As with everything, the trick with interviews, however short or long, is to keep confident and project yourself to the panel. Think of it as being on a chat show, where you are promoting something – not your latest book, TV series or play in this instance, but yourself for the job in question. Watch how people are interviewed on chat shows on television and how they react when unconventional questions are asked (these interviews are rarely rehearsed and can be very revealing – those on Jonathan Ross' shows are a prime example). Also, instead of going into the room desperately needing and wanting the job (which many do, and desperation really shows), think 'How can I help you?' Taking this attitude will relax you, and, even if you cannot help the people concerned on this occasion, you will enjoy it more and have made new contacts that might need your help in the future.

General interviews

Relatively uncommon these days, general interviews are a somewhat strange phenomenon where actors go to meet casting directors or artistic directors, usually in their offices, for a general chat, rather than an audition. 'A chat about what?' you may ask. I couldn't really answer that as in my experience each tends to be different, depending on the parties concerned. You will get on with some people better than others – sometimes you click and sometimes you don't, and, as with any relationship it cannot be manufactured. The real trick with these is to just go in and be yourself.

Like many of my colleagues, I rarely hold general interviews these days as I don't find them particularly useful, far preferring to see artists in action on stage or screen. That said, it is always worth asking, or dropping the subject into a letter. Sometimes it is easier for your agent to ask casting directors to meet you, which they will mainly do if you have recently joined them, are fresh on the scene, perhaps newly out of drama school, or if they know that someone is about to start casting a project for which you would be perfect and should be seen (this is also known as a pre-cast). A casting director is more likely to agree to meet someone who is based far away, or in another country, and happens to be in town for a few days, so whenever you are visiting a new place, it is worth checking if there's anyone you should try to meet.

How long a general lasts can vary dramatically. Sometimes casters may have a day of general interviews, with a whole list of people to be seen at 5- , 10- or 15-minute intervals, like at auditions. Others may just be seeing you and therefore not be so constrained for time. I try to allow time to meet and get to know people, but again it varies depending how well I get on with the actor concerned. My shortest general was 4 minutes with an actor who not only arrived half an hour early but was sarcastic and obnoxious from start to finish, and the longest was an actress who was so entertaining that two and a half hours flew by, inadvertently making me late for a meeting.

Aim to be animated and interesting, having plenty to talk about in order to avoid awkward silences. Remember that a conversation involves two people and it does no harm to let the person you're meeting take the lead. Please also remember that talking about yourself incessantly for hours on end, or exclusively about work can be exceedingly boring. Swot up on the newspapers for possible amusing anecdotes (the *Sun* is great for these). Try to do some research on the person that you're meeting, on the work they have done (have you seen and enjoyed any of their projects?), what they're currently doing (though be careful not to be too pushy) and, if you can, their likes and interests as human beings. Be sensitive to signs that the meeting is coming to an end, leaving promptly with a smile, handshake, thanks for sparing the time to meet you and hopes that you meet again before too long. These are useful social tools that can, and should, also be used at parties, especially those that are Industry related.

If you go to meet a caster whose work is predominantly in commercials, they will undoubtedly be more concerned about your look and general type, perhaps putting you on tape and taking one or more photographs of you as you look at that moment for their records. They may also ask you to complete a form similar to that we discussed in Chapter 19, 'Commercial Castings', so make sure you have the relevant information with you. Those who cast theatre might want to hear a speech and television and film-casting directors might ask you to sight read some script, perhaps on camera, so again be prepared.

So remember to . . .

✓ Prepare answers in advance to questions that might be asked.
✓ Have a short 'Tell me about yourself' speech at the ready.
✓ Paint a memorable picture of your name.
✓ Research the panel. Do you have a mutual acquaintance?
✓ Remember the details of your own career.
✓ Keep everything succinct – leave them wanting more, not less.
✓ Always react positively.
✓ Take weird questions in your stride and play the game.
✓ Be prepared to take the lead, if necessary.
✓ Rise above any distractions, asking to start again, if appropriate.
✓ Think 'How can I help you?'

✓ Try to arrange generals with people based in places you are visiting.

✓ Let the interviewer lead and do not talk solely about yourself or work.

✓ Be prepared to be in front of a camera, sight read or perform a speech.

✓ Be animated, interesting and, above all, yourself.

CHAPTER 26

Awkward Questions

As I've mentioned repeatedly, it pays to be prepared and the same goes for any questions you may be asked. There are two that especially come to mind as being potentially difficult to answer: 'What have you been up to lately?', when the last credit on your résumé may have been years ago, and 'You've not really done anything or have no major credits, why is that?' With both of these it is easy to go into defensive mode or not know how to react, as, while these facts are probably true, they can be negative or demoralising, especially when asked bluntly on the spot. Indeed, the questioner may be looking to see how you react.

As in most aspects of life, honesty pays. Please don't be sarcastic or facetious as this will do you no favours. If you have not done something, then admit it. For instance, when asked 'Are you a trained dancer?' an honest and well backed up answer, such as 'No, I have had no formal training, but I move well and learn quickly/ but am keen and always do my best', is far preferable to 'No mate, I've got two left feet' or 'Dancing? As in you mean . . . dancing?' Keep cool and briefly think through your answers, if necessary before voicing them.

In the case of our original questions, honesty and coolness will again pay dividends here. When asked what you have been up to, it is easy to give answers such as I have been on holiday, renovating my house, walking the dog, earning a living, etc., which may all be true but are not what the panel want to hear. Everyone knows this industry is far from easy and that the vast majority of performers are not in work fifty-two weeks a year, so, if you cannot bluff that you have been busy with projects about which the team won't be able to catch you out, then be honest about it. A well-judged answer, such as 'I have been going to as many auditions as possible, while keeping my skills up to date by taking regular classes' will prove that you are doing all you can and are ready to get back to work. Some people back this up further with phrases such as it's tough, or quiet, but this is really too much, as nobody wants their heart strings tugged, or to be made to feel worse if the job is not going to go your way. Be factual and as upbeat as you can – even if that means acting it.

One audition sticks in my mind, when a young artist who had trained at a good college and was represented by a well-respected agent came in for a musical. After singing and dancing like a dream, the director called her over for a chat. 'I don't understand it,' he said, 'You are so good and yet your CV has nothing on it, even though you left college over three years ago, how come?' I could feel her hackles rising fast and see frustration and disappointment creeping over her face, but she looked him squarely in the eye. 'I have got down to the final two at each of the last three auditions that I've been to, but haven't got the jobs because I was far less experienced than the other girls. All I need is for someone to take that chance on me and give me my first break.' The look of disappointment soon changed to elation when the director told her that he was more than happy to take that chance and she was indeed going to get the break for which she had been striving. It was well deserved as she was excellent in the show and her career is now going from strength to strength, with other employers following suit now she has a mainstream credit on her CV.

So remember to . . .

✓   Be straight and factual rather than defensive and sarcastic.
✓   Stay calm and think before you speak, if you have to.
✓   Keep positive, rather than feeling sorry for yourself.
✓   Always be honest – it will pay dividends.

CHAPTER 27

Is Timing Everything?

There is an age-old belief that the first and last auditionee in any day will not get the job. How true is this and how does timing and where you are placed on the list affect your chances?

Having analysed this over the years, I would say placing doesn't really matter one iota. If you are right for the part and let the panel see what they need to by doing a well-prepared and confident audition, you will receive a recall or even offer. How do we know what the panel need to see? The simple answer is that we don't, as it really depends on the composition of the panel and their mood or perceptions at the time. Sadly, someone who is absolutely perfect or a great actor may sometimes be overlooked, though this often rectifies itself in the future, perhaps after another or several auditions with the same director or producer (maybe for different productions) or perhaps when they have been impressed with your work on stage or screen. Talent will out sounds like a cliché and, while there is no guarantee this will happen, if you believe and keep going long enough, there is no reason why this cliché cannot become reality!

Getting back to timing, there are better times than others. Some say that the second slot after lunch is a good one, as the panel are refreshed. This could be true, and you may well have to make a greater impression later in the afternoon, especially if it has been a long session with a constant stream of people at regular intervals. Indeed, several actors come to mind that I purposely bring in at low points like these, as they have naturally bright and bubbly personalities which can lift the spirits of the panel. In the case of comedy auditions, where laughter from the panel will help you to get the job, it will probably pay to energise more if your appointment is later in the day and the pieces being read have been heard over and over again.

Don't worry what time you are given, though please always inform your agent if you have absolutely unchangeable commitments; be as flexible as you can be and avoid constantly asking for the time to be changed, as this can irritate agents and work-givers very quickly. Lastly, please do not balk at early morning appointments, or make excuses about the early hour or your lack of preparation because of it, when attending them. If you have to get up at 6am to warm up and get there on time, then so be it (it's not a daily occurrence after all), and if you don't want to go and have a chance of the job, there are plenty who do.

So remember to . . .

- ✓ Be flexible about audition times and try not to change them.
- ✓ Go in and give your all regardless of the time of day – it doesn't matter.
- ✓ Be awake, happy and fully warmed up at early morning appointments.
- ✓ Be more energised near the end of the day, as the panel may be jaded.

CHAPTER 28

In the Mood

An actor with whom I talked recently was perplexed. He had just been for his fourth audition for a long-running West End musical and had not been recalled. His disappointment was compounded by the fact that the first and third time he had been in, he was recalled several times and got down to the final two on both occasions, yet the second time he was also not even recalled once. 'I just don't understand it,' he moaned, 'I did nothing radically different on each of the four occasions.' I sympathised with his frustration and explained it could be one of two things. The first was the fact that it was a recast and a suitable part may not have been available this time around (as discussed more fully in Chapter 32). The second, and perhaps less obvious reason, is that the outcome can depend on the mood of the director or panel on the day you audition.

Creatives are humans too and have good and bad days. Some days they are easy to please, others incredibly difficult. I bring people in again and again if I see potential and believe in them, frequently for the same job, and when they get the part on the umpteenth attempt, the powers that be are often surprised that they had not found this amazing person sooner, and don't remember having auditioned them before.

So remember to . . .

✓ Do your best and take each audition as it comes.
✓ Believe in what you do and others will too.
✓ Try again and again, improving every time.

CHAPTER 29

Friend or Foe?

I once heard it said that if someone you know or have worked with previously invites you in to audition, then you will not get the job. I would disagree with this theory, and say that if this is the case, you probably stand just as good a chance, if not better. However, knowing one or more members of a panel may not be as big a bonus as you might expect.

So how should you behave when in an audition situation when one or more people that you know are on the panel? Can you be as friendly as you would normally? Will it help or hinder your confidence? The answers to these questions will, of course, vary from person to person and audition to audition, but a few simple rules should always be observed. Remember no matter how well you know the people concerned, it is still an audition and a job is at stake – which is not automatically yours. Always take the lead from the panel as to the parameters of informality and how far you can push matters. Keep your bright enthusiasm and confidence when you walk through the door, remembering to smile and shake hands, but avoid hugging or kissing unless those you know do so first, and if they do either, respond positively and do not shy away. Have the confidence to judge the situation.

Be careful also about what you say. Some people may test you by bad mouthing others with whom you have both worked to see how you react, especially if they are still unsure of whether or not to employ, or re-employ, you. With people you know, you are more likely to let your guard slip and talk too much, be too pally pally, over confident, cocky or even more negative than you would normally be. It is very easy to talk too much (we have all experienced verbal diarrhoea when we feel comfortable with people) and it is all too tempting to sit recounting tales of the past for too long, especially when you are trying to appear humorous. I know many people who, although good actors and great company, have talked themselves out of jobs without even realising it. Keep in control of what you want to say and how you wish to be perceived. However, should the people you are meeting keep *you* talking, then that's fine (as you will have budgeted the time) and you should never terminate your appointment before the panel are ready.

Negativity can also be more likely to creep in when you know and feel comfortable with members of the panel. Nobody wants to hear phrases such as 'That wasn't very good, was it?' or 'I didn't do as well as I could have', even if they know you can do much better than you demonstrated. Rather than voice these concerns, you could always ask for another try, if you really felt you did that badly. If only one of the panel knows you, they may ask you to repeat something if they know you can do better and want to convince other panellists of their belief that you are worthy of the job. I have often requested, even begged, for someone to be recalled when they have not performed at their best the first time around, as have other members of the creative team, which goes back to the adage that it's not what you know, it's who you know . . . and who knows you. Always keep every audition to the best professional standard, regardless who or what it is for.

As a former actor, I find it far harder when getting my friends in for castings, as it can look like favouritism to the other candidates – especially if the person concerned is overly friendly or kissy towards me when other people are waiting, as this can be demoralising and off-putting to the other auditionees. It sounds strange but I have to be far more convinced that a friend is absolutely right for a role than I do with a performer with whom I am not so well acquainted.

There is an interesting fact to keep in your mind. It is that we are all talked about – in both positive and negative terms – often without our even knowing. I am regularly asked if I know a certain actor, what they're like and whether they would be right for a part, or a worthwhile addition to an agent's list. I am always honest in my response, sometimes non-committal if I don't know the artist that well, as my judgement and reputation is on the line. Much of the time, you will be mentioned by people who know you, or know of you, for various parts, but often this will come to nothing and you will never hear about it (or not be available when checked with your agent), but it is better to be talked about than not! Likewise, I too am discussed by potential employers and recommended for projects. I receive calls from creatives, producers, writers, agents and even fellow casting directors, saying 'I mentioned your name as they are looking for a casting director and you'd be perfect, so you might get a call.' I am sure I am told about very few of these conversations, but even when I have been made aware of the situation, there have been occasions when I hear nothing from the people concerned and am not offered a meeting and the chance to prove my suitability. I just hear at a later date that someone else was employed. Sometimes I am invited to a meeting, which could be with people I already know and can either be very positive or somewhat awkward. As there are often several decision makers involved, who may have differing viewpoints, I will either be offered the job or it will go to one of my colleagues, but as long as I have done my best, then I am happy. Exactly the same will happen to you, more often than you think, especially if you have an agent, who will (hopefully) be frequently mentioning your name and singing your praises to potential employers for their projects.

So remember to . . .

- ✓ Take the lead from the panel on the level of friendliness.
- ✓ Treat all auditions the same regardless – a job is at stake.
- ✓ Keep positive and don't let negativity creep in, about yourself or others.

✓ Be careful not to talk yourself out of a job by talking too much.

✓ Act normally and do not be over the top in front of other auditionees.

✓ Keep positive – you may be being talked about without even knowing.

CHAPTER 30

Actors Who Know Too Much

There are several taboo subjects that when raised or mentioned in an audition situation can be off-putting to the director or other members of the team, and have been known to inadvertently lose people jobs.

I refer to those multi-skilled actors who, while primarily performers, have several other Industry-related strings to their bow. It could be directing, choreography or musical direction, which, while all great skills that keep the pennies rolling in when acting work is lean, are better not mentioned at auditions. I know many people who have been treated sniffily by directors who are fearful that the person they are interviewing might be better than they are, or else try to take over at rehearsals, usurp them or give notes to their fellow cast members. This may not be the case, as far as you would be concerned, but avoid mentioning the subject to be on the safe side – even keeping non-acting skills and credits firmly off your acting CV. If, however, it is brought up by someone else, do your best to brush it off, by saying something like 'Yes, I direct, but today I am being seen as an actor, which is my primary profession/first love, and I know how to separate the two.'

Another sin to be avoided is to tell whoever is reading in with you where they went wrong or give them notes on their performance. Even as a former actor, I don't particularly enjoy reading in with candidates, and sometimes the task is sprung on me at very short notice, leaving me no time to look over the piece, as I am trying to sort out more pressing matters for the session concerned. Several times, as I have taken an artist out of the room and back to reception, asking 'How was that?' the response has been 'Can I give you a note?' Some have followed on with 'That word is pronounced . . .' or 'You should have played that more . . .'. In this situation I always apologise (though sometimes the reader is asked to read in badly to see how the auditionee reacts). I tell them I will try to do better next time – once adding 'As I'd really like to be offered the part of your wife'.

The final cardinal sin is to know more about the play for which you are auditioning than the director. This is not easy to judge, and while it can boost your confidence to be able to reel off facts or complex questions about the piece, the director may feel that you know, or think you know, more than they do, and be dubious or nervous about employing you – however silly or unjustified this may seem. I heard a story some years ago of an actor who pumped the director with specific questions about how she was going to stage various scenes of the play, as well as her viewpoint on aspects of his character and its traits. The director in question – someone with an excellent track record in worldwide theatre – gave somewhat bland answers, before being forced into admitting that, as she was working on three other projects simultaneously, she had not yet had time to read the script. Whatever your feelings about this situation, the director had the upper hand as she already had the job, something which the actor never did. While I am not advocating subservience, always be careful what you say and avoid the temptation to show off in all situations, but especially before the job is yours.

So remember to . . .

✓ Play down skills and experience that compete with the creative team.

✓ Create separate CVs for each of your areas of work.
✓ Never criticise or give notes to those reading in with you.
✓ Avoid showing off, no matter how much you know.

CHAPTER 31

Same Old Faces

'Why do we always see the same old faces on television?' (or working in any media, for that matter). This cry is age old and one we hear time and time again. Many immediately blame the lack of imagination of the creatives and casting personnel, which can be the case, but these days it is very rare indeed. Try putting yourself in the shoes of a director. You have been asked to direct a production of, say, *Romeo and Juliet* at a major repertory theatre, where you can employ a large cast on a weekly wage above the Equity minimum. As a director, you would not only want the most talented people that fitted your perception of each role as closely as possible, but to surround yourself with good, supportive human beings who would simply get on with the job in hand, making your life easier and the experience more pleasurable. While this may sound idealistic, it is possible, and a well-balanced, harmonious and happy company can make all the difference to the finished product as seen by the audience.

So how would you go about assembling said company of actors? You might be teamed up with a knowledgeable casting director to help and advise you, which is great, and good ones really are worth their weight in gold. However, on this occasion you have to cast it all yourself, so where do you start? Well, before you go proclaiming the news in all the casting publications and getting besieged by hundreds of submissions, you would doubtless think of those you know – it's human nature. Your actor friends, the people in your year and the years above and below at college or drama school, or from youth theatre would be your first thought, as would actors you have worked with and those whose work you have seen and admired. Out of those, you could create a wish list of one or two ideal actors for each character, as you see them. As I've mentioned before, it's not what you know, it's who you know . . . and who knows you. While you may immediately know who you would love to give a break and employ in your Shakespearean epic, there would also be some people who you would not wish to have in your company. Perhaps these people might be lazy, unreliable or disruptive, would undermine your authority in the rehearsal room, as they think they know more than you, or simply, in your opinion, not be good actors – that's fine, as you don't have to employ them. So, once you have checked the availability of your wish list and put in offers (if you feel confident enough to do so without hearing them read for the role), you may be fully cast in a matter of days. If so, that's great and word will soon go round, actors and agents bemoaning the fact that they heard absolutely nothing about such a big production. If, however, some or all of your wish list are busy, uninterested in your project or the role you are offering, cannot leave home or afford to accept the money on offer, you will have to cast the net wider.

So why would you immediately think of those you know, to whatever degree, over complete strangers who happen to have performed a good speech or reading and made all the right noises when you chatted to them? The answer is simple – *safety*. The people you know well, or have admired in action, have one thing in common, they are all tried and tested and you know they could do everything that was required of them. In the case of those personally known to you, you have the added bonus of being aware of their temperament and foibles as people and, like compiling a guest list for a party, will have a better idea of who will mix, blend and get on well together (some would say this is half the battle). Though excellent people can be found at audition (directors with whom you have worked may be consulted for advice before a commitment is made), given the choice, most directors will go for what they know rather than go through extensive auditions.

So this is the answer to our question: the same old faces appear time and time again because they are known quantities that are tried and tested by those who personally know them or are aware of their work. *Good work breeds work*. Once directors, casting directors, producers and companies find good, useful actors with whom they click, they will use them whenever possible, and spread the word to others.

When considering whether to apply for jobs and writing the letters for them, put yourself back in the director's shoes. Would you audition and employ yourself? Not just because you believe that you are the best actor who ever lived, but because you are 100 per cent suitable for the brief concerned. If you were on the receiving end of that letter, would it stand out from the others, and, if not, how could you make it do so? Would a director consider their time wasted reading your letter, as you do not fit the stipulated criteria? If this is the case and it would go straight into the 'no' pile, don't send it and wait patiently for something more suitable. Thinking of everyone's point of view, and not just your own, will help you put situations more into perspective, and strengthen your applications, auditions and work.

Another case of the same old faces are the people you will be in competition with at the auditions you go to. You may see the same people on a regular basis, and frustratingly the same person might get the job a large percentage of the time. One of my rivals used to do this regularly, to my great irritation, though gratifyingly he is truly outstanding and has since deservedly won awards for his stage and screen work on both sides of the Atlantic. It can also be easy to be defeatist when up against actors who are more experienced than you for the same role. I have regularly heard actors lamenting 'And then he/she walked into the waiting room and I thought oh well, we all know who's going to get this one then.' Who says they will automatically get it? There's no law that says this must be so. Indeed, if you think that way, your negativity will probably make it come true. Stand your ground, keep your confidence, do your best and go for it – and may the best person win!

So remember to . . .

✓ Put yourself in the director's shoes – would you employ you for a part?
✓ Keep in with employers who respect you – good work breeds work.
✓ Avoid negativity when competing with more experienced actors. Stand your ground, keeping confident – why shouldn't you get the job?

CHAPTER 32

Recasts

When a stage play or musical is first produced, the creative team have a blank canvas on which to mould and craft the production. The actors are the originals, and, if they have been well cast, will be the template for subsequent companies, or even productions of the piece. Recasting, therefore, can often be a harder and more demanding process than finding the originals, as the creatives will often have preconceived ideas of what they are looking for, perhaps seeking exact replicas or wanting a better, stronger or more talented cast than the one before. I know several actors who have taken over in shows as they were not only good performers and right for the part, but exactly fitted the existing costume. It may sound bizarre and even penny pinching, but costumes are expensive to remake and this can sometimes be another deciding factor. Go and see as many original productions as you can so you know if there might be a job for you in the future.

An actress called me once bemoaning her fate, as she had just auditioned and been recalled for a takeover company I was assembling, yet not got the job. This would have been more bearable for her had she not been offered a role in the original cast, which she had turned down in favour of another project. 'How come I was good enough then, but am not now?' she wailed. The fact of the matter was she was no less good than she had been – she was probably even better – but the person who was playing the part she was offered (and who was equally good) had made the decision to renew her contract just after we had held the auditions, so there was no suitable part for her at that time. It turned out the reason she had taken the one job over the other was she thought that the show she took would run for years and ours would not. Ironically, exactly the reverse happened. Sometimes you can never make the right decision!

So remember to . . .

- ✓ Go to see original productions to find suitable roles for the future.
- ✓ Keep in mind there may be no suitable vacancies for you this time.
- ✓ Reapply in future years. Your turn may come.
- ✓ Feel positive about fitting the costume!

CHAPTER 33

The Casting Couch

We have all heard talk of this phenomenon, mostly associated with stories of stardom and rags to riches back in the 1950s and 1960s. It is the constant joke aimed at casting directors (usually delivered with a playful wink or nudge by those intrigued souls who are not in the Industry) and it is indeed what the sofa in my office is jokingly nicknamed. Not as rife as it supposedly was all those decades ago, the practice of offering a job in return for sexual favours does still occasionally occur and while it is not worth worrying about, keep the possibility at the back of your mind. Now far be it for me to moralise or tell any of you how to behave, but it is an abuse of (supposed) power, especially if it gets thoughts of 'what if . . .' going in your mind.

While it is totally your decision what course of action to take in this dilemma, in my opinion, no job is worth that sort of sacrifice or mental torment. You are really worth more than that! I turned down advances myself, as a young actor many years ago – with no detriment to my career, or self respect – and though I may have lost out on a couple of interesting jobs, I knew that the ones I did get were purely on the basis of talent and suitability. Be careful if an audition is in somebody's home or in a hotel room. Always tell someone where you are going, giving them the address and telephone number, which you should ask for in case of emergencies. If you are nervous, ask someone to take you and wait outside and if you are really unsure after speaking with the people concerned, request to meet in a public place – a crowded café or theatre coffee bar – or if you are still not convinced, politely decline.

On the other side of the coin, there are some actors and actresses who flirt outrageously with casting directors, producers and directors, sometimes offering themselves on a plate. While this may seem like a good idea (for whatever reason), it puts everyone concerned in a very awkward position, as the true motive for this action can be unclear. Whenever this has happened to me, I am left wondering if the person concerned likes me for me or for what they believe I can do for their career. Consequently, it has always been met with polite refusal (flattering though the attention may be).

This said, however, there are many cases of performers and work-givers who are mutually attracted and get together, and if that is the case for you, then that's great – just make sure it's for all the right reasons, rather than a one-sided power trip.

So remember to . . .

- ✓ Always ask for a phone number and check it is correct.
- ✓ Tell someone where you are going and give them the contact details.
- ✓ Keep calm and cool whatever the situation.
- ✓ Not be afraid to say 'no'. It will do you no harm.
- ✓ Not be too flirtatious, as it could be misinterpreted.

PART 3

After

CHAPTER 34

Red Letter Days

My greatest memory of auditions as a young and eager actor was the fact that they were there in the diary – both the one in my filofax and the other one in my mind. Sometimes there were lots of auditions for a multitude of jobs (we were talking the affluent 1980s here) and at other times nothing came in for weeks, even months, so those auditions that I was offered were all the more important. When one came my way, often with a week or two's notice for preparation, I would look at my diary regularly at that magic word 'audition' at 3.25 on Tuesday. 'Wonderful!' I would think to myself, as I did whatever preparation was required. As the time went on, I would think about it more, dream about getting the job, whatever it happened to be. The day before, I would be rushing around, trying to make sure everything I could have possibly done was prepared and ready for the big day – which then, often all too soon, arrived.

On the day, I would be very nervous from the time I awoke until after the audition. Don't ask me why – thinking back on it, I lacked much of the confidence I have now and maybe wanted the job too much (believe me, desperation shows!). The allotted time arrived and I would go to meet those all-important people for however many minutes to show them what I could do.

I would come out of the building and then the problem started – *that was it!* All those days or weeks of preparation for a few minutes, during which time I might have shone, done OK or failed abysmally, being stopped a few lines in to what I was doing only to be told 'Thank you, that's all we need to hear today.' All that anticipation and now what did I have to look forward to? A big void of nothing. It used to depress me, until I started thinking of ways to remedy this. I would make sure I always had something planned to do after every audition. Perhaps it would be meeting a friend for lunch (somewhere that allowed flexibility in case I was delayed because my casting overran and they would be waiting alone for hours); maybe a matinee in the theatre, a trip to the cinema, off back to my temp job or straight home to write letters for other auditions – anything that would take my mind off the empty feeling. One actress I know has an audition day ritual which involves heading straight to a top London department store for a glass of champagne and shopping spree. Another, more frugally, hot foots it to the nearest supermarket for an egg mayonnaise sandwich, banana and Diet Coke. You may develop your own, but whatever you do, it will help greatly to make auditions just a normal part of life – like cleaning the fridge or walking the dog – rather than the be all and end all of your week.

Ironically, you will often feel far more confident (and less nervous, if that applies to you) about auditions that come up with little or no notice. When the phone rings asking you to be somewhere on the same day, maybe in just an hour or two, you'll have less time to worry and build it up in your mind. This is where preparation really comes into its own – having those speeches, songs, sight-reading techniques up your sleeve and that audition bag packed – will stand you in excellent stead. It also pays to be as flexible as you can. If you have a day job, are you guaranteed time off for auditions, or can you wangle it, even at the very last minute? Would you be able to start rehearsing that day, if it were necessary, without leaving people in the lurch and risking future employment when times are not so rosy? These are factors to keep in mind, and perhaps discuss with your agent. With mobile communications you can be contactable virtually 100 per cent of the time – and this business is the only one where you can be out of work one day and on the top of the tree the next – so, as always, be prepared for the unexpected, you never know what tomorrow will bring!

So remember to . . .

✓   Keep busy beforehand to combat nerves.
✓   Arrange to do something afterwards, preferably with others.
✓   Keep timing flexible in case of the session over running.
✓   Discuss auditions at short notice with your day job employer and agent.
✓   Always keep your mobile phone switched on (even on silent or pager).

CHAPTER 35

Success

Receiving a job offer is undoubtedly the best part of auditioning for anyone, and making an offer is the part of the process I enjoy most too. There is nothing as satisfying as calling an agent or artist to offer someone a part – especially if they have auditioned several times, working hard to get to the required standard. People take the news in different ways from the contained 'Oh, that's nice, thank you' to deafening screams down the phone or even tears of joy (and all these can be from agents too!). There is an unequalled feeling of elation the moment you hear that a job is yours and you have beaten however many other people to the part.

Keep in mind though that offers can sometimes take time to be made – days or sometimes even weeks after the auditions. This can happen if other roles have to be cast or artists confirmed before you, to ensure the necessary balance of the company, so don't give up hope if your phone doesn't ring immediately, or you hear nothing for a while.

Excited as you may be, ensure you get all the details of the offer confirmed to you – some of these will be already written on your audition log. Check the role you are being offered (it might be different from the one for which you auditioned), covering or understudy responsibilities, rehearsal and performance/shoot dates, as well as the finish date and if they have an option to extend to a later date. Confirm the fees and expenses (subsistence, touring allowance, per diems, etc.), what contract is on offer – Equity or not – and the situation on insurance, should anything happen to you while working or travelling, especially if the job is abroad. You may not need it, but don't be afraid to ask for time to think about the offer or talk it over with your partner or family. Overnight, or the weekend, if applicable, is usually acceptable. Should you need to, and there is scope for it, this is the time to negotiate, having mulled over the offer, rather than diving in straight away.

Another situation which should be treated with caution is when you are offered a job out of the blue. You may be approached directly by a director or producer, perhaps at a party or after a show in which they have seen you perform and asked if you are interested in appearing in one of their productions. This may be something that is scheduled to happen soon, or hypothetically in the future – either way, be careful how you respond. Being freelancers in an over-crowded profession, nobody likes to say no to anything, and being put on the spot really doesn't help matters. If and when this happens to you, the most sensible course of action is to be very enthusiastic and positive about the project, but instead of giving the impression that you are committing, tell the person who has asked that you always discuss everything with your agent and so would they please ring them with the details, mentioning that you had both spoken (you could get some printed cards with your name and agent's details). If you are unrepresented, politely make the excuse of having to check your diary and ask if you can take a number and call them, the casting director or production office the next day for more details (making sure you do so exactly when you promise). This tactic will then buy you more time and you can have a second conversation, away from possible crowds and noise, during which you will be better able to evaluate the situation.

The reason I mention this is that on numerous occasions I have been called by a member of the creative team with whom I am working and told that they were talking to an actor (usually someone famous or up and coming) the night before and had mentioned the project on which we were working. They had asked the actor if they would be interested in being involved or playing a specific part. I have been told that the actor had enthusiastically accepted, and all that was necessary was for me to call their agent to formally make the offer and to finalise the deal. I am always quite cautious when doing this as, not having been there, I'm working on hearsay and do not know exactly what has been said. Usually the agent will not have been primed either. Quite often, the agent will take down the details, and then tell me that the actor simply isn't free for the dates, or there is an overlap which cannot be accommodated. If the artist is available, the agent may not think the project is right for the actor concerned and turn it down on their behalf without further discussion, or come back to me after speaking to their client and tell me that the actor has had a change of heart. Very rarely has the actor been true to their word and ended up doing the job. This is a situation that ends up in disappointment all round, so should therefore be handled with care.

After accepting the job and imparting the good news to family and friends, the nitty gritty really begins. You may have to negotiate your own deal, clear your diary of conflicting engagements, ask for temporary leave (or resign) from any day jobs, sublet or move out of your accommodation (and all the arrangements associated with that), organise child or pet care, book theatrical digs for the following weeks or months, or even pack your bags and get on a train or plane at only a few hours' notice. This can be a daunting challenge, but being prepared for these eventualities will make your life all the easier. Make yourself a list of everything you would need to do if you were offered a job that started rehearsals in a week's time and took you away from home for a year. You can also do the same for a week's filming abroad, flying out tomorrow. Do these now, while you have time and your head is clear, revising the list as and when necessary.

Rehearsal and filming days can be long, busy and stressful, so it pays to do as much as you can before you start, keeping your mind free to fully concentrate on the job in hand. Enjoy and relish every job you do, learning from it and the other actors with whom you are working.

So remember to . . .

✓ Confirm all the details of the offer.
✓ Ask for thinking time, if you need it.
✓ Always be cautious and non-committal when offered a job on the spot.
✓ Write lists of the practicalities in preparation for all eventualities.
✓ Do as much as you can before you start the job.
✓ Relish and learn from it and your fellow performers.

CHAPTER 36

Negotiation

While, if you have one, your agent will do this on your behalf, like everything else we have discussed, it is perfectly possible to effectively negotiate your own contracts and deals. I could write chapters on this subject alone, and indeed many books are available teaching the techniques, but here are a few thoughts if you should ever have to take the reins. First, offers and contracts are increasingly becoming non-negotiable – take it or leave it – and if that is the case, it is rarely worth asking for changes in terms or more money, though not impossible, if approached in a nice way. In theatre, a company wage may be on offer, where everyone is on the same, which is regarded by many as a fairer and easier way to do things.

Money and pay scales usually depend on your level of experience (a graduate on their first job will usually be paid the lowest salary and probably less than someone who has been around longer). You may be offered an 'inclusive deal', where a number of extras, which would otherwise be paid for on top of your basic weekly salary, are bought in as part of the fee. These can include overtime, holiday pay, performance and responsibility fees when understudying and, in some cases, even touring, accommodation and travel allowances. If this kind of deal is offered to you, deduct the costs of all the inclusive items from the gross fee and check you can actually afford to work for the basic salary after you have paid out whatever is necessary.

It may work out to be less than you think, or need. One stance often used is previous amounts that have been earned. You might be offered £300 a week and respond 'Well I was on £350 for my last job, so obviously wouldn't want to be paid any less.' The answer might be positive or negative, and should it be the latter, you then have to decide if you will do the job for less money than before. All negotiation is a matter of give and take, and what you lose on the roundabouts you might gain on the swings. You will doubtless have to concede somewhere, so think of the minimum you can afford to accept and go from there. It really depends how much you want, or need, the work and how much the company concerned wants you. A huge star of the 1960s regularly used to be asked to open shops and make other personal appearances, which were of no interest to him. He got around this by telling his agent to ask for ludicrously high fees, which put many companies off, but if they were prepared to pay what was demanded, he would do them happily, laughing all the way to the bank. Sometimes you can decline and the phone will ring a few hours, days or weeks later with a better offer – it is a risk you have to take and up to you if you can hold out and call their bluff to get what you want. This is easier to do if the company have approached you rather than vice versa; if you are renegotiating a second contract for a long running television series or play, when you have been asked to continue playing a role or are promoted, or you have another job offer on the table. That said, do not ever hold people to ransom by asking for a far greater amount than you were on before, even when you know you have them over a barrel (in other words, for instance, if a further series cannot go ahead without your character). Taking this kind of action will help nobody, let alone you, especially if your agent and the production company or casting director have agreed a fair fee, which you then reject. Keep your feet on the ground and listen to the arguments from your agent and/or the employers as you don't know what future work this may lead to, or indeed lose you, if the people concerned can no longer bear to deal with you. Do not shoot yourself in the foot for the sake of an extra few pounds – it is rarely worth it. If you really feel the need to decline the offer, do it politely, calmly explaining your reasons and thanking them, rather than taking umbrage.

Other aspects that can be negotiated are length of your contract (six or nine months might be more appealing than twelve), or a betterment clause, which entitles you to leave a show, giving several weeks' notice, should you be offered a better part in another production (this will often be offered in the case of understudies). As well as a higher fee or salary, other financial considerations can be mentioned, including a mid-contract pay rise after so many months or when the production has recouped, a royalty (percentage of the box office take when the weekly takings are over £X,000), or perhaps a larger accommodation allowance or booked hotel room. Billing on the poster and outside the theatre, taxis home and solo dressing rooms can also be requested, but most of these items will only usually apply to better-known names and it may be considered cheeky to ask for them until you have a suitable profile.

If you are offered a fringe play for little or no money, and want to do it to invite casting personnel, agents and potential employers to see your work, you should agree some complimentary or, at the very least, reduced price tickets for those you contact before accepting the job. In the case of student or low-budget films, be sure to agree a VHS or DVD copy of the film for your showreel. That said, filmmakers, and even some reputable schools and colleges are notoriously bad at sending these, so keep pestering and kick up a fuss if your agreement is not honoured – with the principal, if necessary. For all low or no pay jobs, you could also try for travel expenses and meal allowances for each day you work.

As I said, this is far easier when an agent does this on your behalf, but I know several unrepresented actors who do a good job for themselves, handling the deal warmly and fairly – perhaps with cheeky humour – and stating valid reasons, rather than yelling, being obstructive and stubborn. Always make sure that everything is agreed before accepting a job, and put all the details of your conversations in writing or an email to the producers to ensure they will be incorporated into your contract. Negotiating retrospectively (after the event) can lead to disagreements and land you in some very sticky situations. Once you have agreed a deal, do not ever go back and ask for more retrospectively, refusing to do the job if your demands are not met (holding the company over a barrel). Some projects or the need to replace an artist can come up at very short notice, so there is little or no time to think matters over as a decision is needed quickly, perhaps there and then. In this situation, you have to think on your feet and decide if the offer is right for you. This can be stressful for the casting person as well as you. Once agreed, however, this deal should be stuck to at all costs, no matter how unhappy you later feel about what has been offered. Bite your tongue and bide your time, because if you are offered further work by the same people (who may remember with gratitude that you have helped them out of a tight spot at short notice), you will have a far stronger case for negotiation. If you don't get your way, accept it and take no for an answer, rather than issuing threats that you never want to work with them again – never is a long, long time!

There is one final and important point that you should keep in the back of your mind. While most jobs go without a hitch and employers honour the agreements that they have made, circumstances sometimes go wrong. In recent years, some companies have gone bankrupt, with their productions folding before the end of the contract and leaving the casts unpaid and owed money. I have even heard instances of artists being offered jobs (often through well-respected agents) only to find, shortly before they are scheduled to start work, that the production concerned was no longer going ahead. Indeed, I know of a case where artists were offered jobs in a production that never actually existed and upon investigation, nobody knew anything about. I hope neither of these scenarios ever happen to you, but there is one simple thing you can do to limit any potential damage – do not spend your fee before doing the job, and wait until the money has cleared in your bank account before spending a penny of it. This can be hard, but it's by far the safest way.

So remember to . . .

✓   Work out the minimum fee you can afford to accept and go from there.
✓   Be prepared to give and take, conceding when you have to.
✓   Ask nicely, being fair and realistic about your worth.
✓   Weigh up the pros and cons as other benefits may make a difference.
✓   Always confirm the agreed points to the other party via email or post.

CHAPTER 37

Rejection

Most of the time, you will be rejected silently – in other words, you will never hear another word about an audition you have done. Harsh though it may sound, most offices simply do not have the time to telephone or write to each individual actor who has auditioned, and, even if they do speak to your agent with the news, you will rarely be told unless you push for an answer or specific feedback has been given. But what should you do if you are given a negative response in person?

I know there are some actors who still think that casting directors are power-crazed individuals and believe rejecting poor downtrodden actors is the best part of our job. From my point of view, nothing could be further from the truth. I hate being the bearer of bad tidings – especially when having to shatter someone's hopes and dreams by telling them to their face that they are not being recalled or have not got the job. We all know this is tough to hear, and as I have mentioned before, anyone who calls you in to audition really wants you to get the job, so it can be equally tough for us too, especially if we were secretly convinced that you would be the one.

While it is never easy, there is only one thing that can be done for the best – take the news on the chin and move on. Tempting though it is, please do not blow your top, be sarcastic, use emotional blackmail or burst into tears. While satisfying at the time, these tactics really will not help the situation. Instead, you will seem far more in control if you just thank whoever is telling you, accepting and taking on board any feedback or criticism you have been offered, and smile confidently no matter how you are feeling. Walk away with your head held high and learn from your experience. There is always next time! Save the moaning, swearing and crying for when you are safely back at home, or at least well away from the people and venue concerned.

There are always incidences where you will feel you have been treated unfairly, but this is a subjective business and a work-giver's idea of a part might be worlds away from your own. If you are really concerned, you can always try asking the casting director or production office for feedback after the event, though this is better done through your agent, as it is easier to be honest, perhaps even blunt, with another person. That said, sometimes feedback is near impossible to give, as you may have done a great audition with no real scope for improvement, but the team just went for someone else who, to their minds, fitted the role better. You may be remembered by the same team for a more suitable role in the future. It always pays to remain positive about a project, despite not getting the job, unlike a friend who wished every production that did not go his way to fail. I always used to go and see shows I had been up for and sometimes I could see why the successful actor was chosen (other times I thought they had made a mistake not employing me!). Either way, I was better prepared for future opportunities with that creative team.

Hard though it may be at the time, be happy for your friends if they are experiencing success when you are not. The story of two actors who trained together comes to mind. At first everything was rosy and both were regularly in work, but later the work dried up for X (despite many auditions over several years), while his friend, Y, had a steady stream of offers. X was supportive, always being the first to congratulate Y on his successes and going to see him in numerous productions. Despite feeling a little jealousy, he was happy that one of them was working. Then some years later, the tables turned and due primarily to persistence, X began to get offers while Y suffered a drought. This was fine for the first job, but as time went on, resentment crept in. No congratulations, no supporting the other's work, just moans of 'I should have been up for that!' In the end, the friendship suffered as X could no longer bear to impart the news of success for fear of feeling bad. I know it is easy to feel like this, but please try not to let this be you. Feel happy for others, after all it is only a job, and with persistence and dedication your turn will come.

So remember to . . .

- ✓ Take rejection and criticism in your stride, keeping your dignity.
- ✓ Learn from your experience.
- ✓ Ask for feedback, if you really feel the need, or get your agent to do so.
- ✓ Keep positive. You may be remembered and employed in the future.
- ✓ Be happy for your friends when they are successful.

CHAPTER 38

Follow Ups

Undoubtedly, the most nerve-wracking part of any audition process is waiting to hear the result. I know it is easy for me to tell you that whenever you finish an audition, you should leave the room and forget all about it, and if you are able to do this near impossible feat, then all the better. Sometimes you will be told at the time if you are recalled or when a decision will be made. Most of the time, if the answer is negative, you will never hear another word (despite sometimes being told to the contrary). It is very tempting to frequently check your mobile and ansaphone for news, or to pester your agent or the casting director concerned on whether a decision has yet been made. The latter is really not a good idea, as not only does it make you look desperate, but can also profoundly irritate. I know people who have lost jobs from pestering members of the creative team – especially on home or mobile numbers, which they have somehow procured. I appreciate that the waiting game is a tough one, but please believe me, if the answer is positive, nobody would keep the information from you for any longer than they have to and you will always be told you have got the job – just make sure that your contact details are correct and up to date.

Whether you got the job or not, it is a nice idea to send whoever got you in for the audition (the casting director, director or your contact at the production company) a card to thank them for seeing you. While this practice is very common in America, not many British performers send them, so by doing this you will stand out from the crowd, as well as also earning brownie points – after all, everyone likes to feel appreciated. Leave it about a week or so after the audition, or preferably until you know the final result. A simple 'thank you' and 'please remember me in the future' are enough. Steer clear of analysing your audition, telling them they made the wrong decision and that you can do so much better given another chance or apologising if you feel you did badly (as the creative team may have thought very differently). If you are given the job, a card is definitely in order. Some actors also send gifts, which, while a nice gesture, some casters can find inappropriate, so it is worth asking your agent's advice before going this far.

Another way of reminding those who have auditioned you that you are still around is by sending Christmas cards. This is an excellent way of keeping in touch while having nothing to say. As with thank you cards, keep the greeting simple, from one person to another, rather than a plea for work. Choose cards that look professional and business-like and are of good quality, steering clear of cartoon Santa Clauses, cards intended for children and those that look and feel as though they came from a pack of fifty costing 99p. Also please avoid sending cards with a photo of yourself on them, and do not enclose your CV or Christmas show performance notice. If you are going to send a mailout for such a show, do it separately, as it will diminish the effectiveness of your festive greeting. If you have not got your full name and contact details printed on the card (which can often be achieved with an ordinary inkjet printer, rather than paying astronomical prices for overprinted cards), please always write your full name in capitals under your signature. Every year without fail I receive at least one card from someone I am unable to identify. Unless you know someone really well, avoid putting 'Lots of love' and including kisses. When done well, a Christmas card is a very effective annual marketing tool. The more ecologically sound among you are probably throwing up your hands in horror at this last suggestion. Emails are indeed the greener, and cheaper, option and used by an increasing number of people, but they really are a far less effective way of communicating your festive message, for several reasons. First, a card requires opening and reading, as does anything sent via the postal service, so more effort is required and it will therefore be better remembered by the recipient, or their assistant. Second, it will more than likely be displayed, and perhaps looked at again before being taken down, whereas an email will be looked at once, before being closed or deleted. Third, because many spammers use the subject heading Happy Christmas or New Year to disguise an email's true content, many, myself included, no longer open such mails from unrecognised senders for fear of viruses. On the plus side, many stores offer recycling boxes for cards after the holiday season, or you can always do what I do and recycle them by cutting them up and making gift tags for next year.

So remember to . . .

- ✓ Try to forget about auditions after you have done them and move on.
- ✓ Not pester and irritate the casting director, or your agent for a decision.
- ✓ Send a thank you card when you know the outcome.
- ✓ Check before sending anything more, such as gifts or flowers.
- ✓ Send professional Christmas cards to those you meet and know.

CHAPTER 39

Turning Down Work

Hard though this may be to imagine, turning down a job can be one of the toughest decisions any artist has to make.

There are various reasons why one might need to do this. It may be a simple question of your availability and a conflicting commitment – whether work or family. The length of contract, amount of money on offer and the suitability or size of the role may also be factors that come into play after you have auditioned. You may also want to change direction (moving from musical theatre to acting roles, or do more television work than theatre, for instance) or hold out for a regular role in a television series, rather than doing one or two episode parts. In order to do this, you may have to turn down the type of work that you are usually offered and wait patiently for what you want. This can be both daunting and financially difficult, but can pay dividends in the long run. Stars sometimes sit 'looking at the wall' for months on end until the right career-advancing script or project comes their way, declining all other offers in the meantime.

No matter how you feel about an offer (flattered, insulted, affronted or otherwise), it is always important to be pleasant, thanking everyone when declining – something taught to me by a big name from television, who did so on a daily basis – as you never know when you might need the people again, or indeed where they might end up.

Before making that final decision, think about where a job could lead, not only from the point of view of that actual production but also future work it could generate elsewhere – as work breeds work – as well as personal fulfilment playing the part. Talk it through with your family, friends and agent, weighing up the positives and negatives. Sleep on these thoughts, if time allows, and as soon as your mind is made up, contact the relevant person with your decision (or inform your agent if they are to do this). If contact has been through your agent and you have not spoken to those concerned, it is a nice idea to send them a card thanking them for their interest, wishing them success with the project and expressing hopes for other opportunities to work together in the future. This method can also be used if you hear that someone has checked your availability for a job that interests you but for which you are unavailable. Both will receive a favourable reaction (even though you probably will not see it) and earn you brownie points.

I remember being offered a long theatre tour that I did not want, as I was determined to stop acting in favour of casting. I was so nervous when it came to calling the producer with my decision, that I actually wrote 'Thank you for the offer and I am very flattered to be asked, but this is not for me at the moment' on a piece of paper in case I panicked and accidentally accepted. The producer was very understanding and we have since worked together several times (with me casting rather than performing).

So remember to . . .

- ✓ Thoroughly think through your reasons for declining.
- ✓ Talk it through, weigh up all aspects – sleeping on it, if possible.
- ✓ Politely thank those concerned, explaining the situation succinctly.
- ✓ Write a telephone script if you are nervous about declining.
- ✓ Send a thank you card for the offer, expressing hopes for the future.

CHAPTER 40

Help!
What if . . . ?

We all have times when events do not go exactly the way we planned and panic sets in. This can be because distractions occur that prevent us preparing as much as we would like, or because of circumstances totally outside our control, such as transport failures.

Whatever the case, the first thing to do is take several deep breaths, calm down and think how to resolve the issue, asking the help and advice of others wherever possible. The less flustered and more accepting you are, the easier matters will be to sort out and the better you will perform when the time comes. Remember, you can only do your best and problems are seldom as bad as they seem.

What if . . .

- *I am offered an audition for a part for which I am not suitable? Should I go?*
  If it is a case of not fitting the brief skills-wise, then ask the advice of your agent or the casting office, declining if necessary. If it is a question of age or looks, I would go anyway, as we all know that the briefs can change.
- *I have been asked to read for a different role from the one for which I suggested myself?*

Do as they request, and then ask if it is worth your reading the original part as well.

- *A friend has an audition for a job for which I have written? Should I gatecrash?*

  If you are totally right for a part in the piece concerned, get as much information as possible and go, politely asking if they can see you and allowing plenty of waiting time.

- *I have been asked to audition for a production that contains scenes that offend my sensibilities? Should I go?*

  As an actor, you should play any part that is thrown at you, as you are in character rather than yourself. However, if you would feel really uncomfortable, it is probably best you decline immediately.

- *I wake up feeling ill on the morning of an audition?*

  If you feel well enough to go, then do so, but do your best and make no excuses. 'Doctor Theatre' could well come into his own. If you really cannot speak, sing or have a physical injury, call your agent or the casting office explaining the situation and ask if they can reschedule your appointment.

- *I am delayed getting to a casting?*

  Call your agent, the venue or casting office, letting them know as soon as you can, even if it means getting off the train. Apologise if you are late, giving an estimated arrival time of 10 minutes later, to allow for further delays. Check they will still be there if your appointment is near the end of the day.

- *I get lost* en route *to the audition venue?*

  Call the venue, tell them where you are and ask for directions, sending apologies if you are running late. Prevent this by carrying a street map or internet mapping printout.

- *My passport has expired?*

  Visit www.ukpa.gov.uk for help and advice on how to renew quickly. Write a reminder in your diary six months before your passport expires so you can renew it without stress.

- *I have an audition for which I have worked hard and spent money preparing, but it is then cancelled?*

These things happen – sometimes even on the day – so don't get angry or upset. Put it down to experience, remembering that the money you have spent is tax deductible, and you will doubtless be in the company's minds for the future.

- *A last-minute audition comes in, but I have a dental appointment earlier that day?*

  Try to reschedule the dentist first, then the audition if the dentist really cannot change. Auditioning when your mouth is numb should be avoided at all costs!

CHAPTER 41

A Diary of an Audition

The old adage 'Never ask anyone to do anything that you're not prepared to do yourself' has always figured highly in my ethos of life. During the latter stages of writing this book, I realised that despite auditioning thousands of actors, I had not faced an audition myself for nearly twenty years. While writing from memory is fine, I felt I should have the experience fresh in my mind, so set about following my own instructions in the hope of procuring myself an audition – and possibly a temporary career change if an offer came my way.

As a member of Equity (under a different name from my own), my first port of call was their Job Information Service, where I found my target – a 'small part' in a play for a well-established theatre company playing a policeman in a murder mystery, which I would not have minded actually doing if it were offered to me. Perfect! I had seen the piece some years before, roughly remembered the plot and fitted the brief as quoted, so set about recreating my acting résumé and writing to the casting director (whom I had never met, so would not be rumbled).

I was very honest about my acting history and wrote a succinct letter explaining that I had been away from acting for over nineteen years and was now keen to explore new challenges. I presented everything corporately, posted the letter and waited for a response, with a little trepidation I must admit. Over the next couple of weeks I bumped into three actors I knew and when the subject of work arose, as it invariably did, all three mentioned that they had auditions for the production concerned – one being seen at the recall stage, having previously worked with the director and company. I got the feeling that they didn't want to see me and was on the verge of looking for something else for which to apply, when, out of the blue, my voice-mail bleeped with a message from the caster inviting me to come in at the recall stage four days later. Listening to the message, I was both excited and completely petrified. Should I take the easy way out and call back saying I was no longer available? It was tempting, but I could not bring myself to turn down such an opportunity, or let down the casting director, who obviously needed to get in more people. Could I actually go there and give it my best shot without losing my nerve? Of course I could!

Now the preparation really started. I searched the websites of several theatre bookshops to check if the script was in stock (as it was somewhat old) and eventually found it at French's Theatre Bookshop, so got on the tube and went there to buy a copy. I started to read it on my way back and eventually found my part, which was indeed small, but quite significant. When I had finished, I went through it, not only highlighting the lines with a marker pen to make it easier to read, but emphasising words and emotions to help the depth and clarity of my characterisation and delivery. I then worked on it by reading it through with a friend, taking their suggestions on board and making notes for inspiration. I looked at the script regularly over the next couple of days until the day of the audition actually arrived.

On the day itself, I decided on the clothes and look. Not having a full policeman's uniform – nor wanting to be sniggered at when I walked into the room – I decided on a black suit, white shirt and dark blue tie to give the impression, and as the play was set many years ago, I slicked my hair back with a side parting to create a more believable effect. I left home with plenty of time to spare – luckily so, as I bumped into an acquaintance on my way who kept me talking for ages – and arrived at the casting venue five minutes before my appointment.

When I entered the building, my heart was in my mouth for fear I would encounter an actor who knew me well when walking into the waiting room and my cover would be blown. I need not have worried – nobody knew me. The casting director was charming, welcoming me with . . . a newly rewritten version of the script! I only had the time while the person before me did his audition to read through it and discover that this version differed radically from the one on which I had worked so hard. All too soon it was my turn and I was ushered into the audition room for what had suddenly turned into a sight-reading exercise (for which I was unprepared). I was introduced to the director and producer, who shook hands and said very little. A third person in the room – whom I later discovered was the assistant director – said nothing, and he and the person reading in the other part were not introduced. The only direction I was given was to play it standing up rather than seated and 'You enter from over there.'

I read the scene as best I could, mentally cursing the lack of direction and not helped by the cumbersome script with which I was unfamiliar and the upstaging antics of the person I was reading with, who ensured that the creatives had an excellent view of my back most of the time. I finished, desperately hoping for a second chance to redeem myself, and waited for some feedback or direction to do it again, which would be so much better and relaxed. Instead of hearing, 'Now try it this way', I was greeted with 'OK, you are free to go.' The temptation to reply 'And thank you too!' through gritted teeth was nearly too much, but I smiled, thanked them all, including the reader, and promptly left the room, warmly thanking the casting director for getting me in, before I left the building. The actor who was in before me left at the same time and we walked to the tube together, chatting – well me asking about him with very little reciprocation ('Me me me' was not just a vocal exercise as far as he was concerned). We parted company at the tube station and, to save brooding on the experience alone, I went to breathe a sigh of relief at a pre-arranged lunch meeting with a friend who was in on my experiment.

A couple of days later, I bumped into one of the actors I knew who had also auditioned, and was told that they had received an offer for a different part on the same afternoon. I checked my mobile for the next few days, in case I was second, third or ninth choice, but nothing came through. So once again I am no longer in competition with any of you and happily back on the other side of the table, with a renewed appreciation of how nerve-wracking the process of auditioning can actually be.

CHAPTER 42

Final Thoughts

Congratulations! You've finished the book, hopefully reading each page regardless of whether you thought it applied to you or not. I hope you found it useful and enjoyable, learning along the way as well as reinforcing other information you already knew.

You now have two options: keep the book to hand, dipping in and out of it and referring to chapters as and when you need to, or file it away safely and forget about it, getting on with your professional life as normal. If, however, you choose the latter option, there is one further thing I would like you to do: make a note in your diary or forward planner to get the book out again exactly one year from today's date and read it through again. This will not only make you realise how much you have retained and used, but also remind you of tips or facts you have forgotten, and give you a chance to reflect on what has happened in the previous year and think of how it could have been improved. Self re-evaluation at annual or more frequent intervals is vital to ensure that you are working towards improvement as effectively as possible and achieving the desired results.

I have saved three other thoughts for last. The first is that everything happens for a reason, when the time is right – the audition that was meant for you, the agent whom you have always wanted to represent you, the life-changing phone call, the job you have always thought should be yours – these will all happen, if and when the time is right.

I first thought of writing this book back in 1993 and made vague attempts to do so, but nothing came of it. Why didn't it happen? Because the timing was not right, and when it was, everything fell into place (thanks also to a lot of hard work and persistence). So be patient, never give up hope or stop believing that whatever you want will happen and it will, when the time is right.

Second, a performer who has been very well known and respected for many decades asked me to share this thought with you – he said 'I am only still working and being wanted because I have remained useful.' Indeed, he is right – usefulness is our strongest asset and often the reason that we are employed (I refer to myself here too). Usefulness comes in many forms, it could be your type or look, a very specific skill or area of expertise, or the fact that you are known for being reliable and easy to work with. Never stop being useful and targeting the right people or companies who would benefit most from what you have to offer.

Lastly, the picture overleaf is the work of Saskia Carter, an extremely promising and hard-working drama student, whom I met in the late 1990s while she was studying at a school at which I adjudicated auditions. As well as working tirelessly at her studies, for which she won several prizes, she would also prepare and cook delicious buffet lunches for the audition panels, which always came complete with a specially designed photocopied place mat. This picture was one of those place mats, which I took as it made me laugh and has been displayed on the notice board in my office ever since, still making me smile every time I see it. I mention this story for two reasons. First, while auditions should be taken seriously, they should also be fun and enjoyed, and can sometimes indeed be a hoot (laugh) for everyone in the room. Second, Saskia was a truly inspirational person. During her studies, she was diagnosed with a brain tumour but she returned to college after treatment, and continued to work courageously towards her dream of being an actress, winning more prizes in the process. Sadly, this was not to be, as she lost her battle before she could graduate and died in May 2001, aged 23. She knew what she wanted

AUDITIONS
THEY
ARE A
HOOT

and went for it, which so many people do not have the courage to do. If you know what you want, and are prepared to work wholeheartedly to achieve it, then *go for it*. The phrase 'Life is too short' could not be more apt – especially in Saskia's case.

Thank you for reading this book and having the desire to learn and improve. If you have found it useful, do please tell all your friends and colleagues, as one positive word from you is worth a million from me. If you have any feedback, comments, suggestions for improvement or success stories, please post them on the Auditions Forum at www.auditionsapracticalguide.com, or, if you'd prefer not to share your thoughts publicly, we would be delighted to receive them via email at feedback@auditionsapracticalguide.com. All will be read with interest by our team, though we're sorry that we cannot respond personally to individual questions or queries.

Here's to your success. Keep focusing, working hard, improving, enjoying what you do and, above all, *believing*, and success will happen. *You can do it!*

Index

Actors Access 7
Actors Centre, The 8, 16, 75, 190
Actors Centre North 8
Actors Inc 7
adaptations 110, 114
Advance Production News UK 7, 156
agent 3–5, 9, 18, 31, 38, 42–4, 46–55, 57, 64, 67, 83, 99, 147, 150, 157, 159, 160–4, 165–6, 168–9, 172–3, 183, 192–3, 203, 206, 210, 213, 217, 223, 235–8, 240–3, 245–50, 252–4, 260; changing and leaving 52–3; obtaining representation with 48–50; presenters 192; seeing your work 43–4, 48–50; voice-over 183
Alton Towers 190
Anderson, Nancy 127
Any Dream Will Do 121
Arnold, Tom 74
arriving early 13, 18, 150, 206
arrogance 18, 65, 101, 119, 155
Arts Educational School 122

Artsline 19
assistants 3, 8–9, 47, 49–50, 57, 59, 73–4, 108, 161, 250, 258
autocue 18, 189

Backstage 7
bag, audition 19, 234
BBC Radio Repertory Company 177; Soundstart 178
behaviour 14, 63, 65–7, 96, 102, 215, 228
Bennett, Colin 152
Bennett, Tom 150
Blackpool Pleasure Beach 190
Blakemore, Michael 127
Bollywood 157
breakdowns 5, 8, 10, 29–32, 47, 109, 154
British Dyslexia Association, The 18
Broadcast 7, 185
Butlins 189
buyouts 165, 180

callbacks 4 (see also recalls)

cards 38, 43, 237, 248; Christmas 50, 55, 249–50; thank you 249–50, 252
Carleton Hobbs Award, The 177
Carter, Saskia 261, 263
Casting Call Pro 7
Casting Directors' Guild, The 12, 48, 165
Casting Workbook 7
Castnet 7
Castweb 6, 155
cattle call 4
CBBC 110
CBeebies 110
Chappell's 127
children and animals 13–14, 109
CITV 110
City Lit 176
client, the 165, 168, 174
Colclough, John 48
Complicite 107
Conference of Drama Schools, The 87
confidence 11–13, 15–16, 27, 49–50, 56, 63, 67–73, 75, 79–82, 84–5, 91–2, 98, 101, 129, 131, 133, 141–2, 171, 176, 191, 198, 202, 205, 212, 215–16, 220, 223, 225, 233–4, 246
Contacts 16, 36, 40–1, 46, 48, 87–8, 108, 155, 166, 171, 173, 178, 183, 192
continuity announcing 184
co-operative agencies 10, 53–4
Co-operative Personal Managers' Association, The 54
Council for Dance Education and Training, The 88
Cowell, Simon 83
Criminal Records Bureau 111, 120
CV (see also résumé) 5, 7, 9, 19, 30, 32–3, 35, 37–8, 40, 46, 64, 177–8, 201, 210, 219, 221, 249

Dahl, Roald 110, 119
dead letter perfect 150, 152
deal 51, 238–43; confirming details of 155, 236–7, 239, 244; inclusive 240
deferred payment 54, 156, 159
Dench, Dame Judi 50
Denys, Chris 112
Disneyland Paris 190
doctor theatre 90, 254
Doollee 114
Doyle, John 137
Dress Circle 127
dressing the part 60, 61, 63, 103, 147, 257
drying 18, 84–5, 92, 184
dubbing techniques 185–6
Dunmore, Simon 12, 114
dyslexia 18, 27

email 6, 8, 18, 28, 35, 43–6, 142, 155, 242, 244, 249–50, 275
emotions 14, 17, 124, 257
energy 71, 83, 85, 113, 120, 124, 136, 192–3
entrance, making an 63, 79–80
Equity 39, 140, 156, 158, 166, 168, 222, 237, 256; job information service 6, 256
excuses 12, 90, 98, 129, 142, 213, 237, 254
eye contact 89, 124, 197–8, 204

Fame Academy 121
film schools 154–5, 159
Finburgh, Nina 16
Find Me A Face 168
first impression 63, 67, 147
focal point 123–4, 151
French's Guide to Selecting Plays, Samuel 114
French's Theatre Bookshop 257

gatecrashing 9, 72, 74–5, 254
Gates, Gareth 122

Gervais, Ricky 175
Graeae Theatre Company 19
Grease Is The Word 121

handshake 79–80, 207
Harris, Chris 112–13
Hollywood 155, 157, 159
honesty 11, 27, 41, 45, 70, 75, 97,
    130, 203, 209–11, 217, 246,
    256
hospital radio 176, 181
*How Do you Solve A Problem
    Like Maria?* 121

I Can theory 68–70
Ibsen, Henrik 93, 118
I'd Do Anything 121
improvisation 84, 110, 138–9,
    143–4, 160, 166, 169–71, 173,
    184, 190, 192
Interact 171
introductions 54, 63–4, 73, 81, 91,
    98, 106, 157, 162, 164, 196,
    258
invitations (to see work) 41–4, 46,
    50

jobbing actor 146, 152

Kher, Anhupam 157
Knowledge, The 173

LA Casting.com 6
Legoland 190
letters 6–9, 28, 30, 32, 38, 41–3,
    45, 46, 156, 181, 198, 206,
    224, 234, 256–7; addressing
    29, 36, 46; paragraphs 28, 36,
    38; keynote plan 32; postage
    38, 40, 46
local, booked as 108, 120
log, audition 56–7, 59, 67, 95,
    175, 236
London Bubble Theatre Company
    137

lying 67, 75

Mackintosh, Sir Cameron 93
Mandy.com 6, 155
Manilow, Barry 127
Manor Pavilion, Sidmouth 108
mark, hitting your 148, 152
McArthur, Anne 16
measurements 38, 166–7, 169
Morley, John 112
Musicality 122
Musicians Union, The 140

name 8, 19, 29–30, 32, 36, 38, 41,
    45–6, 64–5, 67, 79, 91, 127,
    142, 157, 160, 162, 164, 181,
    196–200, 202, 207, 217, 249,
    256; painting pictures 197,
    199–200, 207
National Council for Drama
    Training, The 87
National Theatre 93
negativity 36, 69–71, 74, 86, 139,
    201–2, 209, 216–17, 225, 245,
    248, 252
nerves 13–14, 18, 72–3, 80–5, 91,
    93, 97, 132, 159, 180, 182,
    184, 202, 229, 233–5, 248,
    252, 259
networking 7, 9, 45, 48, 72, 87,
    154
New Shakespeare Company 102
New Wolsey Theatre Ipswich
    137
NY Casting.com 6

Ozanne, Christine 15

PCR 7–8, 108, 155–6, 189;
    Theatre Report 108
pencilling 4, 168
Personal Managers' Association,
    The 48, 54
photographs 7, 9, 19, 27–8, 40–1,
    45–6, 52, 63–4, 73–5, 130,

146, 160, 168–9, 174, 181, 207, 249
playing range 38–9, 61
playregistry.com 114
Polka Theatre 109
Pontins 189
Pop Idol 121–2
Porter, Cole 126–7
positivity 35, 65, 68–71, 82–3, 85–6, 91–2, 95, 98, 110, 123, 144, 165, 182, 197, 200–2, 207, 211, 215, 217–18, 227, 237, 241, 246–8, 252, 263
Potter, Harry 110
power trips 101, 119, 229
pre-cast 206
pre-production 3, 159
projection, voice 100, 103, 119; over projection 149, 192–3
Propeller Theatre Company 102

questions 48–9, 54–6, 70, 74, 82, 85–6, 91–2, 94, 98, 110, 123, 131, 151, 164, 171, 194–6, 198, 201–5, 207, 209–10, 215, 220; awkward 209; obtuse 203

RADA 152, 201
Radio Times 12, 176–7
reactions 96, 106, 124, 150, 153, 162, 170–2 184, 202–5, 207, 209, 215
recalls 4, 9, 52, 61, 66, 69, 85, 87, 92, 95–8, 122–3, 128–9, 132, 135, 139–44, 152, 166, 175, 212, 214, 216, 226, 245, 248, 257; fee 166
record keeping 8, 56, 67, 182
Reid, Beryl 74
repeat fees 165, 180
résumé (see also CV) 19, 27–8, 30, 36, 38, 40–1, 73–5, 130, 209, 256
Right Size, The 107
roleplaying 170–3

rooms, audition 147, 150–2, 158–61, 164–5, 198, 205, 220, 225, 248, 257–8, 261
Ross, Jonathan 205
Royal Exchange, Manchester, The 102
Royal Shakespeare Company, The 83, 102, 104

Salem, Marc 69
Screen International 7, 156
Shakespeare, William 93, 102–3
Shakespeare's Globe 102
sheet music 19, 27, 80, 127, 134–6
Shooting People 7, 155
showreels 41, 44, 64, 154–5, 177, 180–1, 184, 186–7, 192–3, 195, 242
sides 13, 142, 150
sight reading 27, 148, 152, 177, 234
Skill 19
skin work 110
smile 68, 70, 79, 81, 84, 91, 98, 132, 136, 155, 161–2, 197–8, 207, 215, 246, 258
speeches 14–15, 27, 58, 84–5, 88, 92–3, 97–8, 102–3, 105–6, 109–10, 114, 119–20, 148, 162, 196, 198–9, 204, 207–8, 223, 234; anthologies 15
Spotlight 5, 8, 39–41, 45, 48–9, 100, 192; *Spotlight Link* 5, 28; *Spotlight On Presenters* 192–3
stage management 73–4, 111
Stage Pool 6
Stage, The 5–6, 10, 87, 133, 185, 189–90
stand-up comedy 105–6, 189–91
swearing 15, 36, 84, 184, 246

'tell me about yourself' 195, 198, 207

taking the lead 155, 204, 206–7, 215, 217
tax deductibility 43, 50, 138, 255
The Office 175
theatre programmes 12, 127; tickets 43–4, 46, 242
Thomas, Bill 41
Thomson, Peter 69
time, allowing enough 13, 27, 130, 206, 254; of appointments 213
transport 13, 27, 42, 96, 253
Travis, Sarah 137
Tucker, Patrick 15
TV Times 12
typecasting 88, 147, 152, 175; niche 147, 163, 174; playing against type 147; types 41–2, 60–2, 94, 103, 119, 124, 147, 162–3, 169, 173–6, 189, 192, 207, 261

Unicorn Theatre 109

Variety 7
venues, audition 13, 57, 63, 65–6, 73–5, 89–90, 95, 101, 148, 150, 163–4, 246, 254, 258
Video Arts 174
visualisations 69–71
vocal range 32, 39, 134

wardrobe, audition 60, 63
warm up 107, 120, 130, 213
water 91, 130
Watermill, Newbury, The 137
websites, creating 45, 46; social networking sites 45
weekly rep 108
Wilson, Jacqueline 110, 119
workshops 87, 103, 106–7, 110, 112–13, 143, 145, 176–8; leading 111
wow factor 127, 129, 136

X Factor, The 83, 121

Young, Will 122

Related titles from Routledge

Award Monologues for Men
Edited by Patrick Tucker and Christine Ozanne

Award Monologues for Men is a collection of monologues taken from plays written since 1980 that have been nominated for the Pullitzer Prize, the Tony and the Drama Desk Awards in New York, and the Evening Standard and Laurence Olivier Awards in London. The book provides an excellent range of audition pieces, usefully arranged in age groups, and is supplemented with audition tips to improve your acting, and to ensure that you give your best possible performance.

Hb: 978-0-415-42837-8
Pb: 978-0-41542838-5

Available at all good bookshops
For ordering and further information please visit:
www.routledge.com

Related titles from Routledge

Award Monologues for Women
Edited by Patrick Tucker and Christine Ozanne

Award Monologue for Women is a collection of monologues taken from plays written since 1980 that have been nominated for the Pullitzer Prize, the Tony and the Drama Desk Awards in New York, and the Evening Standard and Laurence Olivier Awards in London. The book provides an excellent range of audition pieces, usefully arranged in age groups, and is supplemented with audition tips to improve your acting, and to ensure that you give your best possible performance.

Hb: 978-0-415-42839-2
Pb: 978-0-41542840-8

Available at all good bookshops
For ordering and further information please visit:
www.routledge.com

Related titles from Routledge

Monologues for Actors of Color:
Men
Edited by Roberta Uno

"Presently the best source for minority dramatic material in monologue form in publication, these two volumes [*Women* and *Men*] should be in every library used by students of the theater or actors." – *Choice*

This collection features 45 monologues excerpted from contemporary plays and specially geared for actors of color. Roberta Uno has carefully selected the monologues so that there is a wide-range of ethnicities included: African American, Native American, Latino and Asian American. Each monologue comes with an introduction with notes on the characters and stage directions to set the scene for the actor.

Hb: 978-0-87830-070-9
Pb: 978-0-87830-071-6

Available at all good bookshops
For ordering and further information please visit:
www.routledge.com

Related titles from Routledge

Monologues for Actors of Color:
Women
Edited by Roberta Uno

"Presently the best source for minority dramatic material in monologue form in publication, these two volumes [*Women* and *Men*] should be in every library used by students of the theater or actors." – *Choice*

This collection features 45 monologues excerpted from contemporary plays and specially geared for actors of color. Roberta Uno has carefully selected the monologues so that there is a wide-range of ethnicities included: African American, Native American, Latino and Asian American. Each monologue comes with an introduction with notes on the characters and stage directions to set the scene for the actor.

Hb: 978-0-87830-068-6
Pb: 978-0-87830-069-3

Available at all good bookshops
For ordering and further information please visit:
www.routledge.com